All Things Wise and Wonderful

All Things Wise and Wonderful

A Christian Understanding of How and Why Things
Happen, in Light of Covid-19

E. JANET WARREN

WIPF & STOCK · Eugene, Oregon

ALL THINGS WISE AND WONDERFUL
A Christian Understanding of How and Why Things Happen, in Light of
Covid-19

Wipf & Stock
An Imprint of Wipf and Stock Publishers
199 W. 8th Ave., Suite 3
Eugene, OR 97401

www.wipfandstock.com

PAPERBACK ISBN: 978-1-7252-9203-1
HARDCOVER ISBN: 978-1-7252-9204-8
EBOOK ISBN: 978-1-7252-9205-5

01/12/21

All thing bright and beautiful,
All creatures great and small,
All things wise and wonderful,
The Lord God made them all.

Cecil Frances Alexander and L. Wasson

Contents

List of Tables

List of Figures

Preface and Acknowledgments

THIS BOOK WAS INSPIRED by many friends, colleagues, pastors, students—even *Facebook* acquaintances—who asked or answered questions about causation, stimulating my own questions and responses. Thank you! I cover a wide range of topics and I've attempted to write for the non-specialist, adding some deeper analysis in endnotes. My book is intended primarily for Christians but has enough general information to be of interest to a wide range of readers. The stories I share are based in real-life experience but amalgamated or modified to protect the innocent. Often I've heard the same comments from more than one person, so don't worry if you recognize yourself!

Over the years I have benefited from the many interactions I've had with colleagues from my theological and science-faith networks (the American Scientific Affiliation and the Canadian Scientific and Christian Affiliation). Many thanks to those who offered feedback on earlier drafts of this work: Christian Barrigar, Colin Campbell, August Konkel, Douglas Olena, and David Shumaker. I especially appreciated the detailed feedback I received from Kathryn Belicki and her encouragement to "ditch the high-falutin language." Finally, much appreciation to the team at Wipf and Stock for bringing this project to the finish line.

Note that portions of this book have been previously published as "Pneuma and Pneumonia: Reconsidering the Relationship Between Spiritual and Medical Healing," *Fuller Magazine* 11 (2018) 36–41; and "Providence and Probability," *Canadian-American Theological Review* 9, 1. Also note that references, especially biblical ones, are not exhaustive but intended to be illustrative. I hope that *All Things Wise and Wonderful* increases our wisdom as we walk through our wonderful world.

1

Introduction

WHEN I WAS IN the final phases of writing this book, COVID-19 happened: a pandemic that swept the globe, leaving no one untouched. We learned about the virus that causes this illness and how it spreads. We changed our behavior to prevent getting sick. We learned that there is much that even experts do not know. There is no simple, logical reason why some people get infected and others don't, why some suffer more than others. Many of us felt afraid and anxious. We eventually tired of the jokes about toilet paper and masks (although the two combined could be interesting). Some of us developed explanations for the pandemic that differed from what scientists said. Some believed the whole thing to be a hoax. Some Christians claimed that they didn't need to distance themselves from other people because they were protected by the blood of Jesus. Others thought that God was using the pandemic to judge the world. Practically everyone asked, "How and why did this happen?"

This experience has made it impossible for anyone to ignore the devastating effects of illness, and the complex nature of causation. It also illustrates how much people value explanations. The COVID-19 pandemic serves as a helpful example of cause-and-effect relations in life; the complicated nature of nature, with its many types and levels of causation. It also illustrates human understandings and misunderstandings. And, from a Christian perspective, the pandemic is an opportunity to reflect on what the Bible and theology say about how and why things happen. Questions include: What causes various types of illness, or life events in general? How do we perceive cause and effect, and how accurate are our judgments? What is God's role in illness and healing, or his action in the world generally? Without giving away too much, I'll hint that the answers are far from simple, and not always what we want to hear.

So, who am I and why am I writing this book? I am an evangelical Christian (post-conservative if you must know) who takes the Bible seriously. When I was working on my doctoral dissertation on demonology and deliverance, the topic of discernment of evil naturally arose. As I started researching this area, I realized that discernment is much misunderstood. Christians use the term frequently, but are often unclear about exactly what it is they are "discerning"—God? The devil? Sin? This elicits questions about the causes of evil and affliction, which leads to the more general topic of causation and how we understand it.

I am also a physician and include psychotherapy as part of my practice. In my professional practice, my Christian experience, and personal life, I have encountered many stories of suffering. As a doctor, I am concerned about how much misunderstanding there is regarding the causes of illness, and as a theologian, I am concerned about how much misunderstanding there is regarding the nature of cause and effect in the created world and God's role in it. I am also passionate about integrating faith and science. My aim in this book is to increase our knowledge of how and why things happen from within a Christian perspective. By doing so, we may also become wiser in our judgments and stronger in our faith.

WHY DO WE ASK WHY?

Think about your day so far—how often did you make something happen? How often did you assume that something would happen automatically? Did your new knowledge of how infections, like COVID-19, are transmitted cause you to change your actions? We navigate our days relying on cause-and-effect associations, usually without thinking about it. We flip a switch and the light turns on. We drive to work. We eat to give our bodies energy and maintain health. It is only when things go wrong, when life is disordered, that we think about causation: Why am I sick? Why is my car not starting? Why is the light not on? What caused this war?

How we view cause-and-effect relations affects our actions and our responses to problems. Our beliefs and knowledge about the world generally determine our behavior in the world, whether it is how we respond emotionally, or how we act to change our situations. If I think bacteria are causing my illness, I take an antibiotic. If I believe my headache is caused by banging my head against the wall, I will stop doing this (hopefully). If I believe that a war was caused by another country, I may be angry at people from that place. If I assume that the reason my car won't start is because it has an engine problem, I take it to the mechanic. If I think COVID-19 is caused by mobile networks, I—well, I don't want to think about that. Causation is important not only in everyday life but in most professional and academic disciplines. In the natural and social sciences, experiments are based on hypotheses about what causes events in the world. In health care, physicians base their treatment of a condition on known causes. Historians look to the past to understand causes for historical events, hopefully to prevent similar future events if past events were harmful.

Our thoughts on how and why things happen have important implications for Christian ministry: Are problems caused by someone's sin? God's punishment? Something else? Some beliefs matter more than others—your life does not depend on what you think about how the world was created, but it may depend on whether you believe putting your foot on the brake will stop the car. The idea of causation includes moral responsibility—we are agents who can cause something to happen and can therefore be held accountable for our actions. Of course, sometimes we do things accidentally. We tend not to blame people for unintentional or unforeseen consequences of their actions. Cause and intent are not always identical.

Philosopher J. L. Mackie claims that causation "cements" the universe.[1] Understanding how and why things happen is foundational to human existence. It allows us to function in the world, giving us a sense of stability, predictability, and control. It allows us to plan for the future and figure out the past. We ask questions and seek explanations without always being aware of why or what exactly we are asking. Our questions relate to multiple levels: simple knowledge, practical application, and deep meaning. As soon as children learn to talk, parents quickly tire of the questions. Why is an apple red? Because God made it that way. Because society arbitrarily assigned it that color name. Because light interacts with pigments in the fruit to produce that color. And when parents are especially tired—just because. Most don't bother pointing out that not all apples are red.

Speaking of apples, it is interesting that when the first humans hid from God and he asked (unnecessarily), "Where are you?" they responded with explanations and excuses (Gen 3:9–13). They answered a *why* question rather than the *where* question. Perhaps they instinctively knew that God really wanted to know the *reason* for their behavior. *Why* questions are important to us in many respects; they seem to be important to God too, who is interested in the motivations of our hearts.

Spouses may have noted that when they have different ideas about what caused a conflict, it is difficult to resolve. When we have narrow views of causation, we may avoid personal responsibility: It's all your fault. God planned it. The devil made me do it. Alternatively, we may take on unwarranted responsibility: It's all my fault. If we think that we are just passive recipients of causative powers, we may avoid caring for ourselves, our neighbors, or the environment. There are relational, moral, and ethical reasons to learn about causation. In the legal system, when someone's guilt and fate are being decided, it is essential that we are correct about who caused what.

Questions about cause and effect frequently arise when life is disordered or disrupted. People seek reasons in order to restore some order. As a family doctor, I see pain and suffering daily. Patients always want explanations: Why did I get cancer when I've always looked after my health? What's wrong with me? Some problems are relatively straightforward. A fall from a tree causes a bone in the arm to break, a bullet to the head usually causes death, ingesting poison causes vomiting. However, most problems are more complex. Nasal congestion can be caused by infection, allergies, or irritation; smoking causes lung disease most of the time, but not always; the causes of mental illness are still not fully understood. Sometimes I tell patients that I do not know exactly what their problem is or what's causing it, but I can assure them it's not serious. Most don't like this—they want a *diagnosis*.

Consider sore throats—a swab can confirm if they are caused by a bacterium or a virus. The latter is much more common and less serious, but often patients prefer a positive test because diagnosis and treatment are clearer, or at least seem so, for bacterial than for viral illnesses. People like simple cause-and-effect patterns in their lives. We like life to be orderly and understandable. We want the world to be fair, to make sense. If we can *do* something, anything, that will help, it gives us a sense of agency, autonomy, and purpose. Humans generally don't tolerate uncertainty. We fear the unknown. Explanations, the simpler the better, help us regain some sense of control, and a hope that we can stop, decrease, or prevent our suffering. But, as we will see, our need for simplistic understandings, which are mostly incompatible with Christian thought or the way the world works, has a price tag.

"Why did God allow this to happen?" Christians have extra layers of questions about the cause of problems, especially illness. Suffering might imply that God is absent or powerless, or that life is meaningless. We suffer as a result of suffering. The Bible, between the brief perfection of the garden and the promised redeemed city, is filled with affliction and unanswered questions. Psalmists are blatant: "I am weary with my moaning; every night I flood my bed with tears" (6:6); "How long, O Lord? Will you forget me forever?" (13:1). In Scripture, questions are encouraged, but simple answers are never guaranteed. The story of Job is a classic example of complex and unexplained cause and effect. Job's friends, in seeking an easy answer to his suffering, blame him. Job's wife blames God. God, however, tells Job to accept that there is much that he (Job, that is) does not know about the world.

Because causation is so fundamental to our lives, it is important to understand both the nature of our world and the nature of our understanding of the world. But there is another essential reason: God commands us to do so. Genesis 1:26 calls us to tend creation, which, broadly understood, includes investigating causal patterns in nature. The charge to love and serve one another (John 13:34) involves knowing about human thought processes and recognizing reasons for human suffering. And the command to love and serve the Lord (Matt 22:37) involves us appreciating how he interacts with his creation and creatures. I believe that awareness of the nature of causation in creation and in Christianity is essential for all responsible Christians. Better recognition of the marvels of God's world can increase our faith and inspire worship, better knowledge of creation can increase our knowledge of the Creator, and knowing God is an ultimate aim of Christianity.

HOW DO WE KNOW AND HOW DO WE KNOW WHAT WE KNOW?

Two-year olds quickly learn that a fire is hot, six-year olds eagerly learn to read, sixteen-year olds reluctantly learn algebra, and medical researchers learn about new viruses. They all acquire these different types of knowledge in various ways, such as experience or reason. Humans learn at an amazing pace and there appear to be no limits to the amount of stuff we can know. Most often we do not think about what and how we know. Indeed, it is possible to function well in the world without such information. We may know what a computer is and how to use it, but be unable to explain this knowledge to someone else. We know how to breathe but do not know how we know this.

We all know that we know and know what we know—don't we? I wish it were that simple. In order to understand causation better, it is important to think about what knowledge is and how we obtain it. Knowledge can be viewed as facts, information, and skills that are gained through experience or education. It can be theoretical or practical. There are different types of knowledge and different ways of obtaining it.[2] The toddler who touches the fire learns through sensory perception; in fact, much of what we know of the world is obtained through our five senses. Students gain education through reason and trust in experts, those who have examined and experienced in

the past. Medical researchers acquire knowledge by intentionally manipu-
lating substances to observe a change or produce an effect. These types of
knowledge can be described as *explicit, rational, empirical* (based on observation), or *propositional* (based on logic). They are tangible, generally
accepted, and can be justified or supported by other evidence. Someone else
can touch the fire, other researchers can conduct the same experiment.

However, knowledge can also be acquired without using reason. I can
explain my faith intellectually but deep down I *just know* that Jesus is Lord.
We have all experienced a "feeling" of knowing, or a hunch, without being able to explain it. Our sense of ourselves and our awareness of God
are common examples of nonrational knowledge. We also often use our
imaginations for considering new possibilities. This type of knowledge can
be described as *implicit, tacit, nonconceptual,* or *intuitive*. It is personal and
difficult to explain. Michael Polanyi, scientist turned philosopher, famously
says: "We can know more than we can tell."[3]

It could be said that all knowledge is causal, because things relate to
each other in space and time.[4] I know that there is coffee in my cup because
I prepared and poured it. I know the ground is wet because I watched rain
falling from the sky, and I remember from previous experience that rain
causes wetness. I know that there are gravitational forces on earth that have
causative effects because I've seen things fall, and also trust the many scientists who support this theory. Knowledge relates to *inference*—we deduce
facts from connections between events, and memory. It is solidified with
repeat occurrences. Causal knowledge can be both explicit, involving conscious awareness, and implicit, lacking such awareness.

There are differing levels of knowledge: we can know something is
a chair, but also know its composition, its approximate dimensions, and
how we plan to use it. Knowledge relates to time—we can roughly know
the past and the present, and some aspects of the future, such as the sun
rising tomorrow, our plans for a vacation when pandemic restrictions lift,
or Christmas occurring on December 25. Our knowledge of the world also
depends on when and how we interact with it. People in China had a different experience of COVID-19 than people in Canada, because, when they first
experienced it, they did not know what it was. We only have access to parts
of reality that are presented to us in particular places and at particular times.
In other words, the "real" world is sometimes different from the "observable" world. There is often more than one "correct" way to know the world.[5]
This should encourage us to be open to different perspectives and the possibility of being wrong. And, of course, we can't even observe all aspects of
reality, such as the spirit world.

Spiritual Knowledge

The great theologian Karl Barth allegedly summed up his lifelong learning thus: "Jesus loves me this I know, for the Bible tells me so." Because God wants to be known, he has unveiled himself in various ways. Barth mentions the Bible as one way. Another way is through nature: we can understand the Creator by observing his creation.[6] A third way is spiritual revelation.[7] This is a type of nonconceptual or tacit knowledge, a way to know "things that are not visible" (Heb 11:3). In Scripture and throughout history, people have reported mystical visions and dreams, hearing an inner or audible voice, and developing sudden insights. Such revelatory experiences are typically transient; they are difficult to describe but profoundly meaningful.[8] Paul suggests that we can know God through the "eyes of [our] heart" (Eph 1:18); that is, in a nonrational manner. We have all heard stories of people being slain in the Spirit, receiving visions, and hearing the voice of God.[9] These experiences are subjective; therefore, difficult to evaluate. But the sheer number of such reports compel us to take them seriously. And they may help us understand how and why things happen.

In sum, we can acquire spiritual knowledge in both rational and nonrational ways. We can know spiritual reality through mystical experiences, intuition, and imagination, but can also know it through reason and authority, such as by studying the Bible and Christian theology. Some Christians favor one method over the other, but I think both are necessary and, indeed, often interrelated. I suggest that spiritual knowledge is perhaps best obtained through a blend of experience and education. Interestingly, Augustine referred to knowledge as involving both *scientia* (analytic, rational means) and *sapientia* (wisdom from God).[10]

Spiritual revelation is usually experienced as direct and immediate— an encounter with God that is only thought about afterwards. It can be considered *preconceptual*; the experience comes before the words and ideas. However, it is important to recognize that all experience is mediated. Even divinely-inspired Scripture passes through the pens of its authors, who in turn have been influenced by their own language and culture. Indescribable spiritual experiences similarly pass through biological beings; they produce patterns of activity in the brain.[11] God does exist and does speak, but the way we investigate and explain this is limited by human nature. This is difficult to comprehend because the feeling many Christians have is that God communicates directly to them, often without words. But it is impossible to separate this knowledge of God from the way that we receive it, or the words we use to relate our experiences.

Language and Knowledge

Covid-19 taught us a whole new language: physical distancing, self-isolation, flattening the curve. It was needed to communicate new concepts. However, language is not always straightforward. Have you ever had an occasion when you cannot find the right words to describe something? Or when you're a few minutes into a discussion and realize that you and your conversation partner are talking about entirely different subjects? Language can be unclear and complex. Consider some common English oxymorons: original copies, open secrets, clearly confused, militant pacifist, larger half, act naturally. And some other amusing word facts: monosyllabic is not monosyllabic, misspelled is not misspelled, unpronounceable is not unpronounceable. Yet language is essential for conceptualizing and communicating cause and effect in our lives. The words we have and use influence and restrict how we understand the world, including how and why things happen. And language is in turn influenced by education, experience, and culture.

Recall that knowledge can be obtained through both logical, explicit means and intuitive, implicit means. Language reflects this. It can be classified in many ways. Two common types are *literal*—the simple, primary meaning of language, and *figurative*—language that uses figures of speech, such as metaphors. In the past, only literal language, which is associated with logic and rationality, was considered to reflect "true" knowledge.[12] Figurative language was dismissed as merely decorative. However, according to contemporary linguists, figurative language can reflect *truths* about the world. In philosophical terms, it has *semantic power*.[13] Unlike philosophical or scientific language, figurative language is not analytical but provides a picture that can increase our depth of knowledge. It is more flexible than literal language and allows for ambiguity and multiple meanings. Indeed, metaphors often convey meaning better than literal language; they are more than just figures of speech. Metaphors are especially useful, essential even, when we are talking about religion and spirituality. Try and explain the "breath of God" or the "light of the world" in literal terms. Metaphors help us understand difficult ideas by using words and images that we are familiar with. They use what's known to reveal the unknown.

Jesus is described as "living water" and "bread of life." Metaphors can be conceptual, based on ideas, and cluster together to form a system or model. Water and bread both point to the idea of Jesus as providing spiritual sustenance and nourishment. Models offer a framework through which to view the world, and are sometimes presented as diagrams. Later we will review some models that describe relations between cause and effect, and some that help us understand the relationship between God and the world.

Multiple metaphors provide multiple snapshots of the world, enabling us to better comprehend it. When a concept is abstract and difficult, we often need more than one model to describe it. Because knowledge has limits, figurative language is especially helpful in increasing our understanding of how and why things happen.

Limits of Knowledge

Can we know the real world? The answer may seem intuitively obvious. After all, we manage to function quite well on a daily basis using our five senses—at least most of the time. However, our brains (the source of our beliefs) are locked in a small bony box, with little access to the "outside" world. It's humbling to know that many animals can hear sounds that humans cannot. We cannot see all sides of a cube but are confident in its existence. We also believe that Paris is real, even though we may never have been there (pity). What about things like dreams, consciousness, and spiritual experience? They are not perceived by the five senses but seem very real. And what about scientific concepts like numbers and subatomic particles? We use math every day as if it is real, but it is only an abstract, though helpful, linguistic tool. There are many allusions to the elusive nature of reality in arts and literature. Think of Lewis Carroll's classic, *Alice in Wonderland*, in which things fade in and out of existence. Science fiction often depicts computer-generated artificial reality in contrast to the reality of humans whose brains are connected to machines.

Some ideas are notoriously difficult to grasp. Try and think about nothing right now (sorry). Many concepts are inherently vague. What defines baldness? (How many hairs does one need to lose to be labeled bald?) Is a person standing in a doorway inside or outside the room? Is sixty-three a large or small number? How many grains of sand constitute a heap? Philosophical paradoxes nicely illustrate the limits of knowledge.[14] The liar paradox is attributed to Epimenides, an inhabitant of Crete, who asserted, "All Cretans are liars" (a statement shared by the Apostle Paul; Titus 1:12). Similar examples include: "This sentence is false" and "If you try to fail, and succeed, which have you done?" The dichotomy paradox describes someone moving from one point to another: first you walk halfway there, then halfway more, then halfway more . . . but you can never arrive (maybe go to Paris instead).

Other limits relate to perceptions and perspectives. What we know depends on what we see, hear, or feel. A classic story describes three blind men describing an elephant through touch. The man at the trunk will describe "reality" quite differently from those at the tail or leg. When I'm out hiking, I may think I see a snake and move closer (just a little) to confirm the accuracy of my knowledge. But how do I know that what I see is a snake, especially if it is a rare type that I have not seen before? I rely on knowledge gained through my previous experiences, and the knowledge of others. But how do others know that this is a snake? This an example of what philosophers call *infinite regress*—reasoning that goes on forever.

Our beliefs about the world also affect our knowledge of it. If we think snakes are in the area, we are perhaps more likely to see one; if we think too much though, we are likely to think we see snakes, even if they are not there. Sometimes our beliefs are reasonable even if inaccurate. You can believe your alarm will ring every day because you set it, but if the power goes out, it may not ring. That belief is wrong but understandably so. We can also believe something that is only coincidentally true. I see my friend in a crowd but, on closer look, realize it is not her; later I discover that she was indeed part of that crowd, just not the person I saw. We sometimes have irrational beliefs, such as horoscope predictions, that may on occasion be true. The connection between belief and truth is complicated.

Some philosophers are skeptical about whether we can know anything with accuracy, because of the problems we just discussed: circular reasoning, infinite regress, unreliable testimony, and inaccurate interpretations of experience. However, our own common sense and experience, as well as the beliefs of most scholars, suggests that knowledge is possible, even if somewhat limited. Our senses are generally trustworthy, as is the testimony of other people. I suggest that whenever possible we rely on many types and sources of information. And we always need to be mindful of the nature of our knowledge, and the limits of the language that we use to communicate it.

WHAT IS CAUSATION?

The novel coronavirus causes the disease COVID-19, which usually produces a fever and a cough. But not everyone gets the same symptoms, and not everyone who has a cough has COVID-19. Cause-and-effect relations are complex. Consider a car that skids on ice, narrowly avoiding an accident. Contributing causative factors include bad weather, poor road conditions, bare tires, mechanical problems, driving too fast or distracted, demonic interference, and/or divine intervention. Or consider the story of the Gerasene demoniac (Matt 8:28–34). Jesus encounters naked, loud, violent men who are apparently inflicted with evil spirits. They yell and beg Jesus to send them into some nearby pigs. Jesus obliges, the pigs run into a lake, and the men are restored to normalcy. What caused the men's behavior? Mental illness? Evil spirits? Social exclusion? All of the above? Did the pigs drown because Jesus ordained it? Because the demons made them act irrationally? Because water prohibits breathing?

The term *causation* is usually used to describe a process that produces change, the making of an effect. *Causality* is used by philosophers to refer to such processes, or discuss the association between cause and effect. In many ways, causation underlies all knowledge. The world is dynamic and almost everything affects something else; events are interrelated. Because of this, we often think in terms of cause and effect to help us navigate life. In fact, the word *because* relates in an obvious way to causation and explanation. We connect the dots between things that happen, or, as psychologists say, we view the world through an implicit causal framework. As well as being part of our daily lives, causal concepts are important in many scholarly disciplines, although some hesitate to use the term *cause*. Scientists prefer words like associations and risk factors, because of the difficulties involved in proving causation.

There are many different types of questions about causes and explanation, and they require different responses. "Why does the light turn on when I flip the switch?" is answered very differently for a two-year old, a physics student, and an electrician. "Why did mommy die?" is answered very differently for a child, a physician, and a theologian. Some questions are more important than others. Most answers depend on our perspective and needs. The big *why* questions are different from the basic *how* questions. The latter are of a mechanical, practical nature, whereas the former relate to meaning and purpose, and tend to have emotional impact.

Causation is a deeply intuitive notion that enables us to function in daily life. It links our experiences together, so our days run relatively smoothly. It helps life make sense by predicting and explaining events. It is present in young children and is so instinctive that we usually only think about it when something goes wrong. It is ingrained in our minds and culture. This is especially true in Christianity, which has a coherent worldview of a Creator-Redeemer God. We understand that God "caused" the world to come into existence, that human sin "causes" many problems in the world, and that God sent Jesus to "cause" our healing and salvation.

WHAT ARE SOME ASPECTS OF CAUSATION?

We have seen a few examples that hint at the complex nature of causation in our wonderful world: novel viruses, light switches, car accidents, cancer, falls, wars. There are factors great and small, superficial and deep, accidental and intentional, mechanical and moral. Philosophers have long pondered the nature of causation and offer some helpful insights.[15]

Causal Levels

Aristotle described four aspects or levels of causality. He used a bronze statue to illustrate these, but I will use the wooden desk I am sitting at, because it is more familiar to us.

- *material*: inherent, pre-existing properties; the nature of a thing; the wood that the desk is constructed from
- *formal*: systematic, interactional aspects; causes that operate through intrinsic forms; the wood becomes a desk, not a chair
- *efficient*: the mover, agent, or initiator of the process of change; causes that act on objects; the carpenter who builds the desk
- *final*: purpose, reason, or teleology; causes that pull the object toward perfection; my work at the computer that sits on the desk.[16]

This classification helps us think about the various types or levels of questions on causation. Each category provides a different perspective and addresses different questions. The first three focus on *how* questions and are usually aspects that we can observe and study. The last aspect addresses *why* questions and can be very subjective and personal.

The first level, material, is relatively straightforward. But note that it has limits—wood would not work well in the construction of clothes. Many materials have an inherent possibility or potentiality to move or change: ice melts easily, sand squishes.[17] In the natural world, causation is often described as *dispositional,* meaning that things have a natural tendency toward a particular type of action: a smooth round stone is more likely to roll than a ragged square one, delicate glass has a tendency to shatter easily, ice is usually slippery. These tendencies do not change and can limit the ability of forces to act on them. It can be difficult to make ice non-slippery, or a smooth stone rough. If something is predisposed to change in a certain direction, an agent will struggle, or find it impossible, to make it change in an opposite direction.

Aristotle's formal level describes the shape a material assumes. It explains why something is one thing and not another. A desk and a chair may both be composed of wood, but they are very different in form and function. Efficient causation is more interesting and is what most scientists and philosophers focus on. It describes the causative force that acts upon something to produce an effect. We mostly think about personal agents who deliberately cause something: God creates the world, I build a desk, the cat on my desk obscures my view. But causative forces are not always personal: a fire can accidentally burn my desk, gravity can cause things to fall. Often many different efficient causes can produce one effect.

Final causation is similar to the term *explanation*, which is a justification given for an action or belief. It is perhaps the most difficult level to figure out because it can be very subjective. People use desks for different purposes. On a grander scale, final causation relates to our personal belief systems. We want to know the overarching reason for things that happen. Aristotle thought there was an ultimate cause, a being above all others. He used the term *unmoved mover*. Christians would use the term God.

Note that all categories of causation may interrelate. The light switch question can be answered by referring to material and formal levels (a discussion on electricity, the generative mechanism), an efficient level (because an agent flipped a switch), or a purposeful level (it's dark and I want to see; an explanation).[18] However, not all four factors are present in every causal situation. Materials can change, forms are not always readily identifiable, agents are not always necessary, and not everything has an ultimate purpose. This does not mean that God is not involved with his world, just that he does not directly cause all things. The COVID-19 pandemic has occurred partly because of the nature of viruses (material) to live in people (material), and consequently cause symptoms (perhaps both material and efficient), without malicious intent. There is no final level. This interconnection of factors can be dizzying.

Causal Relations

Consider the following causes and effects: viruses and pandemics, ice and car accidents, demons and crazy behavior, smoking and cancer, flipping switches and illumination. We'll use this last example to illuminate some philosophical terms that describe causal associations:

- *contiguity*: cause and effect are related in space; my hand is physically close to the light switch when the light goes on, meaning I likely caused the illumination

- *temporality*: cause and effect are related in time; there is a very short period between me touching the switch and the light turning on

- *agency*: a personal being acts upon an object or situation to bring about a change; I, the agent, plan to turn on the light using my hand to do so; as a result, there is illumination.[19]

These broad concepts are helpful for understanding connections between events. Sometimes things are related in space but not time, sometimes in time but not space. Many causes can have effects on things far away. This is common in our digital world when a text message to someone far away can cause them to perform an action. Temporal associations can have variable time intervals, and patterns are sometimes surprising—before water "suddenly" boils, there is a slow and steady rise in temperature. Agents are not always necessary when change occurs naturally. Plants often grow even when humans neglect to water them. Dead wood decays over time.

Contiguity and temporality are often related, and the term *constant conjunction* describes processes that regularly occur together. This is common in nature: water freezes at fairly predictable temperatures and time intervals. Constant conjunction can also occur without a cause-and-effect relation: whales are always mammals but being a whale does not cause one to be a mammal. Conversely, a causal connection can occur without constant conjunction: smoking often causes lung cancer, but not everyone who smokes gets cancer. In sum, although cause and effect are frequently related in time and space, the connection is neither certain nor uniform.

With respect to agency, there are many aspects to consider. I am writing this book with intent and control, and I could be said to be a direct cause of it. But I have also been influenced by other people and hopefully the Holy Spirit, who are indirect causes. Our actions in life are usually intertwined with the actions of others. I may plan to "cause" my book to sell 100,000 copies, but this outcome depends on other people's "plans" to buy it (thank you).

These philosophical categories are useful for theology. Divine causation can be viewed as direct (God intentionally and explicitly makes something happen) or indirect (since God created the world, everything that happens is sort of caused by him). Some streams of Christianity claim that God is the primary, direct, and ultimate cause of everything that happens. This view is often broadly and uniformly applied: people do not always distinguish between God healing cancer and God telling them what socks to wear. Other Christian views include causative agents other than God. Human beings have genuine freedom or independent agency. We are responsible for working with God in causing things to happen. Caring for and developing the world includes understanding the nature of cause and effect in creation.

Sometimes us agents have little control over our actions simply because of the nature of the world: the knee-jerk reflex is involuntary; we cannot change the temperature at which water boils. Sometimes failing to act can cause an event: plants die if not watered (guilty). In a machine, a broken part (something missing) or an interference like dust (something added) can cause operational failure. These situations do not require an agent. A person, an impersonal force, or random things like dust can produce effects. When there does not appear to be an agent acting in a situation, we often use the terms coincidence or accident.

The ideas of *necessary* and *sufficient* conditions are also valuable in understanding causation. Few causative factors are both necessary and sufficient. Air is necessary for life, but it is not sufficient because we also need food, water, and love. To travel across the country, taking a flight is sufficient, but not necessary because one could also drive. Developing COVID-19 requires exposure to the virus, but this is not a sufficient cause, because not everyone who is in contact with the virus develops the disease.

To complicate things further, usually no single cause can explain an effect. An effect can have more than one cause: a sunburn occurs because of hot sun, sensitive skin, and lack of sunscreen (oops). Two or more effects can have the same cause: the sun causes my sunburn and my feelings of heat and thirst. Two events may be related because they are both caused by a third independent factor, or they have a common cause: I have a sunburn and eat ice cream because of the hot sun, but ice cream, fortunately, does not cause a sunburn.

There is often redundancy or *overdetermination* in causation; many effects have numerous distinct, unrelated causes. A car accident can be caused by ice on the road, worn tires, or a distracted driver, among other things. None of these is necessary for an accident to occur, each may be sufficient, but usually they work together. The concepts of immediate or *primary* versus remote or *secondary* are helpful. With the car accident, the primary and immediate cause is the car colliding with an obstacle, but remote or contributory causes include the ice, the tires, and/or the distracted driver. When someone sadly dies from COVID-19, the immediate cause of death is heart-lung failure, but the original cause is infection with the coronavirus. It is also useful to distinguish between *specific* (this car accident was caused by bad weather conditions) and *general* (car accidents are frequently caused by bad weather and impaired driving) types of cause-and-effect relations.

In sum, connections between causes and effects are important, but often involve many different causative factors that are associated in different ways. This makes it difficult to evaluate causation, but our understanding can be aided through the type of language we use.

Metaphors and Models of Causation

Reports on the 2020 pandemic used the language of warfare: We are fighting a war against COVID-19. Health care workers are soldiers in this battle. The implication is that the disease is caused by an enemy that attacks human health. As an aside, I'm not sure warfare imagery is ideal in a world in which war is a reality. Nevertheless, this example shows how the linguistic tools we discussed earlier can help us understand, describe, and evaluate cause and effect. Because we cannot *see* causation, metaphors and models are invaluable.

Life is complex and constantly changing, so it is not surprising that movement and direction metaphors are commonly used to describe causation: lead, follow, block, shape. When we have problems, we refer to being "derailed," or "running into brick walls." When events occur in rapid succession, we refer to the "domino effect." At deeper levels, we talk about life as a journey, following truth, walking along the right path. Such metaphors are often better than philosophical terms because they can be used in different ways. Biblical writers compare the Holy Spirit with a wind that brings about change. Since a breeze is different from a storm, the image is flexible. Metaphors help us to express uncertainty and blend different causative factors.

Speaking of blending . . . I enjoy baking. This involves many ingredients and different causal steps with a delicious result. But not all processes occur in a stepwise fashion. To understand causative processes, philosophers have developed some helpful models and images.[20] Some are straightforward and depicted as lines, chains, circles, and forks (Figure 1.1). In a *linear* model, there is only one cause, one effect, and one direction by which they are related. Falling from a tree is unidirectional. In a *chain*, there are many causes and effects, but they are still connected in a straight unidirectional way. Flipping a switch to turn on a light involves numerous steps between the first action and the final effect. A chain model can help us distinguish between the remote and immediate causes we discussed above. For a cake, the oven is an immediate cause and buying ingredients is a remote one.

When shopping, one can usually save money by buying in bulk; however, you have to already have enough money saved to buy the large quantity. This process, like many in life, is circular. A *circle*, or causal loop, occurs when the first cause is affected by the last. Causal effects still go in one direction but reconnect so that every cause is also an effect. Both chains and circles allow us to see how we can intervene in the process at any point, by breaking the connections or changing their direction. They illustrate that it is often difficult to know when processes begin (recall the problem of infinite regress). When baking cookies, does the process start when I plan the activity, buy the ingredients, mix the dough, shape them, put them in the oven, take them out, or serve them (assuming I haven't eaten them all already)? *Fork* models of causation are used in situations where one effect may have more than one cause—a cough can be caused by an infection or an irritation, or one cause may have more than one effect—the coronavirus causes fever, cough, and fatigue.

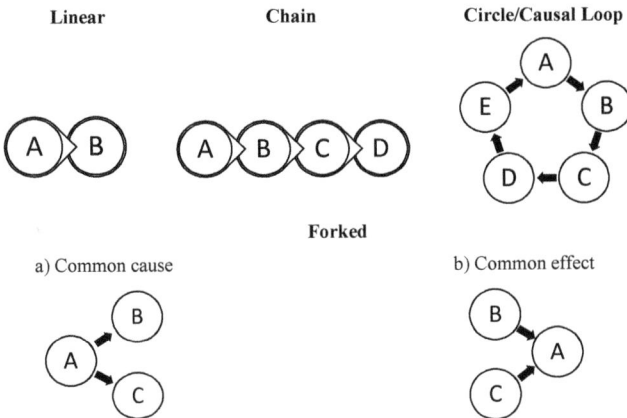

Figure 1.1: Simple Models of Causation

Simple models are common and intuitive; relatively easy to grasp and usually predictable. Many people only think of causation in terms of two-item linear models: God caused the pandemic, the coronavirus caused it, China caused it. When we add chains, forks, and circles, our understanding of causation in the world expands. Simple models may be helpful at times; however, as we have seen, most events have many levels of causation, and causes and events interact. Straightforward models are perhaps more useful at the theoretical level than at the practical, everyday-life level.

Almost daily the weather report is uncertain: There is a 10 percent chance of rain today. Most life events involve numerous elements and little predictability. Probability models use statistical tools to analyze what happens when multiple causative factors interrelate. Probability reasoning helps us to make judgments about future events based on what has occurred in the past. We can revise our views when we receive new information. However, such models are not always easy to grasp and require many instances of an event to be able to detect patterns; they depend on group data. Knowing some probability concepts is important for our understanding of how and why things happen; we will explore this topic further.

Of course, the most common type of model is the most complex. Network or web-like models can be thought of as chains, forks, and loops multiplied and superimposed (Figure 1.2). They reflect situations where causation occurs in multiple directions and involves many different factors. Web diagrams are commonly used to describe disease causation. A model of the COVID-19 pandemic would include things like viral exposure, close contact with an infected person, age, location, presence of other illnesses, and, for conspiracy theorists, evil foreign powers. Such models illustrate not only the complexity of causation, but also the idea that it is practically impossible to know all possible variables involved in events.

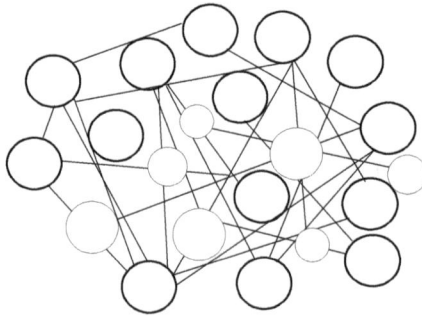

Figure 1.2: Network Model of Causation

Evaluating Causation

Why did I get sick? What caused my plants to die? Why is my car not starting? We all want to know why, and in our eagerness, are sometimes too hasty in our conclusions. It is perhaps easier to think that God caused the pandemic than to think about many small causes that acted together. Because we are surrounded by causes and effects, we sometimes assume that things are causally connected when they are not. We mistake *correlation* for *causation*. Winter weather is associated with eating less ice cream but does not cause this. People who attend church may be healthier than those who do not, leading Christians to conclude that religious practices cause good health. But very sick people are unable to leave their homes, and church attenders may also make healthy lifestyle choices. There may be associations, but these can have many possible explanations. False, or spurious, correlations are common and often humorous: graphs showing the divorce rate in Maine closely match those describing per capita margarine consumption.[21] It is usually very difficult to figure out underlying causal structures, and often the best we can do is infer the likeliest explanation; for example, there is a probable cause-and-effect connection between a broken window and a guilty-looking child.

Analyzing and discerning causation is complicated. There is usually guesswork and bias involved. Some philosophers even argue that there is no such thing as causation, mostly because we cannot see it.[22] However, we can only function in the world because of our intuitions about cause and effect—whether or not we are aware of these. The good news is that we have an innate ability to detect causation. We can tell the difference between a pile of rocks that have randomly rolled together and a cairn, which has been deliberately placed.[23] The bad news is that our perceptions and intuitions have major limitations, as we will see. More good news is that we can avail ourselves of guidance from philosophers, scientists, and the oft-neglected Holy Spirit.

Scientist-philosopher Judea Pearl has long explored the nature of causation. He notes that causal intuitions are often sufficient in daily life, but not always, and suggests some strategies we can use to evaluate causation. *Observation,* asking "what is going on," allows us to make associations between things that are related. *Intervention,* asking "what if I did something different," allows us to make changes to situations in order to test theories about causation. *Imagination,* asking "why this and not that," allows us to consider other possible explanations.[24]

If we see a pile of rocks and want to know what caused it, we can carefully inspect the context, or surrounding area. We should consider the agent (if any), the material nature of the specific object, other elements in the environment, and the person interpreting the situation. We sometimes forget that evaluators, ourselves that is, are part of the causal network. Some outcomes may be interpreted differently by a Christian and an atheist—the latter would not consider God as a possible causative agent.

Scientists commonly use interventions in their research. They change, add, or remove a factor in a causal chain and observe the effect. Establishing a causal mechanism adds strength to causal explanations.[25] However, given the numerous variables in the world and the fact that we can seldom control the variables of life, scientific techniques are not applicable in all situations.

We often ask *what if* questions when we regret an action. This is not usually helpful. But, when evaluating causation, it *is* helpful to ask such questions and imagine possible answers. Philosophers use the concept of *counterfactuals*—things that did not happen but might have—to analyze causality. They ask *what if* and *why* questions, and examine all possible explanations and outcomes. Someone may die in a car accident; however, if they received medical aid immediately, or if they were wearing their seatbelt, they may not have died. Someone may contract COVID-19 and blame the friend they visited recently, but not consider all the other people and places they had been in contact with. Christians may claim that God answered their prayer for rain, but seldom think about whether or not it would have rained anyway.

I am always amazed how quickly children learn about cause-and-effect relations. Through personal experience, we develop automatic frames and categories to help organize and understand the world.[26] All animals that bark are dogs; being a dog causes barking. There is usually ice in winter that causes falls. These strategies for evaluating causation work most of the time, but not always. For convenience, we often oversimplify and apply causal categories broadly, using them in situations where they don't apply. We may call a seal a dog because it barks. People can fall in winter when there is no ice. Ice sometimes persists into spring. More serious errors in causal thinking can occur. During the Medieval period the bubonic plague was believed to be caused by God; priests proclaimed divine judgment and called for repentance. It was later discovered to be an infection carried by rats, and the affliction ended when rat poison was used liberally.[27] Note the important connection here between our beliefs about what caused something and our actions in changing it.

In general, it is wise to ask multiple questions before making conclusions. It is my hope that by the end of this book you will have a better understanding not only of the nature of causation in our wonderful world, but also how to evaluate it with more accuracy and wisdom.

HOW DO WE COMMONLY THINK ABOUT CAUSATION?

I once taught basic medical care to Burmese volunteer medics. In the evenings we had devotion times, and I was asked to teach some counseling skills. The scenario for role-playing was a person dying of cancer. When "patients" asked what caused their cancer, students uniformly pronounced, "God." They seemed to have forgotten the lesson earlier in the day during which we had discussed smoking and other causative factors that contributed to the development of cancer. They perhaps used different causal frameworks because the situation appeared different, or perhaps were implicitly addressing different levels of causation. Recall Aristotle's recognition of the human need to know and to ask why. Except that frequently we do not know what it is we are asking. Perhaps my students were thinking that God used smoking to inflict cancer, but mostly, I suspect, they were not aware of the complexity of causation.

Cause and effect in daily life is a common topic in Christian circles, especially at a personal level. People often assume that God causes all occurrences, evident in many clichés: "God has a perfect plan for my life"; "When God closes a door, he opens a window." A popular poem claims that what we see of our messy lives is only the underside of a tapestry that God is perfecting. Here are the first two verses:

> My life is but a weaving
> Between my Lord and me;
> I cannot choose the colors
> He worketh steadily.
>
> Oft times He weaveth sorrow
> And I, in foolish pride,
> Forget He sees the upper,
> And I the underside.[28]

Although this poem may be comforting to some people, I am not convinced it is an accurate reflection of causation as experienced in the world or as understood in Christian theology. More on this later.

Many people, including famous ones like Marilyn Monroe and Albert Schweitzer, think "the universe" has a purpose, and "everything happens for a reason."[29] In general, we all need meaning and purpose in our lives. Cause-and-effect relations offer explanations, thus providing meaning. We like to be in control of our lives, for things to make sense. Even those without any religious affiliation believe in providence. Popular discussions on this topic often confuse reason and response. We can choose to *respond* to tragedy by learning from it or creating something meaningful, but this does not mean that the actual *cause* of the tragedy involved a specific reason. When things don't make sense, or if our beliefs about causation are challenged by new information, we are not happy. No one likes being wrong, so we either insist on our original view or make up extra explanations to justify our beliefs and help things make sense.[30] There is a lot of inconsistency between what we believe and how we act. Some people readily claim that evil spirits caused their illness, but they happily seek medication or surgery to treat it, seemingly unaware of the discrepancy between their beliefs and their behavior. Physicist Stephen Hawking observes, "I have noticed that even people who claim everything is predetermined and that we can do nothing to change it look before they cross the road."[31]

Christians' misconceptions and inconsistencies about causation are compounded by theological misunderstandings. A well-meaning friend once told me that if a certain tragedy hadn't happened, I would never have grown in my faith. I remember thinking that God is God: surely he's flexible enough to teach us lessons without making us suffer. And, just because God may bring good out of circumstances, does not mean that he caused the situation in the first place. On another occasion I was shedding tears of stress in church, being in the midst of an overwhelming move. The kind pastor counseled, "I don't know why God allowed this to happen." But moving is typically stressful for everyone—no theological explanations needed.

In my psychotherapy practice, I commonly encounter people who attribute causation directly to God, and sometimes use bizarre justifications for this belief. A woman with depression insisted that she was "where God wants her." I wisely resisted asking why she was taking medication for depression if this was something God wanted. Another, whose son died tragically, stated, "No-one leaves this earth a minute too soon." I wonder if this pronouncement and its implied meaning, that God planned the death, was her way of justifying the event and avoiding the work of grief. I have also heard many sermons that have causal assumptions. One pastor claimed that God made us "fat or thin, with gray hair or not." I think the message was about trusting in God's control, but the physician in me knows that gray hair develops with age, and weight is affected by diet, exercise, and other factors.

People often rely on hindsight to help them feel better, and can be quite confident in their claims about how and why things happened. A recently-divorced acquaintance stated that God only wanted her to be married for two years (perhaps a convenient way to avoid responsibility). A science colleague shared that when his book was rejected by one publisher, who also gave a long critique, he revised the manuscript and published it elsewhere. He thought the result was better and attributed this to providence. However, it's also the normal process involved in the book publication process.

Some people believe that all good things are from God, and all bad things are from the devil. They forget about human sin, and the many other causative factors that affect life. Our desire for simple causal explanations frequently leads us to adopt false dichotomies. Some people think that either God micromanages everything or that life is completely random and purposeless. Perhaps this helps them make sense of the world, but they neglect the gray areas of causation and the nuances of interpreting it.

A woman prays for sunshine at her party but forgets about the farmer next door who needs rain. People may think that they did not get COVID-19 because they take care of their health, implicitly judging others who *did* get the disease. A recent social trend is sports teams who pray for a win—do they think God has favorites? We tend to be self-centered in our assumptions. Whenever I question people about their causal beliefs (irritating of me, I know), they often change their responses, but the inconsistency remains. I doubt that many people believe that there are profound reasons for burning supper, losing keys, or being stuck in traffic. But how do they decide which events have deep reasons?

Many of these examples are trivial. However, there can be some serious consequences for having simplistic beliefs about causation. I have heard many stories of people feeling deeply hurt by fellow Christians who assured them that God intended their suffering. They often feel blamed. When we find a "cause" or a reason for someone else's problem, perhaps secretly thinking they deserve it, it helps us feel better. Such views feed prejudice. Our beliefs on why things happen can also absolve us of responsibility. If I think that God "made" me lazy, I will accomplish little in life. If I think that God "planned" my marriage failure, I will not learn from my own mistakes. Some people abandon their faith because they have only been taught that God causes everything. This perspective does not help them make sense of the suffering they see and experience, so they reject Christianity.

To be fair, not everyone has inconsistent or oversimplified beliefs about causation. I recall hearing one pastor, when he requested prayer for a friend with lung disease, advise the congregation, "Don't smoke." Clearly, he thought that cigarettes, not God, caused the disease. It is also likely that people do have more nuanced views on causation but do not express themselves well. My anecdotes have many possible complex psychological and theological explanations, but they nevertheless serve to illustrate the misunderstanding and inconsistency that exists surrounding how and why things happen.

WHAT ARE SOME PROBLEMS WITH HOW WE VIEW CAUSATION?

Those who believe that COVID-19 is a hoax, or that the blood of Jesus protects them from contracting the disease, may not follow preventive measures recommended by public health agencies. Consequently, they have a higher likelihood of contracting the disease. This is just one example of how important it is for us to have a good understanding of causation in creation and Christianity. Yet we don't. Creation is complex, humans are complex, and God, especially with respect to his interaction with the world, is complex.

The problem is not so much that we lack information, but that we insist on simplistic explanations. We also tend to separate our experience in the world from our Christian faith, making glib comments about God causing all things without thinking about how this works in creation. Furthermore, our brains are wired to seek meaning. We do not like it that causes cannot always be found or that sometimes stuff just happens. And, as sinful beings, we are often self-serving, wanting to be in control.

As we will learn in subsequent chapters, the world that God created is majestic but multiplex. From teensy particles to glorious galaxies, everything intertwines in webs of causation and consequences. Much of the natural world is self-sustaining. It includes uncertainty and randomness that contribute to its beauty and proper functioning. But, when multiple causative factors are involved, sometimes things go wrong. Humans are perhaps the most complicated of all creatures. The only ones to even be thinking about issues discussed in this book. Our minds are efficient in evaluating the world, but sometimes we oversimplify and/or jump to the wrong conclusions. And most of us have difficulty admitting when we are wrong.

The triune God is mighty and mysterious; evident in both Scripture and experience. He lovingly cares for his creation and his creatures, but engages with the world in variable and complicated ways. God has gifted his creation with tremendous freedom, and with this comes tremendous responsibility. He wants us to join him in caring for creation, and in developing our characters as creatures made in his image.

We don't like problems such as when God "answers" one person's prayer and not another's, or when good things happen to bad people. We like to think that we know what happens and why. But the problem is that we assume the issue is with God whereas, most of the time, the problem can be explained by either the complexity of the world, and/or the complexity and usual operations of our human minds. It is our assumptions that are usually incorrect. Life, perhaps especially the Christian life, is not simple. Truth is rich and deep.

Overall, there appears to be a mismatch: causation is complicated, but our judgments of it are simple. Our minds are designed to find meaning, the result being that often we find meaning where there is none. We need to acknowledge the complexities of creation and the foibles of human reasoning. This mismatch is a problem not just because it is an inaccurate reflection of reality, but because it can have important consequences for our choices and actions. As I mentioned above, misconstruing causation, especially from a Christian perspective, can result in us responding insensitively to suffering, or neglecting personal and social responsibility.

For those who believe in a sovereign God who created, cares for, and sustains his world, issues of causality become more complex, and perhaps have more personal meaning. I suggest three issues that are important for a Christian understanding of how and why things happen:

- the complex nature of a created world that has inbuilt causal processes

- the complex nature of humans who reflect on causation, especially with respect to discerning God's action in the world

- the complex nature and degree of God's involvement and interaction with the world.

Another problem is that there is little Christian writing on causation in everyday life or on how we think about it. There is much written on the problem of evil, the nature of God's action in the world, and the varying views of divine sovereignty and providence. These relate to causation only indirectly. In the science-faith dialogue, the topic of causation has focused on arguments for the existence of God and how he created the universe. There is little discussion on cause and explanation at the level of our everyday experience. I believe that viewing some of these issues through the lens of causation may benefit both Christian belief and practice. And, of course, viewing causation through the lens of Christianity is what we are called to do. As Christians, we need to consider cause-and-effect relations in the world carefully and seriously, recognizing the presence of God's Spirit in the world and within us.

HOW WILL WE ADDRESS THESE PROBLEMS?

I'm writing this book to address these and other questions about how and why things happen, from within a Christian perspective. To more deeply understand the many natural, human, and spiritual forces that impact our lives. To increase our wisdom about all the wonderful things in the world. In the first section of this study, we will consider biblical and theological writings about cause and effect, because the Lord God made everything. Then we will address all creatures great and small—namely how causation is understood by mathematicians and scientists. (Hint: it's complicated.) In the next section, we discuss the wise and wonderful things pertaining to the human mind-brain and our perception of how and why things happen. This includes thinking errors and moral failings. Psychology and Christianity offer some tips on how to improve our evaluation of causation. We conclude the book by considering ways we can apply this knowledge in our daily lives in order to live as faithful and wise servants of Christ. It is my hope that not only will we be better informed about this important topic, but also that our Christian lives and ministries may be enhanced.

Throughout the book, I will use information gleaned from many different disciplines, illustrating this with everyday examples and stories. I will especially use examples of cause and effect in illness—this is common in the Bible and in our experience and is also a common reason why people ask questions about causation. I endeavor to write with wisdom, humility, and humor, somewhat resonating with the author of Ecclesiastes:

I . . . applied my mind to seek and to search out by wisdom all that is done under heaven; it is an unhappy business that God has given to human beings to be busy with.

ECCL 1:13

ENDNOTES

1. Mackie, *Cement of the Universe*.

2. The philosophy of knowledge is known as *epistemology*. Primary types of knowledge are propositional (knowing that), procedural (knowing how), locational (knowing where), and acquaintance (knowing a person). Robert Audi suggests four basic sources of knowledge: perception, memory, consciousness, and reason (*Epistemology*). See also Evans and Smith, *Knowledge*.

3. Polanyi, *Tacit Dimension*, 4. He notes the importance of individual perspective and emphasizes *knowing* rather than knowledge. Polanyi, *Personal Knowledge*. The category *nonconceptual* applies if content cannot be represented conceptually, or if listeners don't understand or can't articulate the concept. Gunther, *Nonconceptual Content*.

4. Steven Sloman states, "causal relations hold across space, time, and individuals; therefore, the logic of causality is the best guide to prediction, explanation, and action" (*Causal Models*, 11).

5. This is the philosophical approach, adopted by many scientists, of *critical realism*: the view that there is an actual, objective reality "out there," beyond ourselves, but that we can only comprehend this reality by interacting with it and interpreting it. E.g., Bhaskar, *Realist Theory*, 12–20; Pearcey, *Total Truth*, 295–302.

6. The idea that we can understand God through observations of creation is known as natural theology and was developed by William Paley in the nineteenth century (*Natural Theology*). See also McGrath; *Science of God*.

7. Other types of revelation are general/natural (our experience of and reasoning about the created world) and inspired or historical (the Holy Bible). E.g., McIntosh, *Discernment and Truth*, 215–55.

8. Religious experience can be defined broadly as "any experience by which a religious belief is acquired, deepened or confirmed." Clouser, *Knowing with the Heart*, 12.

9. When asked to explain how they can be certain that the voice is God's, the usual response is nonanalytical: they "just know" or "it feels right." For anecdotes see Jersak,

Can You Hear Me?; for empirical studies, see Parker, *Led by Spirit,* 20–38, 62–116; Luhrmann, *God Talks Back,* 39–71.

10. Tornau, "Saint Augustine." See also Davies, *Creativity of God,* 5–8, 20–8.

11. E.g., McNamara, *Religious Experience;* Sears, "Nature of Experience."

12. Premodern scholars, such as Origen, Augustine, and Aquinas, referred to imagination, reason, emotions, and religious experience in knowledge. However, in the eighteenth century it was thought that the highest nature of humans was to live as rational beings, with passions subdued. The last few decades have witnessed a recovery of scholarly interest in emotions, imagination, and figurative language. E.g., Avis, *God and Imagination;* Coakley, "Introduction"; Davies, *Creativity of God.*

13. E.g., Ricoeur, *Rule of Metaphor. Conceptual metaphor theory* was developed by George Lakoff and Mark Johnson (*Metaphors We Live By*) and has been very influential. They argue that metaphors are based on conceptual correspondence between ideas, not simply similarities. Metaphors are largely irreducible and non-translatable; they are neurological not just linguistic, permeate thoughts and actions, and reflect our worldviews.

14. Paradoxes are absurd or self-contradictory statements of concepts that often occur when we misapply rules from one realm to another. E.g., Pearl and Mackenzie, *Book of Why,* 189–218; Yanofsky, *Outer Limits,* 15–64.

15. E.g., Psillos, *Causation and Explanation;* Sloman, *Causal Models;* Mumford and Anjum, *Causation:* Paul and Hall, *Causation;* Pearl and Mackenzie, *Book of Why.*

16. Falcon, "Aristotle on Causality." Aquinas adopted his theory; see Clayton, "Natural Law."

17. Aristotle used the term *entelechy* to denote an internal principle of growth and perfection that can guide an object or organism to actualize its potential qualities. Cohen, "Aristotle's Metaphysics."

18. John Polkinghorne similarly considers why a kettle is boiling: because of electrical factors or because I want a cup of tea ("Is Science Enough?").

19. Hume originally noted the importance of resemblance, contiguity in space and time, and causality in making associations. See Vyse, *Believing in Magic,* 75–100.

20. Sometimes referred to as causal structure. E.g., Sloman, *Causal Models;* Hitchcock, "Causal Models." These are also noted in psychology. Kim et al., "Centrality of Causal Cycles."

21. Vigen, *Spurious Correlations.*

22. Hume believes that we cannot see causation—all we know is a series of events; there is no direction, correlation only. In contrast, Thomas Reid thinks we can see aspects of causation, such as a person bending the springboard before diving.

23. Kirkpatrick uses this example with respect to discerning divine action (*Mystery and Agency,* 139).

24. He suggests that we need an inference engine that incorporates inputs and outputs. Pearl and Mackenzie, *Book of Why,* 27–31, 259–98.

25. E.g., Chambliss and Schutt, *Social World,* 106–11.

26. E.g., Sloman, *Causal Models,* 101–15. Discussed further in chapter 6.

27. Philip Yancey, *Prayer,* 261–4

28. Benjamin Malacia Franklin, "Just a Weaver," public domain.

29. E.g., Navilon, "Everything happens for a reason."

30. Two common practices are to assume cause in the context of necessity (finding other conditions to explain failed causal relations) and to assume cause in the context of probability (assuming a cause based on prior belief in its likelihood). Harré, "Discourse Frame."

31. Hawking, *Black Holes,* 170.

PART 1

The Lord God Made Them All

IT MAY SEEM STRANGE to begin with the last line of the refrain that forms the title of this book, but I think it is the most important. As a Christian, I like to base my views on biblical and theological understandings. When we wonder how and why things happen in the world, we are also asking the question of how, when, and where God acts. Yet we often forget to integrate our questions. God made all things wise and wonderful; in order for us to appreciate these better, we need to think about why and how he made them, and indeed, continues to do so.

In this section, we first look at what we can infer about cause and effect in the Bible, especially with respect to illness and healing. Scripture mentions many factors that make things happen in creation. In chapter 3, we discuss some aspects of causation within Christian theology, such as God's character, presence, and activity. The sovereign Lord is big enough and flexible enough to interact with all the complex causes in his world. We also consider some models that help us understand divine action. We ask: What are some agent and non-agent causes in the Bible? Is there only one cause or many? What is our responsibility in the world? Does everything happen for a reason? What are some ways we can envision God's interaction with creation?

2

What Does the Bible Say
about Causation?

ONE OF MY COUNSELING clients was convinced that God had a particular plan for her life, with it turning out exactly as she wanted, and that he would punish the people who had mistreated her. She cited Proverbs 16:4: "The Lord has made everything for its purpose, even the wicked for the day of trouble."[1] However, Proverbs is poetic in style—such literature tends to use hyperbole and is not meant to be read literally or applied to our individual circumstances. When read in context, the point of this proverb is to encourage faithfulness, wisdom, and righteous living. The reference to punishment of the wicked is likely an example of a general cause-and-consequence principle, not applicable to every circumstance. And we always need to consider the entire Bible, which, as we will see, describes multiple types of cause and effect.

Many Christians are guilty of citing a few favorite verses to support their views on how and why things happen. One common view is that God causes everything that happens, including pandemics. Consider this example from an apologetics website. Using Job 37:6 ("For to the snow he says, 'Fall on the earth'") and the few verses following, the author concludes that God causes the weather. But biblical scholars view the book of Job as wisdom literature; poetic and not meant to be interpreted as a description of scientific phenomena like the weather. The author of this article insists that God has a reason for all happenings, although he somewhat confusingly notes that actions have natural consequences, and doesn't explain how causes can be both divinely ordained and natural.[2] Another writer also uses Job to support the common claim that everything is sifted through the fingers of God.[3] I'm sure these authors intend to encourage faith, but our trust in the Lord should not depend on simplistic interpretations of his Word.

I love the Bible. There is so much that happens and so many layers of meaning in each passage. Although considering how and why things happen is not a priority in God's Word, if we evaluate it carefully, it can provide guidance for navigating the complexities of life. What we believe about biblical teaching on causation will affect how we act in the world. A proper understanding may help us to exercise our faith more responsibly.

I should point out that Scripture focuses more on the nature of the triune God and his interaction with humans, than on the nature of nature and God's interaction with it. It does not describe an explicit, scientific, or logical account of causation. Biblical authors are more concerned with questions of *why*, not *how*, or, as Aristotle may say, *final* causes rather than material or efficient ones.[4] They ask questions related to meaning, their relationship with God, his presence, and his absence. When the psalmist laments, "Why, O Lord, do you stand far off?" (Ps 10:1), he is rhetorically expressing grief, rather than asking a literal question.

Nevertheless, information about how and why things happen can be *inferred* from biblical texts. It is present in stories of healing and other miracles, in teaching about suffering, and in words of lament. It is present in discussions about God's care for his creation. The Bible discusses outcomes caused by the direct action of personal beings—divine, human, and sometimes even demonic. It also mentions events caused by factors in nature. And it sometimes describes happenings that have no specific explanation or are caused by many different things.

Illness and healing are common occurrences in biblical stories. Being physically and mentally unwell is such a frequent source of lament in Scripture that it is often used as a metaphor for suffering. David writes, "Be gracious to me, O Lord, for I am languishing; O Lord, heal me, for my bones are shaking with terror" (Ps 6:2).[5] His poetry is filled with figurative language. Illness is also a common source of questioning in our current world. Therefore, examining how the Bible depicts causation in the world and God's interaction with it can help us develop a Christian perspective on how and why things happen. It may also inform our response to global disasters.

HOW SHOULD WE UNDERSTAND
AND INTERPRET THE BIBLE?

The Bible does not explain COVID-19. Instead, it tells the story of God creating a world filled with creatures with whom he lovingly interacts. It teaches about God's care and involvement with his creation. The Word of God is presented primarily as a story. It is in narrative format, incorporating metaphor, myth, parable, and poetry—recall how important figurative language is for revealing complex truth. So, when psalmists describe mountains trembling and the earth melting (Ps 46:3,6), or Behemoth, a mythic monster (Job 40:15) not a dinosaur,[6] they are not referring to the scientific nature of creation. Like poets today, the psalmists use illustrations from nature to reveal truths about the nature of God.

As well as noting the literary genre of a biblical passage—poetry, history, parable, chronology—we need to consider its context.[7] This can include editorial aspects, such as its relation to passages before and after, and even its placement in the canon of Scripture. Historical and cultural contexts are also important. Think about the world in which biblical authors lived and what was important to them—in many cases, their style of writing and the things they are concerned about are different from ours. Finally, we need to remember that practically every word in the Bible serves a larger theological purpose. Stories of Jesus healing people are not simply historical reports, but show that, by his actions, he is the promised Messiah (Matt 15:31).

Some biblical texts are frustratingly fluid and ambiguous: "Lord" and "Angel of the Lord" are sometimes used interchangeably (Gen 16:7–14; Exod 3:2–6); in the Exodus story, both God and Pharaoh are said to harden Pharaoh's heart (Exod 7:3, 8:32); in the story of the deliverance at Gerasa, Matthew states there are two men, whereas Mark and Luke only mention one. Biblical authors freely interchange references to individuals and groups: both Solomon and thousands of laborers are said to have built the temple (1 Kgs 5–6). They understood precision differently from contemporary Western Christians.

In addition, the Bible relates many unique, theologically significant occurrences. When God causes wet wood to catch fire, it is to prove his superiority over false gods (1 Kgs 18:20–40). When Jesus speaks spectacularly to Saul on the road to Damascus, it is to call him to spread the Gospel to the Gentiles (Acts 9:1–18). These experiences are exceptional and not meant to be taken as normative.[8] We need to be cautious about generalizing and extrapolating biblical stories to fit with all situations in life. Furthermore, Old and New Testament authors view cause and effect differently, partly related to the times they lived in. The Israelites inhabited a culture that worshipped many gods; therefore, biblical teaching emphasized monotheism—Yahweh being the only true God, the ultimate cause. In contrast, the Gospels were written in a culture that accepted natural and demonic causes of events in addition to divine causes. We need to remember this in our interpretations.

Ambiguity can be challenging for those of us who like clear, simple, scientific-like explanations. Contemporary Western society tends to favor rational and logical approaches over imaginative ones. It's helpful to compare methods of scientific inquiry with those of theology. Scientists use empirical strategies to investigate creation, forming and testing hypotheses, then developing theories based on their findings. Some of these last; others are replaced by new theories. Biblical scholars use literary, linguistic, and historical methods. They rely on insight from the Christian tradition and inspiration from the Holy Spirit. Their observations have validity two millennia later. Science is a methodology and a body of knowledge; it does not address questions of meaning and ultimacy. Christianity teaches transcendent truths, offering personal hope, comfort, and challenge, as well as communal relationships and a body of knowledge. Despite these differences, we inhabit the same world as biblical authors did, albeit in different cultures and contexts, and learning about causation is possible. We merely need to be responsible in how we draw conclusions from the Bible.

WHAT ARE SOME NATURAL CAUSES IN THE BIBLE?

The second verse of the well-known hymn "Great Is Thy Faithfulness" includes a reference to God's promise to Noah: "seedtime and harvest, cold and heat, summer and winter, day and night, shall not cease" (Gen 8:22). There is natural order in the world depicted in Scripture. Seasons happen without a direct cause, or the involvement of an agent, but simply because nature has inbuilt regularities. The Bible also refers to random and unknown or unspecified factors that are a part of creation and can cause things to happen.

Order, Cause, and Effect

Consider a classic text on original creation: Genesis 1 focuses on order and separation, the creation of a holy space, set apart from the darkness of the world.[9] A place where God can live in his creation and walk with his creatures. The Creator separates and organizes light and dark, land and sea (Gen 1:4, 9); he then gifts these spaces with the ability to produce vegetation and living creatures (Gen 1:11, 20, 24). Already we can see that God allows for some independence in creation; it is to be self-perpetuating. He does not need to directly *cause* every new being—he designed the world so that it can multiply on its own.

Genesis describes creation as *ṭôb*. However, rather than a Western idea of perfection, the biblical term implies purpose and order, functional goodness.[10] This implies that there is room for improvement. Humans are given responsibility for caring for creation, making it better (Gen 1:28). This idea is developed further in the biblical story: the temple and laws for Israel provide structure for keeping life orderly; followers of Christ are instructed to develop the church as a way to order the world, by evangelizing and practicing charity.[11]

God "gives the sun for light by day and the fixed order of the moon and the stars for light by night" (Jer 31:35). People die "natural" deaths (Num 16:29). These and other texts imply a creational infrastructure—an inbuilt foundation in which cause and effect occur naturally, without intervention. Recall dispositional or intrinsic causation: aspects of the world are self-causing. Biblical scholar Terence Fretheim points out that God does not have to maintain the world on a daily basis. The created order itself, through propagation for example, participates in the act of creation. God does not micromanage but uses constraint and restraint; he lets creation be.[12] We could say there is a season to everything (Eccl. 3:1), but not necessarily a reason.

"The sun rises and the sun goes down" (Eccl 1:5). "When clouds are full, they empty rain on the earth; Whether a tree falls to the south or to the north . . . there it will lie" (Eccl 11:3). Biblical authors and their audience, although they did not use contemporary scientific categories, observed regularities in nature, such as weather cycles and gravity. The psalmists praise God for nature, for making grass grow and providing rain (Ps 147:8). When Jesus teaches about loving one's enemies, he points out that weather is independent of character: "He makes his sun rise on the evil and the good, and sends rain on the righteous and on the unrighteous" (Matt 5:45). Although God is described as the cause of the weather in this and other texts, it is in a general, indirect manner. As Creator, he cares for his world, but this does not mean he *directly causes* every sunrise. Often there is no reference to God; weather is assumed to be a natural phenomenon, caused by seasons and wind (Prov 25:23; Ezra 10:9; Jas 5:7).

"The locusts have no king, yet all of them march in rank" (Prov 30:7). Proverbs often describe order in creation, with no causal assumptions. In fact, many apparent cause-and-effect statements in the Bible are simple observations about the nature of the world. They are not necessarily accounts of God's causative action in the world. Paul uses a farming example to illustrate how human behaviors have natural consequences: "you reap whatever you sow" (Gal 6:7). Cause-and-effect assertions are typically descriptive, not explanatory. They are closer to Aristotle's material or efficient levels, not final levels. It is also important to note that statements about how things happen are not definite promises. The proverb "Train children in the right way, and when old, they will not stray" (Prov 22:6) describes a general pattern of action that will most likely produce a positive result.[13] As most parents know, there is no guarantee as to how their children turn out.

Biblical scholar Frederick Gaiser investigates cause and effect in the Bible, focusing on weather. He notes that "sometimes, it just snows" (2 Sam: 23:20) and "sometimes it just rains, and even the disciples will get cold and wet" (referring to Paul's experience on Malta; Acts 28:2).[14] He suggests that multiple views of causality are helpful: empirical knowledge can balance moral perspectives, complexity and uncertainty can balance mechanistic understandings, and mystical views can balance pragmatic ones. I agree that the more different viewpoints we have, the better we will understand how and why things happen. We need to examine many different biblical texts to learn about causation. When they seem to contradict each other, we need to accept ambiguity and complexity.

Disorder and Chance

The ostrich "deals cruelly with its young" (Job 39:16), severe famines occur without warning (Gen 12:10), and the wilderness contains "poisonous snakes and scorpions" (Deut 8:15). There is much in the Bible that we don't like—messy, ugly, unpredictable things. In short, disorder. Most of this is attributed to human sin and evil forces, or God punishing disobedience. However, some of it seems to be a normal part of life. In ancient cultures, the *deep*, *darkness*, and *waste* commonly symbolized chaos and disorder. When he creates the world, God does not eliminate this chaos, but separates it.[15] Elements of disorder remain. There is both birth and death, war and peace, mourning and dancing (Eccl 3:2–8). Biblical authors seemed to accept that disasters occurred in life—earthquakes and fire (1 Kgs 19:11–12), storm and shipwrecks (Acts 27:13–44), vipers (Acts 28:3). Paul teaches that suffering is inevitable (Rom 5:3; 8:18); indeed, all of creation is in "bondage to decay" (Rom 8:21).

The Genesis 2 creation account tells the legendary story of Eden. In this garden, the first humans would have observed cause and effect in nature, both good and not so good. They would have experienced rain, possibly hurricanes and droughts. They may have discovered rotten apples. If Adam fell out of a tree, he would have injured himself. Accidents would have happened. When the humans are cursed, God tells the woman her pain in childbirth would be multiplied (Gen 3:16). This suggests that there was already pain—a natural and sometimes beneficial, if unwanted, effect of childbirth. Not everything was blissful: as one author puts it, there were "mosquitos in paradise."[16]

Those living in the ancient world also seemed to be aware of the concept of chance or *randomness*—qualities, situations, or events that have no pattern and are unpredictable. They used methods that involved chance, such as casting lots to make decisions (Josh 18:6–10; Jon 1:7). The Bible also states that some things occur by chance, not the hand of God (1 Sam 6:9), and that much is uncertain: "In the morning sow your seed, and at evening do not let your hands be idle; for you do not know which will prosper . . . "(Eccl 11:6). Jesus rebukes his audience for thinking that the men who died "when the tower in Siloam fell on them" were more guilty than others (Luke 13:4). He clearly does not connect their death to their behavior, and he seems to imply that this was a natural occurrence or a random accident.

Fretheim thinks that biblical teaching is compatible with the ideas of chance and imprecision. The world is reliable, but it is not static; there are elements of unpredictability and novelty. He suggests that God created the world with some disorderliness in order to allow for human participation and creativity.[17] I think that the COVID-19 pandemic is a good example of disorder in the world. According to biblical principles, humans are mandated to use our God-given abilities to restore order, through scientific (developing a vaccine, finding treatments), social (caring for others), and spiritual (praying) means.

WHAT ARE SOME PERSONAL CAUSES IN THE BIBLE?

When Jesus heals a blind man, he tenderly touches him and spreads saliva on his eyes (Mark 8:23). This causative action is direct and intentional, dependent entirely on Jesus's behavior. Agents can also affect things indirectly, by influencing situations and people. It is not always easy to distinguish between direct and indirect causation; however, the style of language can give us some clues. When authors use the passive voice, this usually signifies an indirect cause: Ruth "happens" to wander into the field belonging to Boaz (Ruth 2:3)—I suspect that God guides her, but the text is unclear.[18] Let's now look at some personal agents that make things happen in biblical stories. It is important to note that, despite my subdivisions, humans and evil spirits are created beings—not in the same category as the triune God. Their abilities have been given to them by the Creator.

God

As the hymn says, "The Lord God made them all." Indeed, the Father, Son, and Holy Spirit have causative abilities. God creates the world with a series of "let there be" statements (Gen 1:3–27); Jesus expels demons "with a word" (Matt 8:16). Some biblical verses are clear about God's causative activities. However, before we glibly conclude that God causes everything, we should carefully evaluate what the Bible says about how, when, and why God acts. Divine causation is related to the nature of God and his love for his creation. He is motivated to act because of this love. Although God is all powerful, he does not use his causal powers arbitrarily or unilaterally. He is present within his creation and within those who love him; consequently, he primarily acts from within these locations. God's actions are not random but related to his purposes for his people and his kingdom.

First, let's consider the nature of God as revealed in Scripture. He is holy and almighty (Rev 4:8) but also loving and forgiving (John 3:16; 1 John 4:8, 16). He abounds with compassion and is slow to anger (Ps 30:5). God is flexible in his dealings with wayward Israel; he changes his mind (Exod 32:14) and regrets his past actions (1 Sam 15:11). He is also extremely responsive to his people, expressing disappointment, anger, and sadness (Jer 3:19,20; Matt 21:12, 23:1–39; Luke 19:41).[19] The Bible depicts a God who is more concerned with people than with events, with holiness (Eph 1:4, 5:27; 1 Pet 1:15, 16) than with happenings, with character (Rom 5:3–5; Col 3:12) than with circumstance, with care than with control. Incidentally, this partly explains why the Bible teaches little about causation: God has different priorities.

Second, because action and presence are naturally related, it is important to consider what Scripture says about God's presence in creation. He fills heaven and earth (Jer 23:24), is nearby (Jer 23:23), "not far from each one of us" (Acts 17:27), and is present wherever two or three are gathered in his name (Matt 18:20). His majesty and provision are present in nature (Isa 40:12; Matt 5:45; Heb 1:3). However, Old Testament writings are fluid and ambiguous regarding the dwelling place of God: heaven (Pss 2:4, 53:2, 80:14), the temple (1 Kgs 8:10–13, Ps 11:4), eternity (Isa 57:15), Mount Zion (Pss 20:2, 65:1, 74:2).[20] They also suggest that divine presence is stronger in certain people, places, and times than others, such as Samson (Judg 13:25, 14:6,19, 15:14) and Saul (1 Sam 10:6,10, 16:13). God even withdraws his presence on occasion (Ezek 8:6, 10:18).[21] In the Gospels, Jesus, as the Spirit-filled son of God, embodies divine presence and action. He has authority to forgive sins and heal people. After Christ's ascension, his followers are given the Holy Spirit, who acts within the Christian community to inspire, teach, and heal. The indwelling Spirit means that God's presence is stronger in followers of Christ. This presence inspires godly action.

A few years ago, a local Christian organization built an impressive reproduction of the biblical temple for people to physically experience. However, the temple in Scripture also has symbolic significance, a connection between heaven and earth. As the primary place where Israelites encounter God, the temple contains degrees of holiness. Building on this, biblical scholars suggest that all reality can be understood as graded or hierarchical.[22] Places and people closest to God are most holy; those furthest from him are least holy, or evil. Holiness, tied to the presence of God, is not uniform. It exists on a continuum. Fretheim claims that "God is present on every occasion and active in every event," although there are indications of "varying intensifications of the divine presence in the world."[23] In other words, at certain times and places God is *more* present and active than at other times and places. Biblical theologian Michael Welker goes further and suggests that divine absence is possible: "the Spirit is present in that which is *held together* and *enlivened* by God—but not . . . in that which is decaying to dust . . . through falseness and unrighteousness human beings can grieve and banish God's Spirit."[24] This is important for understanding how and why things happen. If God is far away or even absent at times, we cannot claim that he directly causes everything that happens. Things can happen apart from his presence. We need to evaluate causation differently in situations where God is honored than in situations where he is rejected.

Third, let's look at what the Bible says about God's causative actions. He creates and sustains the world (Ps 104). Much divine action involves restoring the order of creation that was lost because of sin and the actions of evil spiritual forces. God provides structure to Israel by separating clean and unclean aspects of the world. Jesus restores order by expelling evil spirits and healing people. Numerous stories show God directing his people. When God needs something done, it happens: his promise to Abraham, his covenant with Israel, his deliverance of Israel, the incarnation, crucifixion, and resurrection. His Spirit acts generally in the world, convicting people of sin, offering forgiveness, and guiding towards goodness. However, there is no biblical evidence that the Lord acts *all the time in all things*. God directs particular people for particular purposes: Moses, Jonah, Mary, Paul. Jesus heals and delivers people to demonstrate that the kingdom of God has arrived (Matt 12:28; 15:31). As biblical scholar Bruce Waltke notes, when God intervenes in human history, it is primarily to reveal truth (Paul's experience on the road to Damascus; Acts 9:1–19) or to save his people from intolerable situations in order for them to spread the Gospel (freeing disciples from prison; Acts 12:6–11, 16:25–29).[25] We need to keep these principles in mind when considering God's action in our world today.

The Bible depicts God speaking and acting in many and various ways: from whirlwinds (Job) to whispers (Elijah), from drama (the Exodus; the story of Jonah) to dreams (Joseph, Daniel), from tongue-lashing (Matt 23:1–36) to tender touch (Matt 20:34; John 13:1–20). God often uses other beings to do his will: he sends angels as messengers (Judg 6:11–21; Acts 8:26) and protectors (Ps 34:8; Acts 10:22); he uses pagan nations to punish the Israelites (Hab 1:6); and he empowers humans to act (Bezalel and Oholiab, Exod 35:30–35; the disciples, Luke 9:1–6). It is clear that God gives his creatures causative powers, and want us to use them responsibly.

Humans

During the Covid-19 pandemic we saw people acting in ways that help humanity and honor God, and ways that . . . are not so helpful. The Bible has similar examples. David praises the Lord with exuberance (1 Chr 29:10; 2 Sam 6:14) and also commits adultery (2 Sam 11:2–5). Many biblical characters cause things to happen—both good and bad. Fortunately, Scripture provides some guidance about how we should act.

First, humans are charged with caring for creation and one another; we are "created . . . for good works" (Eph 2:10) and are called to rule over the earth (Gen 1:28). This implies both humble, hard work and commanding authority. Creation is undeveloped—we are responsible for its development. Like priests, we are to represent God and exercise faithful stewardship (1 Pet 4:10).[26] The Lord gives the Israelites detailed instructions about moral behavior and purity laws (Exod 20; Lev 5–7). Jesus provides his followers with commands that surpass the law—their righteousness must exceed that of the Pharisees, and even lust is considered adultery (Matt 5:17–48). James gives practical instructions to "care for orphans and widows" (Jas 1:27). Moral and societal responsibility mean that humans have an independent ability, indeed responsibility, to cause things to happen.

Second, since we are created in God's image, we are capable of acting as creators and of being in relationship with God and one another. But we are not God; we can *choose* whether or not to follow him. This freedom can be good, bad, or neutral. God gave the first humans freedom to eat from any tree except one; they were not told what to have for supper on any particular day or how to prepare it. Their choice to eat from the one prohibited tree was a bad one, but their choice of what to eat for supper was neutral.

Third, the way in which the Bible commands human responsibility is through action: we can choose the ways of righteousness or wickedness (Deut 5:33; Prov 2:12–15, 15:19–24), we can "enter" the kingdom or the narrow gate (Matt 5:20, 18:3,8,9), and choose the "way" (Mark 10:52; John 14:4–6). Our choices have consequences, and our action or inaction produces effects. Recall what happened when the first humans disobeyed God.

Fourth, Scripture includes many *therefore* and *if-then* statements: "If you heed these ordinances, by diligently observing them, the Lord your God will maintain with you the covenant loyalty . . ." (Deut 7:12). Human action has effects. Proverbs is full of action-and-consequence statements: "A slack hand causes poverty, but the hand of the diligent makes rich" (Prov 10:4); "A soft answer turns away wrath, but a harsh word stirs up anger" (Prov 15:1). There is much biblical teaching about rewards for obedience, primarily blessings, and punishment for disobedience. In the Exodus story, God gives Pharaoh many opportunities to "let my people go" and warns him about the plagues that would follow disobedience (Exod 9:1–6). The Israelites are held responsible for obeying the law: "If any of you sin without knowing it, doing any of the things that by the Lord's commandments ought not to be done, you . . . are subject to punishment" (Lev 5:17). In the New Testament, Jesus teaches that those who follow his commands will enter the kingdom of God (Luke 18:18–30). The book of Acts contains many examples of the disciples using their agency responsibly. They preach the Gospel (Acts 4:8–12; 7:2–53), care for those in need (Acts 2:45), and heal many people (Acts 3:7; 9:40; 19:12).

Finally, the Bible suggests that humans are responsible not only to obey but also to work with God. The author of Hebrews notes that "every house is built by someone, but the builder of all things is God" (Heb 3:4). Paul teaches the Corinthians that they are coworkers, planting and watering seeds, but overall God is to be praised (1 Cor 3:6–9). The Israelites defeat their enemies when Moses holds up a staff as commanded by God (Exod 17:8–13). Divine-human cooperation is often assumed. The most helpful interpretation of the much misunderstood and misapplied statement in Romans 8:28 is in a footnote of the NIV translation: "in all things God works together with those who love him to bring about what is good." God works *with us* more than for us. There appears to be a reciprocal relationship between divine and human action, but exactly how this works is unclear, as in the statement, "The human mind plans the way, but the Lord directs the steps" (Prov 16:9). The Lord guides us but we are responsible for listening to him, following him, and working with him, according to the grace and gifts he's given us.

Of course, human causation is complicated. In many biblical stories people make sinful choices that affect themselves and others. Humans may have multiple motives, and their intent is difficult to discern. As Paul states, "I do not do the good I want, but the evil I do not want is what I do" (Rom 7:19). Human sin complicates our understanding of cause and effect; this is complicated further by the influence of evil spirits.

Evil Spirits

At the beginning of the novel coronavirus outbreak, the Chinese president called it a demon that must be controlled.[27] He likely meant this metaphorically, but I think that the action of evil spirits is something to take seriously. Interestingly, scholars seldom consider demons as causative agents; indeed, they debate the existence and nature of evil spirits.[28] The Old Testament rarely refers to demons as direct agents, but includes commands not to consult them, through witchcraft and divination (1 Sam 28:3–25; Lev 19:31; Deut 18:10–11). This suggests that they have causative powers. The New Testament includes many examples of evil spirits influencing people psychologically through oppression, deception, or enticement toward sin (Acts 10:38; 1 Cor 7:5; Jas 3:15, 1 John 4:1–3; Rev 12:10).[29]

Demons can act in opposition to God and goodness, often by inflicting harm on his creatures. However, this does not mean that their agency is on the same level as that of God or humans. Their abilities are limited— they do not have creative powers, only destructive ones, and are sometimes viewed as anti-creational forces. Evil spirits mostly inflict harm on people who have a vulnerability, such as sinful practices or thoughts. They can be considered parasitic on human sin; anger may give the devil a "foothold" (Eph 4:26, 27; 1 Tim 3:6).[30] In fact, infectious agents are an apt metaphor for evil spirits. Like viruses, demons have little ability unless they enter a human host. And, although miniscule and unseen, in large numbers they can inflict serious harm. Demons of course are subject to the authoritative commands of Jesus, having been destroyed, at least in principle, through Christ's death and resurrection.

WHAT DOES THE BIBLE SAY ABOUT ILLNESS AND HEALING?

How should Christians deal with Covid-19? Did God cause it to punish people? Did demons cause it? Many Christians have thought about how biblical teachings may apply to COVID-19. Scripture does not specifically mention pandemics, but there is nevertheless much that we can learn about causes of illness and how we should respond.

"The father of Publius lay sick in bed with fever and dysentery" (Acts 28:8a). The Bible mentions many different types of illnesses that are familiar to us: blindness, deafness, paralysis (the term used includes lameness and neurological disorders), hemorrhage (probably heavy menstrual bleeding), fever, seizure disorders, and skin disease. It is important to note that these stories of illness and healing are told to make a theological point, not to provide a scientific classification. Some writers have attempted to use current medical categories to describe biblical afflictions, such as Paul having bipolar disorder.[31] However, I think that this approach is misguided and can lead to misunderstanding. We need to remember the original context of the Bible and avoid applying contemporary categories to ancient texts.

To reiterate, biblical authors have no scientific interest in illness. They are more interested in agents (usually God) that cause an illness than in medical mechanisms behind an illness.[32] They don't ask questions about the origins of diseases, and tend to use descriptive names. Seizures are mentioned frequently—sometimes these are caused by evil spirits, other times no cause is specified. Writers often make broad statements, without details of what, how, and why: "Hezekiah became sick" (2 Kgs 20:1). In many of the healing stories, no specific cause is identified: "they brought to him all the sick, those who were afflicted with various diseases and pains . . . and he healed them" (Matt 4:24). As Adolf von Harnack pointed out over a century ago, "Jesus says very little about sickness; he cures it."[33]

Illness

"Lord, he whom you love is ill" (John 11:3). Lazarus's sister sent this message to Jesus; as is common, the illness is not explained. However, at times Scripture does offer explanations. We can use our fourfold classification of natural, divine, human, and demonic factors to gain some insight into the biblical understanding of illness causation. These causes are often interrelated. Remember that God is the creator of all causative factors, but he has made a world that has some "self-causing" abilities, he has given some freedom to evil spirits to afflict people, and he has given responsibility to humans to obey him and to care for creation. Also recall the importance of context when interpreting biblical verses on illness.[34]

First, natural or biological causes are implied in the cases of the man born blind (John 9:3), the man born crippled (Acts 14:8), and the many general statements about illness, in which a cause is not mentioned. Biblical scholar Peder Borgen notes that "blindness, paralysis etc. are usually described in a 'naturalistic' way, as backgrounds for healing."[35] He suggests that injury should also be considered thus. It appears that, in the Bible, sometimes illness just happens.

Second, in some instances God directly causes illness. He inflicts the Egyptians with boils (Exod 9:8–12) and strikes the disobedient Israelites with plague (Num 11:33), fever, and consumption (Lev 26:16). The Deuteronomist warns Israel: "The Lord will afflict you with consumption, fever, inflammation, with fiery heat and drought, and with blight and mildew" (Deut 28:22). The Gospels and Acts also record some instances of God causing illness. The angel of the Lord tells Zechariah that he will become mute (Luke 1:20). God strikes down evil Herod (Acts 12:21–23) and blinds the false prophet Elymas (Acts 13:11). However, note that these afflictions all occur as divine punishment for sin. The events also occur at theologically significant moments for the people of God. There is no indication that God causes illness on a frequent and ongoing basis; indeed, Jesus never lectures people about the meaning of their illness. Consequently, there is no reason to conclude that God caused the 2020 pandemic.

Third, with respect to human causation, as we just saw, illness is sometimes linked to sin. This is usually indirect. After healing the man at Bethsaida, Jesus advises "do not sin any more, so that nothing worse happens to you" (John 5:15). In the story of the paralytic, he obtusely states, "Which is easier, to say to the paralytic, 'Your sins are forgiven,' or to say, 'Stand up and take your mat and walk?'" (Mark 2:9). The theological point is that Jesus has authority to forgive sin, not necessarily that God punishes sin with infirmity. Paul warns the Corinthians about their thoughtless disregard for each other when they celebrate the Lord's Supper: "For all who eat or drink without discerning the body eat and drink judgment against themselves. For this reason many of you are weak and ill, and some have died" (1 Cor 11:29–30). Unfortunately, he does not elaborate on exactly how their sin caused their illness. The Bible also suggests that illness is connected to communal sin.[36] Jesus focuses on healing marginalized and oppressed people, whose illness is compounded by social factors. He condemns the Pharisees for neglecting justice and mercy (Matt 23:23). In sum, human sin *sometimes* results in illness, but the association between sin and sickness is variable and vague.[37]

Fourth, demons commonly cause illness: muteness (Matt 9:33), seizures (Matt 17:15–18; Luke 9:42), physical handicaps (a woman crippled by a spirit; Luke 13:11; a paralyzed man; Matt 9:2–8), and behavioral/mental illness (the Gerasene demoniac; Mark 5:5; Luke 8:27). Interestingly, demonic attribution is far more common than divine attribution in the Gospels.

Jesus rebukes demons and heals illness. As Episcopalian Morton Kelsey notes, "Jesus seemed to believe that a primary cause of sickness was a force of evil let loose in the world which was hostile to God."[38] Jesus's teaching and actions show that illness, like demons, is incompatible with God's kingdom. Of course, this does not mean that every affliction is caused by evil spirits.

Did evil spirits cause the COVID-19 pandemic? No, because they do not have creative abilities. However, this crisis has made many people feel vulnerable. Given what we know, it is quite likely that demons whisper misinformation in someone's ear, or feed on their fear and pain. They may incite conspiracy theories or encourage people not to follow medical advice. Although we cannot know for certain, it is important that we consider the role of evil spirits when evaluating how and why things happen.

In sum, biblical texts suggest that illness can be caused by natural factors (intrinsic properties of nature, such as regularities and randomness) or personal factors (the triune God, created humans, and created evil spirits). However, we also noted that the Bible does not explain many occurrences, that causation is frequently indirect, and that causative factors overlap and intertwine. It can be difficult to know exactly how illness occurs.[39]

Recall that biblical language is frequently fluid and flexible. Some of this apparent ambiguity could be explained by the multiple causative components that are involved. In the test and punishment for an unfaithful wife, three "agents" (or intermediaries) can be identified: the Lord "causes miscarriage," the priest puts her under a curse, and the water "causes bitter suffering" (Num 5:11–31). The book of Job names God, Satan, foreign armies, and natural forces as causes of Job's suffering. In addition, God's creative work often implies a chain of causation. He creates water that then allows trees to grow and birds to nest (Ps 104:10–18).[40]

We saw that sin and God's punishment for it are frequently intertwined. In one of David's laments, it appears that both God and David's own sin cause his physical ailments: "There is no soundness in my flesh because of your indignation; there is no health in my bones because of my sin" (Ps 38:3). Sin and evil spirits as causative factors also often cooccur. Ananias lies, but Satan is implicated in influencing his sin (Acts 5:3). Paul attributes his mysterious thorn in his side to both God and Satan (2 Cor 12:7–10).[41] And, in an example of God, Satan, and sin as causes, Paul teaches that God "gives up" wicked humans to their sinful desires (Rom 1:24–28) and advises turning over sinners to Satan (1 Cor 5:1–5; 1 Tim 1:20). I think it should be clear by now that the Bible does not give a simple account of causation. Instead it appears that many different causes can work together in many different ways to cause illness. The phrase *sometimes but not always* may be helpful: sin only sometimes leads to punishment by illness, demons are not always the cause of illness.

Healing

The story of Publius's sick father has a happy ending: "Paul visited him and cured him by praying and putting his hands on him" (Acts 28:8b). In fact, biblical texts usually focus more on divine *healing* of illness, than divine *causation* of it. The Lord offers healing and renewal (Ps 51:2, 7; Zech 3:5). He raises the dead: two widows' sons (1 Kgs 17:17–24; Luke 7:11–15), Jairus's daughter (Matt 9:18, 24, 25), and Lazarus (John 11:1–4). Jesus heals those with skin disease (Matt 8:1–3) and bleeding problems (Matt 9:20–22).[42] Significantly, when Jesus heals the sick, the blind, the deaf, and the lame, he announces the activity of the Holy Spirit (Isa 35:5–6; Matt 12:22–28). Overall, sickness is contrary to God's will for salvation and life. In fact, health in the New Testament is associated with salvation, life, peace, and wholeness.[43] To reiterate, Jesus did not heal everyone; his primary purpose was to announce the arrival of the kingdom, overcome evil, and restore the world to right relationship with God.

Humans also have responsibility for regaining health. Faith is sometimes a factor in Jesus's healings, although it is not required. Jesus commends the Canaanite woman for her faith, and her daughter is healed (Matt 15:21–8); he tells both the hemorrhaging woman and the leper that "your faith has made you well" (Luke 8:48; 17:19). Other healing stories do not mention faith. In general, God's action in a negative manner is always in response to sin and disobedience; however, his loving, restorative action is independent of human action or faith. Sometimes God heals in response to prayer: Isaac and Zechariah pray for children and their wives conceive (Gen 25:21; Luke 1:13). Physicians are mentioned in the Bible, and Paul offers "medical advice": "take a little wine for the sake of your stomach" (1 Tim 5:23). Jesus teaches his disciples the importance of feeding the hungry and taking care of the sick (Matt 25:31–46), and gives them authority to heal the ill and cast out demons (Matt 10:1). The book of Acts tells many stories of how the disciples enacted this responsibility.[44]

Finally, and perhaps most importantly, followers and disciples of Christ are given the Holy Spirit (John 15:1–27; Acts 2:1–47; Rom 8:9). God's Spirit within encourages and enables us to work with him in bringing about his kingdom through praying, caring for the sick, and offering various types of healing. The Bible emphasizes divine-human cooperation. Indeed, the Spirit of God relies on the faithful to do his work. His presence and action are strongest within the community of Christ-followers. Our responsibility in causing relief of suffering is humbling and has implications for our response to the COVID-19 pandemic. In many ways, we are God's hands, feet, and face. This is aptly summarized by the title of a recent statement by the science-faith organization BioLogos: "Love Your Neighbor, Wear a Mask."[45]

CONCLUSION

In his recent book, *Christ and the Coronavirus*, John Piper claims that "Not one virus moves but by God's plan."[46] He bases this conclusion on Isaiah 46:10 ("My purpose shall stand, and I will fulfill my intention") and his belief that God decides everything; nothing happens outside his will. God's sovereignty "rules in sickness." Piper suggests that God's purposes in the pandemic include a call for repentance and a recognition of the horrors of sin. Some infected people are also being judged for their sin. Although Piper helpfully reminds us that God comforts the suffering and encourages Christians to care for the sick, I do not think his theology about divine control fits with what we have seen about biblical ideas of causation. Recalling principles of interpretation, it is a stretch to use a prophetic verse (Isa 46:10) directed at the wayward nation of Israel to conclude that God is omni-causal.

I prefer N. T. Wright's views in *God and the Pandemic*.[47] He points to the model of Christ who experienced unjustified suffering and exemplified humble sovereignty and servant leadership. Specifically, there is no evidence that God is judging the world through the pandemic or has orchestrated it for any specific purpose. We need to consider the nuances of the entire Bible and avoid assuming that there is a straightforward causal link between ill behavior and ill fortune. Wright uses an example from the early church as a guide to how Christians should respond to COVID-19. In Acts 11:27–30, the disciples hear about a global famine (not caused by God) and send relief to those in need. Wright also points to the faithful responses of Christians during previous pandemics, such as building hospitals and remaining in town to nurse the sick.

Although the Bible has limited teaching on causation, our overview of areas where it is implied offers some perspectives on how and why things happen. There are natural processes in creation, regularities in the world, with intrinsic cause and effect. There are also divine and created agents that cause things. Often these overlap and interact; in particular we saw how humans are called to cooperate with God in his work.

In the Exodus 14 story, divine action is intermingled with human agency and natural causes: God parts the waters (possibly taking advantage of naturally occurring tides and wind), an angel assists, and Moses stretches out his hand.[48] Scott Shauf, in his examination of Acts, observes that "the divine spirit works, angels act, and humans perform miraculous deeds, all expressed without any doubt and without offering alternate explanation."[49] Causation appears to be complex, intertwined, multifactorial, and often unexplained. This fits well with the nature of the created order; a world that is filled with potentialities and probabilities.

Biblical scholar Ellen van Wolde points out the complexities of causation in the Bible. She acknowledges our human need for coherence and the Western preference for linear models of causality. We like simple cause-and-effect relations. Yet, much of Scripture is presented in a nonlinear manner. In Genesis 1, light is created before the sun. The Genesis 2 creation story depicts a beginning; it does not logically follow from Genesis 1:31, which describes the end of God's creative act. Cause-and-effect stories and statements usually relate to broader contexts and perspectives. Sometimes texts zoom in on specific contexts; "They do not provide general answers valuable for every time and place." "Causation is a continuous process, in which certain possibilities among a multitude of possibilities are selected and realised."[50] There are often many causative factors in any occurrence; these are limited by previous events and in turn may limit subsequent ones. Van Wolde's points confirm the need for us to be aware of our often-simplistic assumptions when we interpret the Bible, and to be aware of the complex nature of cause and effect in the Bible.

The beauty of creation reflects the beauty of God; what we see in the world and what we learn through Scripture and the inspiration of the Holy Spirit reflect the nature of God and how he interacts with his creation. The Bible is clear that God is sovereign and has created all things. However, he has gifted both the natural world and human beings with the ability to effect causation. In the case of humans, it is not only an ability but a responsibility. Although we may never fully understand why and how things happen, we are called to work with God in doing good, as empowered by the Holy Spirit.

Therefore I have uttered what I did not understand,
things too wonderful for me, which I did not know.

JOB 42:3B

ENDNOTES

1. See discussion on this and many other misunderstood verses in Boyd, *Satan and Problem of Evil*, 394–416.
2. Slick, "Does Everything Happen?"
3. Nichols, "Fingers of Love." See also Warren, *Purpose Driven Life*, 194.
4. Eric Eve points out that biblical authors were more interested in knowing "what

agent caused this" rather than "what mechanism" (*Healer from Nazareth*, xiii–xxi). Biblical authors occasionally addressed some *how* questions from a prescientific viewpoint, but this was not their primary concern. Fretheim, *God and World*, 27–28.

5. See also Psalm 102. Fredrik Lindström notes that it is difficult to know if an illness is genuine or not; he also points out that multiple metaphors are used (*Sickness and Suffering*, 26, 429–65).

6. E.g., Senter, "Leviathan, Behemoth."

7. E.g., Fee and Stuart, *Read the Bible*.

8. E.g., Waltke, *Will of God*, 15–20.

9. The verb *bārā* (typically translated "create") connotes separating and ordering. Walton; *Ancient Near Eastern Thought*, 183; Wolters, *Creation Regained*, 13–51; Smith, *Priestly Vision*, 79, 87–89.

10. E.g., Dumbrell, *Search for Order*, 17–22. Good can also mean free and peaceful (Ps 104:28; Isa 45:7). Fretheim, *Creation Untamed*, 16; Smith, *Priestly Vision*, 62.

11. E.g., Beale, *Temple and Mission*.

12. Fretheim, *God and World*, 7–8; *Creation Untamed*, 26. Further, because the world is dynamic, it is not risk free. Fretheim, *God and World*, 108–11. Note that verses often used to support the idea that God micromanages, such as death when God withdraws his Spirit (Ps 104:29; Job 34:15), appear in poetic literature, used hyperbolically to illustrate a point.

13. Other examples include the Genesis 3:16–19 "curse," and Jesus's statement about blasphemy from the Holy Spirit (Matt 12:31); these are not necessarily divine judgments but descriptions of life apart from God. Warren, *Cleansing the Cosmos*, 114–17, 190–91.

14. Gaiser, "Why Does It Rain?" 9.

15. Smith, *Priestly Vision*, 51–71; Warren, *Cleansing the Cosmos*, 101–106.

16. Aurelio, *Mosquitoes in Paradise*.

17. Fretheim, *God and World*, 7; *Creation Untamed*, 21.

18. David Daube notes a correlation between direct causation and the presence of intent, and vice versa (*Deed and Doer*, 10–20, 29–30).

19. E.g., Boyd, "Open Theism"; Rice, "Biblical Support."

20. Beale, *Temple and Mission*; Warren, "Pneumatology Meets Demonology."

21. Burnett, *Where is God?* 157.

22. There is a range encompassing very holy, holy, clean, unclean, and very unclean. The sacred, or very holy, is associated with God, temple, life, being, and order. Jenson, *Graded Holiness*, 58–62, 210–15. The ideas of order, structure, classification, and grading originated with Mary Douglas's seminal work, *Purity and Danger*.

23. Fretheim, *God and World*, 23, 25.

24. Welker, *God the Spirit*, 161.

25. Waltke, *Will of God*, 160–72. Fretheim similarly comments on a verse that seems to imply that God causes all things: "I make weal and create woe" (Isa 45:70). Weal and woe relate to judgment and restoration in history; therefore, this does not mean that every event is caused by God. Fretheim, *Creation Untamed*, 99.

26. E.g., Fretheim, *Creation Untamed*, 10–36; Wolters, *Creation Regained*.

27. Zheng et al., "Wuhan coronavirus."

28. E.g., Warren, *Cleansing the Cosmos*, 14–17, 220–22.

29. Fee, *Empowering Presence*, 761–71.

30. Fee, *Empowering Presence*, 712–13. The relation between sin and demonization in the Bible is complex, but there are clear semantic and experiential associations. E.g., Warren, *Cleansing the Cosmos*, 137–38, 223–29, 269–76.

31. E.g., Wilkinson, *Bible and Healing*.

32. Contemporary cultures believed the same. E.g., Eve, *Healer from Nazareth*,

xiii–xxi; Shauf, *Divine in Acts*.

33. Harnack, *Mission and Expansion*, 101.

34. Later Judaism and Greek culture viewed most illness as having demonic origin; "treatment" involved exorcism rituals and appeasement of deities. However, there were also physicians in the ancient world and the beginnings of empirical medicine; illness was considered both naturalistic (due to injury, germs, or the weather) and personalistic (due to sin or demons). Greco-Roman views were more naturalistic, although disease was always considered more than just a bodily ailment. Around the time of Christ, there was likely much syncretism. In general, if a condition was mysterious, a spiritual cause was assumed. E.g., Kee, *Medicine, Miracle*.

35. Borgen, "Miracles of Healing," 101. He classifies biblical causation as naturalistic or personalistic.

36. Mark Biddle notes sin's wide range of meanings, including the concept of sin as a collective phenomenon with cosmic effects; it is "a nexus of cause-effect-cause" (*Missing the Mark,* 115–19, 136). Fretheim similarly points out the complex interaction between causative factors; people's sinful actions affect themselves, others, and, when sin accumulates, the cosmic order (*Creation Untamed*, 112–16).

37. Lindström notes that in the psalms, there is no causal chain between sin and sickness (*Sickness and Suffering*, 25, 429–65). Borgen states "Jesus therefore to a large extent breaks with the idea of divine retaliation commonly current at that time" ("Miracles of Healing," 101).

38. Kelsey, *Christian Healing*, 75. See also Gaiser, *Healing in the Bible*, 134–35; Thomas, *Devil, Disease*, 297–303.

39. Gaiser thinks it is impossible to make sharp distinctions between illnesses that have demonic origin and those that have natural origin (*Healing in the Bible*, 134).

40. E.g., Langford, *Providence*, 40–60.

41. E.g., Thomas, *Devil, Disease*, 73, 305–15.

42. Healing included restoration to purity and therefore society; healing, cleansing, salvation, and exorcism are also intertwined. E.g., Twelftree, *Miracle Worker*, 118–19; 167–88; *Name of Jesus*, 132–55; Gaiser, *Healing in the Bible*, 3–126; Warren, *Cleansing the Cosmos*, 192–205.

43. E.g., Gaiser, *Healing in the Bible*, 103–5, 177; Seybold and Mueller, *Sickness and Healing*, 130–48.

44. Twelftree, *Name of Jesus*, 57–77, 289–91.

45. BioLogos, "Love Your Neighbor." This organization was started by Francis Collins, director of the National Institute of Health, who currently leads a team working on finding a vaccine for COVID-19.

46. Piper, *Christ and Coronavirus*, 49.

47. Wright, *God and Pandemic*.

48. Langford, *Providence*, 42–45.

49. Shauf, *Divine in Acts*, 186. He further notes that, in biblical historiography, there is a notable lack of theorizing with respect to causation of events (207).

50. Van Wolde, "Limits of Linearity," 380, 391.

3

What Does Christian Theology
Say about Causation?

CONSIDER THIS WELL-KNOWN REFRAIN:

> *I know who holds the future,*
> *And I know he holds my hand;*
> *With God things don't just happen*
> *ev'rything by Him is planned.*[1]

Some Christians believe that God planned the COVID-19 pandemic. This idea that God is in direct control of everything may provide comfort in troubling times. Indeed, the creator God made all things wise and wonderful; the God of comfort is always with us. But this does not necessarily mean he directs all things that happen. We have just seen that biblical views on causation are nuanced and diverse. Humans are able and commanded to make things happen. In addition, creation is beautiful and has amazingly complex cause-and-effect patterns. This often results in surprise and uncertainty. As responsible Christians, we need to carefully consider truths about how and why things happen, even if they make us uncomfortable.

Theologians seldom directly address the issue of causation in the everyday world. However, they indirectly address it when discussing evil and suffering, providence, divine action, and the God-world relationship. Most theologians point out that we need to accept the limitations of human knowledge and the mystery of God. But our Creator wants to be known.

As Frank Kirkpatrick states, God is mysterious enough that he cannot be understood, but also personal enough for us to relate deeply with him.[2]

Remember the importance of asking the right question or questions. If we ask, "Did God cause the pandemic?" we are inviting a yes-or-no answer. But the question, "In what ways is God involved in the pandemic?" may encourage us to think about many possible aspects of divine interaction. Also recall that there are different levels of reality and different types of causation. If we want to know how vaccines work, we are asking a scientific question (Aristotle's efficient causal level). But if we pray for God to guide and inspire scientists who are working on a vaccine for COVID-19, then we are assuming that there is interaction between final and efficient levels. There are different categories of causal questions, but they can be considered together. I believe that God is involved with all levels of reality and that our understanding of how things happen in the world should be integrated with our Christian faith.

Someone once suggested to me that studying theology would ruin my faith. Fortunately, I've found quite the opposite. Theology is important because how we understand the nature of God will inform how we understand his action in the world, how we understand causation in general, and how we act in life. If we believe that God is not involved in the world, we may work agonizingly to prevent getting COVID-19 or we may resign ourselves to suffering. If we think that God has a loving but hidden purpose in the pandemic, we may silently suffer, trusting in his plan, and not working to heal the world. If we think that God wants us to share responsibility in caring for the world, we may take food to our neighbors and wear masks. Of course, there are many other variations of beliefs and behavior, and these are not always consistent, but the point is that we can develop our faith by learning more about the nature of God and his involvement in creation.

WHAT IS GOD LIKE?

A popular worship song describes God thus: "You're rich in love and you're slow to anger; Your name is great and your heart is kind."[3] Sometimes music and poetry are better able to depict the Lord than dry theological language. Sometimes even these fail. But if we want to know God's role in how and why things happen, we need to think about what kind of a god he is.

God's Character and Sovereignty

"I am God Almighty; walk before me faithfully" (Gen 17:1). God is authoritative and powerful, the supreme causative agent, originator and sustainer of the world. He is also passionate and compassionate, the *Most Moved Mover*.[4] He suffers because of and with his people. He is more interested in godliness than goings-on, in care than control. The Almighty is both immanent and transcendent, both close to us and way beyond us.

His character is consistent, but his actions can vary depending on the situation. As a wise parent may treat children differently at different ages and stages, the wise God may treat people and situations differently at different times. As we saw in the last chapter, he has higher expectations for the nation of Israel and followers of Christ, and he favors the poor and downtrodden. God's actions are always true to his character. It makes no sense that he would cause a pandemic, in particular, something that affects the poor and elderly more than others. As philosopher Wilton Bunch states, "the idea that God actually intends for people to undergo extreme physical or mental anguish is cruel and incompatible with the scriptural account of a God who loves his creatures."[5]

"How great you are, Sovereign Lord!" (2 Sam 7:22). The Bible is clear, and Christians agree, that God is *sovereign*. This term relates to kings and rule, power and authority. But Christians understand divine sovereignty in different ways. One model portrays God as an aloof monarch, a dictator, or a puppet master. This theological view claims that God's sovereignty is specific and all-encompassing. He ordains every detail of life and meticulously controls all events; his desires are never thwarted.[6] People who claim that God planned the COVID-19 pandemic likely hold this perspective.

However, other models view God more like a *servant* king, who respects his subjects and allows them to participate in decisions and actions related to the kingdom. This means that sometimes his people do things the king doesn't like. In this theological view, God exercises a more general type of sovereignty, in which some things happen that are outside of his will, like people refusing to obey him.[7] He is all-powerful but chooses not to exercise his power in all times and places. As a wise king, God's activities are seldom one sided.[8] He neither dominates nor coerces, and chooses to give freedom and responsibility to his creatures. I believe this second view is more compatible with what we see in the Bible and in the world.

Both views emphasize the love of God. The first implies a controlling type of love, and in fact care and control are often confused and conflated. Just because God deeply cares for sparrows (Matt 10:29) does not mean that he controls their every action, like causing them to fall and die.[9] The servant-king view implies a risky type of love. God desires input from his creatures, and delicately balances his authority with his respect for the freedom that he has given to creation. This means that sparrows, and people, can do things against God's will. But of course, God is big enough to handle it. He has more than one plan, and intervenes on occasion in order to bring about his kingdom—the sacrifice of his son being the prime example. Gregory Boyd points out that love entails risk and God chooses to experience risk; in fact, it takes a stronger and more secure God to relinquish some control. He summarizes: God "does not need to be meticulously controlling on the level of free agents to ensure that his sovereign plan for the world will be accomplished."[10]

It is important to think about sovereignty in light of the big picture. We tend to relate divine sovereignty to our personal lives, but God's priorities may be different from ours. Recall from the last chapter that his dealings with individuals usually relate to his overall plan for saving and reconciling the world to him. As Stanley Grenz notes, sovereignty is primarily an eschatological concept, related to God's larger plan for fulfilling his kingdom.[11] He helpfully suggests we distinguish between present and future, between overall and specific, and between principle and actual. God will act to bring about the future fulfillment of his reign, where every tongue confesses that Jesus is Lord (Phil 2:11). His universal plan will be accomplished, but not necessarily his plans in every specific situation in our daily lives. God reigns over creation in principle, but this does not mean that everything that actually happens is in accordance with this reign. As we know, many people do not follow him, there is much in the world that is tainted; indeed, the whole creation groans (Rom 8:22).

Our view of sovereignty should be compatible with our experience in the world. Since we live our daily lives making conscious free choices, and since we see much that is chaotic and harmful in our world, our views need to reflect this. Theologians Fringer and Lane summarize the character and sovereignty of God well:

> What kind of God initiates actions that awaken possibilities of evil? A good God! What kind of God does not seek to control everything? A servant God! What kind of God refuses to dominate and instead gives in to the domination of a cross? A suffering God! What kind of God creates with purpose but also with possibilities? A loving God![12]

God's Love and Limits

"Can God make a rock that is too heavy for him to lift?" This is usually said jokingly but has some serious undertones. God has limitations. Some Christians may be shocked to think this, but it has important implications for how we understand God's role in making things happen in the world.

First, God is unable to do things contradictory to his nature. Because he does not have a physical body, he cannot climb a mountain or experience fatigue. When he was incarnate, it was as a male; therefore, he could not have born children. God cannot lie, sin, or cease to exist.[13] As Paul points out, "if we are faithless, he remains faithful—for he cannot deny himself" (2 Tim. 2:13). Scientist-theologian John Polkinghorne summarizes nicely: "The good God cannot do evil deeds; the rational God cannot act irrationally. The God of love who has given a measure of independence to creatures will not arbitrarily withdraw that gift."[14]

A second type of limitation relates to the nature of creation. When God creates something, by definition, it is not something else. Water is wet, not dry. Viruses replicate inside, not outside, human hosts. God cannot make a square round. One creative action eliminates the possibility of many others, by default. Sometimes one action may have an undesired consequence, or side effect—recall forked models of causation in which one cause can have two effects. If God grants a job to someone, that means someone else does not get the job. If God were to stop a hurricane in one part of the world, the weather everywhere would be affected. In the movie *Bruce Almighty*, "God" said yes to everyone's prayers to win the lottery. Needless to say, no one was happy about winning pennies.[15]

A third aspect of divine limitation relates to the freedom that God has gifted creatures, and the responsibility he has delegated to us. There are many views on the nature of free will, but I believe it represents a genuinely reciprocal relationship between God and his creatures.[16] Freedom allows us to choose to cooperate with God or not. The Holy Spirit may guide us, but our thoughts and actions are ultimately free. Our options are somewhat limited by our contexts (our bodies, the climate we live in, the family we born into), but we nevertheless have countless choices.[17] In most situations, such as a career path or vacation destination (post-pandemic!), we have many possible selections. Boyd suggests that "God sets the parameters in which all free activity must take place . . . but within these parameters he allows free agents room to make their own decisions."[18] We could view God as having overall responsibility, and humans having responsibility within their smaller, designated areas.[19]

Should I eat fruit or cookies? Should I attend church today? We live our daily lives making free choices that have a large effect on how and why things happen. Decisions can be complex, interacting with each other. We can sometimes avoid sickness because we choose to eat healthily, exercise, and wear a mask. We are free to pray, and prayer can bring about real changes in the world. Our choices are affected by our previous choices. This is especially evident with drug addictions. Each wrong choice limits subsequent ones and the further along a pathway we move, the harder it is to return.[20] We become the choices we make.

Finally, since God respects our freedom, he must suppress his desire to intervene. In other words, God imposes limitations on himself. This understanding is related to the theological notion of *kenosis*, which describes how God humbled and emptied himself when he became a man (Phil 2:6–8).[21] He gave up his status and power, and through his weakness and sacrifice effected our salvation. In the same way, God acts in the world today. Out of love and respect for his creation, he often applies the brakes, allowing humans to act freely, and letting things be. He wants people to *choose* to love him, rather than coercing them to do so. Jürgen Moltmann argues that the very act of creation involves a contraction of divine presence.[22] Since God is present everywhere, he first has to make room for the world by creating a space from which he withdraws himself and restricts his power. Self-imposed divine limitations fit well with a world in which there is genuine freedom, and with a God who reigns as a servant king.

HOW DOES GOD ACT?

Recall John Piper's assertion that not a single virus moves unless God plans it. But like many people who believe that God orchestrated the COVID-19 pandemic, he is a little short on details. Piper does not specify exactly how God created the novel coronavirus, or how he spread it around the world, or how he gives some people symptoms and not others. I'm not suggesting that we can ever know every detail about how God acts, but there is much that we can learn. However, if cause-and-effect relations in the world are challenging to figure out, understanding how a divine being causes things is immensely more so.

The Bible and Christian experience show that God cares for the world, draws people into relationship with him, and invites them to be co-creators with him. He has causative powers. His actions have effects. He acts within the world but is much bigger than it. And, although perhaps obvious, we should remember *why* God acts: because of his deep love, he wants to save and redeem his creation and creatures, drawing all things to himself through Christ. Divine nature, divine action, and divine purpose interrelate.[23]

"God's ways are not our ways." Some people claim that we cannot know anything about divine action. I agree that there is always an element of mystery, but I think that we are called to understand God and his world better. If God's action is completely unknown, then we cannot be confident that he acts at all.[24] And I also don't think that it's within God's character to be deceptive and hide his activity.

Most theological discussion about how God interacts with his creation uses the broad category of *divine providence*. This term refers to the general governance and guidance of God: "the ways God acts to promote our well-being and the well-being of the whole world."[25] There are many models of providence, but we will discuss the two major ones that are most relevant to our understanding of how and why things happen.[26] These are similar to the two views on sovereignty that we discussed earlier.

The first view argues that God acts directly and specifically in all things at all times, according to his prearranged plan. In philosophical terms, this view is *deterministic*. God exercises omni-causality and meticulous control, like a dictator king.[27] He even chooses his followers. Human free will is considered compatible with divine determinism; we only feel and act like we have freedom but really don't. Cause-and-effect relations are linear and simple because God causes all things. Divine purposes are often thought to be hidden and mysterious, but we can be assured that everything that happens, no matter how bad, happens for a good reason. This is why Piper describes the COVID-19 pandemic as "bitter providence."[28]

Admittedly this view has some variations and nuances, but I see many problems with it.[29] First, it does not mesh with the biblical picture of a God who is flexible and responsive to his creatures; indeed, he changes his plans at times and not everything goes according to plan. Second, it does not match our experience in a world in which the way things happen is affected by many variables. Because this approach denies the possibility of randomness, it can border on fatalism. Third, deterministic views, especially in extreme forms, are difficult to reconcile with human agency and accountability. In fact, such views may lead to magical thinking, seeing God as a "superhero" who absolves us of responsibility.[30] If God is controlling everything, we don't have to work. People sometimes find it comforting to believe that God controls all things, but I think this denies rather than honors. When we simply accept what happens, we may fail to learn about the nature of causation in God's world. People who don't practice physical distancing, believing that COVID-19 is God-ordained, may regret it when they get sick. If we don't learn to suffer alongside God and accept uncertainty, we may not grow in our faith. I agree with Bartholomew that we should be concerned with "what is true not what is comforting,"[31] although the two are not always incompatible.

Finally, deterministic views typically lead to inconsistent and illogical thinking, as we saw in some examples in chapter 1. People often believe that providence is deterministic (God controls everything) but that salvation is dependent on free will.[32] This makes no sense. A scientist colleague once pronounced: "God decides, we measure." This may be true sometimes but, as we shall see, our measurements in fact can affect outcomes. And we are given much more responsibility in developing creation than simply measuring. Recall the people who believe that God planned the pandemic. When I ask what possible reason God would have for inflicting suffering on innocent people, they usually back down, or engage in convoluted reasoning, saying that God knew it would happen. And when I ask why God would not prevent it if he knew it would happen (I know, irritating of me), they often change the subject.

Philosopher Caleb Cohoe points out the problems implicit in assuming that everything that happens is because God wills the best for us: "If it is good for your body to be nourished, then God will nourish you even if you do not eat. If it is good for you to be in a certain place, then God will place you there, even if you do not go there yourself."[33] Because God created the world, we can praise, or blame, him for absolutely everything. However, this is unhelpful: if God is the agent of everything then he is also an agent of nothing in particular.[34] In which case there is no point in discussing causation. If God causes absolutely everything, then there is no need for us to ask how and why things happen, and you can stop reading this book (please don't).

The other major view of providence emphasizes freedom and divine restraint.[35] Not everything is predetermined; philosophically, this view is *indeterministic*. God usually acts generally, preserving creation and empowering creatures, but also acts directly and specifically on occasion. He is omnipotent but respects the integrity and freedom of the world he created. Proponents of this view emphasize a God who prioritizes love and relationships, and is willing to risk unpredictability and the possibility that his will be thwarted. Thomas Oord describes an "adventure model of providence," with calculated risks, free decisions, and some randomness. This view best fits our world of "genuine good and evil, randomness and regularity, freedom, agency, disappointments, and even miracles."[36]

A free-will, indeterministic model is compatible with human experience and a world that has multiple causative factors. It is also compatible with the biblical description of an intimately involved Creator. Of course, it does not solve the difficult question of why God intervenes on some occasions and not others. Examining some issues related to how God acts to cause change in the world may help us address this question.

The Realm of God's Action

Where is God in the pandemic? The short answer is "everywhere." The domain of divine action is the entire universe. But remember the importance of asking the right question and asking more than one question. What we perhaps mean by this question is where specifically is God acting in the pandemic. Recall that just because God is present within and to his creation does not necessarily mean that he is directly—at all times, in all places, and all manners—involved in every aspect of it. Indeed, he has chosen to restrain his power, and to focus his attention on Christ followers.

Some people believe that all nature is sacred; trees are temples, the universe is God (such views are known as pantheism). However, in Christian thought, God and world are neither identical nor completely separate. God is not present within every tree and water molecule on earth, indistinguishable from the world; he is in a whole different category from his creation.[37] Neither does he sit above the world occasionally dipping his fingers in to stir things around. God is simultaneously inside and outside of creation; immanence and transcendence are intertwined. Many people use the terms *natural* and *supernatural* to describe where and how God acts in the world, but these terms can be confusing.[38] Natural connotes areas where God is not involved; supernatural implies that God only shows up on rare occasions. This does not fit with what we learned about causation in the Bible, which, incidentally, does not contain the term supernatural. Instead we saw that, although God has created the world to be self-sustaining, he is continually present and acting within it, although not in a uniform manner. There are no sharp divisions between "natural" and "supernatural," but many shades of grey.

In Christ, "all things hold together" (Col 1:17). Through the pre-existent Word, the world can be seen as sacred. Just like God is mysteriously present in the bread and the wine we use for communion, so is he present in creation.[39] Terry Wright suggests that we focus on God's faithful presence in the world, embodied by Christ, rather than try to figure out mechanisms of divine action. Through Christ, providence is made flesh; sovereign presence is an active presence.[40] The triune God is transcendent, beyond the world, but also immanent within it through his Spirit: "God's breath is everywhere, reaching out and touching people."[41] The Holy Spirit is given to certain people but also "benefits their spatial and temporal, proximate and distant environments."[42] On a hot day, we may feel the breeze from the fan of someone sitting next to us. Because of the presence and providence of God in the world, all of creation profits. Believers and unbelievers alike receive the undeserved goodness that is a side effect of God's presence. This is known as *common grace*.

However, recall that God's action always has relevance for his broad purposes—to reconcile humanity and build his kingdom. In other words, although the domain of God's action is broad, he chooses to limit it. Because he has created the world to be self-sustaining, and because he has given freedom and responsibility to his creatures, it is not necessary that he act everywhere, all the time. As Bartholomew points out, "God does not need to be directly involved in any events whose outcomes have no relevant consequences for his wider purposes."[43] This idea can be liberating. I once had a patient who was anxiously seeking God's guidance in whether she should move homes or not. She felt quite relieved when I suggested that God trusted her to decide where to live, and would be with her whatever she chose. In a similar way, I think that God trusts us to decide to wear masks to minimize the spread of COVID-19.

Also recall that God has chosen to focus his attention on the community of Christ. The domain of God's action is the world in general, but more specifically the church. In the Bible we saw that holiness can be viewed as graded. There is variability in the extent of divine presence and action. In particular, it intensifies in relation to Jesus, the church, and the indwelling Holy Spirit. The Spirit is like the wind: sometimes a gentle breeze, sometimes a howling gale, and often somewhere in between. Clark Pinnock argues that the Spirit is "more present" in humans and "more effectively present" to those who know the risen Christ.[44] Divine action is strongest in those domains that are closest to the triune God, the holy center of the world, the one who holds all things.

So where is God in the pandemic? His Spirit comforts and inspires both those suffering and those working to treat and prevent COVID-19. He is working through those who volunteer to deliver groceries to the housebound, the healthcare workers who take on extra shifts, and the person who refused a ventilator so someone younger could have it. He is not specifically within viral particles. And he is likely only weakly present with those who act selfishly or seek to harm others by their action or inaction. The domain of God's action is theoretically unlimited. However, in reality, God holds back his action and respects the freedom he has granted to humans and the created order.

The Nature of God's Action

In the movie *Bruce Almighty*, "God" answers prayers electronically. If only real life was that simple. As I mentioned, it is difficult to know exactly how God acts, and I think it's more important to know *that* he acts rather than *how*. But we can learn something about the nature of divine action by considering things like governance, miracles, and the nature of freedom. The question of how God acts relates to how Aristotle's four levels interact; how a final cause—the Spirit of God—affects material, formal, and efficient causes. It also points to the importance of integrating our faith with our lived experiences. God and world are intertwined.

Recall the problems with the natural/supernatural distinction. Well, the problem of dichotomies arises again in discussions on divine action. This is often classified as general/special, ordinary/extraordinary, or indirect/direct. Such divisions can sometimes be helpful ways to frame the issues, but can also limit how we understand God's action, which is much more variable and nuanced than these categories imply. Problems arise with extreme views, both when we conflate the categories and when we separate them too much.

Some Christians believe that God never intervenes in creation, and miracles no longer occur. They discount the possibility of direct, extraordinary divine action. A subtler variation on this view is that God's activity is only spiritual in nature. God inspires and persuades but does not directly cause things to happen in the world.[45] These interpretations emphasize general divine action; God's relation to the overall process, the whole world, but not particular incidences in it. I don't think these views fit with the biblical witness or Christian experience, which show that God works specifically at times. At the other extreme, some Christian perspectives emphasize special divine action. Those that view God as directly causing and controlling absolutely everything have difficulty discerning when God is acting in a special manner. If everything occurs through God's direct action, the term miracle becomes meaningless.

Christians in charismatic denominations are sometimes accused of focusing excessively on extraordinary acts of the Holy Spirit. They assume that gifts and manifestations of the Spirit signify a higher level of spirituality, and they may neglect the work of the Spirit in guidance or discernment.[46] Such views separate general and special divine action too much, and imply that God is not much involved in the ordinary, natural world. Perspectives that sharply distinguish between general and special divine action risk viewing God as a capricious, arbitrary intervener. As William Pollard notes, "If a miraculous event could only happen outside the natural order of things, then it would necessarily imply that it would be unnatural for God to exercise providence over his creation. Such an idea is, however, clearly un-biblical."[47]

God's action in a general sense is often described using terms such as *governance, ordinary sustenance, preservation,* and *common grace*.[48] Because God cares deeply for his creation, he watches over it but does not need or desire to create everything anew at each point in time. Alternatively, he creates continually, but in a general sort of way, working with the material world but not intervening in natural processes. This idea of continuing creation fits with some biblical themes: original creation, creation after the flood, Jesus as the new creation, the church as a new creation, and the promised new creation.[49] As we saw, God created the world to be self-sustaining; there are regularities in nature that benefit everyone, and do not require specific divine intervention. He oversees creation, but commonly leaves things to take their natural course. The Lord offers grace freely but generally refrains from intervening because of his respect for the freedom that he has given to creation. His action is self-limited.

We have already discussed human free will and the relative freedom of evil spirits to act destructively. Interestingly, forces of nature can also be considered to have freedom. Anglican Austin Farrer, writing about the 1755 Lisbon earthquake, suggests that God does not impose his action on natural forces: "The will of God expressed in the event is his will for the physical elements in the earth's crust or under it: his will that they should go on being themselves and acting in accordance with their natures."[50] In other words, sometimes bad things that happen in the world are simply a side effect of processes that are created for optimal functioning. Polkinghorne expands on this idea and explains negative events in nature through what he calls the free-process defense. Just as humans are free, so is nature free—to cause disease through random mutations, or to cause earthquakes through random shifting of tectonic plates.[51] And to cause a novel and vicious coronavirus to develop. Polkinghorne points to the complexity of the world in which order and disorder, perfection and imperfection, intersect. This overlap and intertwining of good and bad in nature give us a clue about how God acts.

Many of us prayed for miracles during the COVID-19 pandemic, perhaps without being sure exactly what we were asking. Miracles are an example of special or direct divine action and are much misunderstood. The Greek terms that are translated *miracle* usually mean sign, power, and wonder. They are broad and do not specify how God acts. Miracles are sometimes viewed too narrowly and sometimes too widely. They have classically been described as violating the laws of nature, or causing something to happen that cannot be explained by science.[52] However, I think that this view is too narrow, implying, as we discussed above, an artificial distinction between natural and supernatural. More importantly, it would not have been the way biblical authors understood miracles. Remember that the Bible is focused more on *why* than *how*, on agency rather than scientific mechanism. Miracles are an act of God, not a breach of nature. In Scripture they are signs and have theological purposes: to demonstrate the power of the one true God over pagan gods, and to affirm Jesus as the promised Messiah. Miracles carry "the signature of God."[53] In addition, if we view miracles as unexplained events, then we are assuming that this is only because we don't have enough scientific knowledge yet, and have to defer to God to fill the gaps. This implies that eventually we will have no need of God. Clearly this is not a biblical perspective.

Some Christians view miracles too broadly. I have heard people claim that God miraculously caused it to rain on their dry crops, or that he healed their cold virus. When something is personally favorable, it is easy to forget that both rain and cold viruses are common in the world. This sort of claim does not fit with biblical teaching associating miracles with advancing the kingdom of God. When we see too much as miraculous, the concept is diminished and may be trivialized. We risk disrespecting God and the nature of the world he has made.

I think that our view of miracle needs to emphasize its significance in pointing to the presence and action of God in the world, and the advance of his kingdom. There are some guidelines for judging whether events are miraculous or not.[54] Miracles should be verifiable, consistent with God's character as depicted in the Bible, have spiritual/theological meaning, inspire awe and wonder, and be counterintuitive. Of course, we can never be certain whether God has intervened in the world or not, but perhaps this is a good thing as it keeps us humble. We need to be cautious in using the *term* miracle, but this should not stop us praising God for the wonders of the ordinary or seeing his majesty in nature.

A miracle is a highly unusual event but is not necessarily incompatible with natural processes. In fact it is possible that some miracles require the involvement of humans and nature. God may guide people to act, but they have to listen to him. Jesus healed the lame but did not replace missing limbs. Someone receiving chemotherapy may not have any white blood cells that God can use to heal their infection. This leads us to the question of exactly how God might act in the world.

The Mechanisms of God's Action

I heard a story once about a traveler hearing a bell that drew him into a church and led him to put his faith in Christ. We have all heard stories about

God healing diseases, giving guidance through a book or movie, putting significant people in our paths and so on. And we know the cliché: God works in mysterious ways. But we still speculate: Did God move atoms to ring that bell or did he use it coincidentally? Does God heal by changing cells in the body, by accelerating natural processes, or by working through doctors? Does God act from outside the world or from within it? Let's look at some of these aspects of exactly how God acts.

Recall that I don't find dichotomies helpful: immanence and transcendence are not identical but also not easily distinguished, natural and supernatural are artificial categories, God's presence and activity are intertwined. Since the triune God created the world and its inhabitants to be in relationship with him, it makes the most sense that he acts from within and through the created order. Rather than intervening in the world through occasional lightning bolts, God works through natural processes, "within the grain of nature."[55] He uphold and directs creation internally.[56] Reality is flexible and intertwined, dependent on divine presence and activity. Everyone benefits indirectly from the Holy Spirit who swirls through the world. Moltmann suggests that we eliminate the language of causality because it implies a one-way relationship. He prefers terms like indwelling, accompanying, reciprocity, and mutual cooperation. God's involvement with the world is "an intricate web of unilateral, reciprocal, and many-sided relationships."[57] However, I think that the language of cause and effect in theology can be helpful as long as we don't assume linear, unidirectional connections between the two.

In the Bible, God acts to restore order, to renew creation and creatures, rather than radically change them from the outside. Jesus acts from within the family and culture into which he was born in order to bring light into the darkness. The Holy Spirit, although gifted from beyond, acts through followers of Christ. Godly reality has boundaries, but evil, darkness, and disorder continually infiltrate this reality and require ongoing cleansing. God's action is subtle and continuous. Instead of breaking into the world, it uncovers the true reality that is already present but hidden in creation. God works through the church and in miraculous ways to remove the grime of the cosmos and reveal pristine reality.[58] Recall that miracles do not breach the natural order of things. They can be viewed as occasions in which divine action is stronger and more visible than usual. Thomas Torrance suggests that miracles involve *recreation* of original order in situations where decay and disorder have occurred, rather than *suspension* of natural order.[59] As I mentioned before, COVID-19 is a good example of disorder; it is not compatible with God's good creation. By finding ways to treat and prevent it, we can help restore order.

In terms of detailed mechanisms of God's action, those working within the science-faith intersection have made some proposals that we will discuss in chapter 5.[60] A challenging problem is figuring out exactly how spiritual and material realms interact, or finding a causal joint between God and the world. I am not convinced that this will ever happen, but this does not mean that spiritual-material connection is not possible.[61] Speculations are interesting and stimulate thought, but God may act in ways completely beyond our comprehension. I also think it's helpful to consider his action, and his relationship to the world generally, in nuanced and metaphorical terms. Recall the concept of gradations of holiness and that the focus of God's action is the church. One of the ways he works from within creation is through his creatures.

Human Cooperation with God's Action

During the 2020 pandemic, many of us prayed for God to guide healthcare workers, scientists, public health leaders, and even politicians. We assume that God talks to people. In our discussion on causation in the Bible, we noted that a primary way in which God works is through intermediaries: priests, prophets, the church. We also noted ambiguity; at times both God and humans cause the same thing, implying an overlap and intertwining. And, of course, the primary means by which God acts in our post-ascension world is through the Holy Spirit. It is God's Spirit who indwells believers and is active in creation. This Spirit, who is both a quasi-impersonal force and a personal agent, speaks to our hearts and minds to act causally in the world.[62] Recall that God's activity is always mediated. Even spiritual-religious experiences are associated with brain activity, and our interpretation of them is dependent on our language and culture. The Spirit works through our created mind-brains.

Theologians refer to the idea of God and humans working together as *double agency, accompaniment, cooperation,* or *concursus.* This last can be defined as "the concurrent action of two or more causes that lead to a particular effect."[63] Note the similarity to the philosophical concept of two causes having a common effect. There are different types of concursus.

A first variation, known as *prior concursus,* views God as the powerful, primary cause who directs free will; humans are only secondary causative agents. This view is deterministic. It suggests that people are mere tools in God's hands.[64] He uses us to accomplish his purposes, but we have no choice as to whether God uses us or not. This view, like other views of God as omni-causal, has many problems. It minimizes the distinction between

Creator and creature, limits human action to submission, negates human responsibility, and does not explain what happens when humans refuse to cooperate with God. Theologian Joshua Reichard points out that "a logical quandary exists between relying on God as a primary cause or precondition to human action and holding human beings personally accountable for their actions."[65] Viewing people as mere puppets of God does not fit with biblical concepts or our everyday experience.

The second category, *conferred concursus*, claims that humans have genuine freedom, although God may orient human will toward positive action. There is divine-human collaboration rather than humans simply being tools used by God.[66] The Holy Spirit enables and encourages people toward obedience but does not impose his will on them. Divine will is a *contributory* cause to human agency but not a *sufficient* cause. Wright suggests that "God acts, creatures act, but sometimes these two lines of activity entwine, with God's line allowing the creaturely line to share its space."[67] At times we work closely with God; other times less so. There is ebb and flow and overlap between human and divine causation.

On occasion when paddling, I sneak up behind another boat and hold on for a free ride (it's usually brief). The front canoe is doing the work, but I'm still required to hold on. I can choose to let go, but I do better if I accept the help. This experience offers an illustration for the truth that God and humans do not have equal causative powers, but we are more than just puppets. Reichard notes that "God is always and at once persuading all things, including human beings, toward the common good, but determining nothing . . . the question is whether human beings recognize and identify with God's cooperative activity."[68] In other words, we are responsible for participating in God's work. Cause and effect intertwine.

No doubt we all pray at times, even if we don't fully understand it. Prayer is probably the most common way in which Spirit and spirit work together. God craves communication with his creatures. He has also granted us the ability to ask him to act; known as petitionary prayer.[69] I suspect that the primary nature of divine action is mental revelation, spiritual guidance, inspiration, insight, and comfort. And, because God values free cooperation, I suspect that the manner of his action is primarily, though not only, through persuasion.[70] Gentle urging accords well with a God of love. It also fits with human free choice and divine guidance as attested to in Scripture. At times God nudges, but at times he can present people with offers that are practically impossible to refuse. Many Christians tell stories of how, before they committed their lives to Christ, God's Spirit pursued them, convicting them of sin, and providing them with the gospel message in many and various ways. We can only find God when he first finds us. In theology this is known as *prevenient grace*; divine love always comes before human decision.

I suggest that, although he may directly use human agents on occasion, mostly God tasks humans with responsibility, desires collaborative interaction, and guides us along the way. But remember, causation is complex. Our lives are also affected by multitudes of people who don't want to follow God, evil spirits that seek to thwart God's will, and natural processes that have causative powers. COVID-19 is a good example of something that happens apart from both God and humans, since it is something that neither desire. Before we discuss these complexities, let's reconsider the language we use to describe how God acts in the world.

Models of God's Action

In George McDonald's classic story, the princess rescues her friend from goblins by following an almost invisible silvery thread that her grandmother (who represents God) provides.[71] God is depicted as acting by subtly guiding a faithful follower. Divine action may be better understood through metaphors and models than through philosophical/theological language. Our knowledge of the Bible, and our knowledge and experience of the world are the basis for metaphors and models—using what we know to illuminate the unknown. We have already alluded to some models; now we expand on these and consider others in order to broaden our perspective and understanding of divine causation.

One set of analogies uses human relationships.[72] We have argued against God acting unilaterally through micro-management and direct control. Therefore, models that view God as a puppeteer, dictator, or engineer are unhelpful. However, the healthy parent-child relationship nicely illustrates how God lovingly cares and guides his creation while allowing it freedom to develop. In fact, Jesus compares himself with a mother hen (Matt 23:37) and the Holy Spirit is sometimes likened to a mother.[73] A baby in the womb has independent movement but is still dependent on its mother. Parents give children freedom but with specific parameters. Similarly, a wise prime minister or a servant king exerts general governance without being responsible for all that goes wrong in his country.[74] A hostess of a large family dinner may oversee the occasion without doing everything herself. Others bring food and mingle freely. At a successful party, the hostess may also impart a warm ambience to the entire group, without guests being able to specify exactly what she did. Finally, the doctor-patient relationship can be compared with the God-world relationship. People have responsibility for maintaining their health but turn to physicians when things go wrong. When I delivered babies, I mostly felt "in charge" of the situation because I knew what was going on and had some interventions available if needed. But often all I did was guide a natural process. New mothers sometimes found my mere presence with them reassuring.

Nature metaphors also help us understand God's action in the world. Like the sun, God steadily sustains the earth, and we are naturally drawn to him. The Bible is replete with light imagery for God and goodness; Jesus is the "light of the world" who gives the "light of life" (John 8:12). Like the wind, God's action is ubiquitous and unpredictable. Both Hebrew and Greek terms for *spirit* can also be translated as breath or wind. John likens the Holy Spirit to a wind that "blows where it chooses" (John 3:8). Remember that the wind varies from whispers to gales. Finally, like ocean tides, God's action is steady and foreseeable, but only in the long run.[75] Anyone who has swum in the sea knows that cooperating with waves is essential. I think using sun, wind, and tides together can give us a good picture of how God acts in the world.

A final set of metaphors relies on games and the arts. God is viewed as a creative artist rather than a construction engineer.[76] He is like an expert chess player who is confident in his superior skill, wisdom, and knowledge of the other player, but may not know exactly what moves the other player will make or how many moves it will take to win the game.[77] There is both superiority and a respect for the freedom of the weaker player. God is like a novelist whose characters take on a life of their own, doing things he may not like, but he writes the overall plot and the ending.[78] He is a potter working with clay that does not always cooperate, and a designer who uses multiple methods to create. He is the director of a choir and conductor of a symphony, in which membership is optional. Each instrument is independent but, through obedience to the conductor and attunement with the Spirit, beautiful music is produced that resonates throughout the world.[79] God is also a playwright: Pinnock describes the world as "a theatre where the divine purposes are being worked out by the resourcefulness of God in dealing with the surprises of a significant creation."[80]

Using a combination of models is most useful; different ones resonate better with certain situations and certain people. Each offers different snapshots of how God acts in the world. This approach encourages us to think in less certain terms, allowing for theological flexibility while ensuring biblical and scientific compatibility. It may shift focus away from our circumstances and toward our relationship with our Creator and Savior. Overall, I think the language of metaphor and analogies is more accessible and perhaps more helpful than the language of philosophy or science.

WHAT DOES THEOLOGY SAY ABOUT
ILLNESS AND HEALING?

A few years ago, I had not one but two papers to present at a theology conference. The week before I had contracted a nasty cold virus; the continual hacking cough proved hazardous to my vocal cords and rendered me literally speechless. When I arrived at the conference, the first person I encountered said, "*Someone* doesn't want you making that presentation" (subtext: the devil caused the laryngitis). Someone else suggested that maybe God wanted me to lose my voice so that my presentation on the voice of God would have more impact. Others offered advice for taking care of myself, perhaps implying I was responsible for my healing. I whispered in response, "It's just a cold." Of course, many people prayed for me, without sharing their thoughts about causation, but implying that they believed in divine healing. (For those who need to know, I got through both presentations and eventually recovered my voice.)

These comments illustrate how some Christians understand the causes and cures of illness: God, the devil, people, or—at least in my view of what caused my laryngitis—natural and random elements. We have seen that all of these are causative factors present in biblical texts, and in fact often intertwine. We have discussed how God acts in flexible, variable ways, and gifts creation and creatures with freedom and responsibility—to cause illness and bring about healing. The idea of multiple factors and agents that make things happen in the world is implied in Christian theology. We'll consider some general issues first.

Recall that in the God-world dyad, cause-and-effect relations are not linear and unilateral, but usually reciprocal, dependent on human cooperation. God can more effectively govern the world when people are attuned to his Spirit and follow his direction. We need to align our actions with divine purposes.[81] Reichard suggests that "theologians may need to move beyond archaic theories of linear causation and focus instead on subjectively interpreting the ways in which human beings may be said to interact with God." We should not be obsessed with finding a "causal link" but move toward "a scientifically informed understanding of the multiplicity of causative factors, including both God and human beings."[82] I agree, and suggest we include evil spirits and natural processes as potential causes.

Events, like the fall of the tower of Siloam, can happen without God or humans causing them. The Bible depicts elements of disorder and randomness in creation. Causal chains intersect and accidents occur. To complicate things further, evil spirits can influence human actions and possibly also "natural" evil events, like tornadoes.[83] Orthodox theologian David Bentley

Hart suggests that the 2004 Asian tsunami was caused by the movement of ocean tectonic plates, a normal process in creation that at times causes disaster. Interestingly, he also attributes some responsibility to spiritual powers, those alienated from God and holding the world hostage. Using a God-as-artist metaphor, he is clear that there is no simple "causal relation between a cosmic machine and its divine artisan."[84] It is reassuring to know that, although events in our world are sometimes arbitrary, we can trust that God's purposes will prevail in the long run and that he is always present with us.

In sum, Christian theology affirms that things happen in the world as a result of many different causative forces (remember, all except the first are created by God): the Holy Spirit working in the world to draw people to the cross, to God, and goodness; humans exercising their free will, either responsibly or irresponsibly; evil spirits seeking to destroy God's good creation; natural elements of creation, acting according to their nature.[85] In addition, these forces frequently interact—humans are influenced by the Spirit of God, evil spirits, and our own sinful natures. God is sovereign and, in his wisdom, has created a world that is complex and sometimes "self-causing." He deeply desires human collaboration in fulfilling his kingdom plans.

So, what about my laryngitis? Your friend's cancer? Global pandemics? Both the Bible and Christian theology view afflictions as being caused by multiple different factors. We saw that God occasionally causes illness as punishment for sin, but Jesus views it as something contrary to God's will, to be resisted and counteracted. Illness in the Gospels is primarily caused by evil spirits. Sometimes it is not explained or assumed to be caused by natural factors. Karl Barth insists that sickness "like death itself, is unnatural and disorderly, an element in the rebellion of chaos against God's creation."[86] This clearly contradicts the idea that God caused COVID-19 in order to punish sinful people or teach us a lesson. Remember that our perceptions of what causes things impact our responses. If we assume that God caused the pandemic, we may not work to counteract its effects. If we assume that evil spirits caused it, we may not change any of our irresponsible behavior. It is always important that we consider all possible causes.[87]

Some people who offered opinions about the cause of my laryngitis seemed to focus only on one factor. When the condition is more serious than a cold virus, comments like those I received are not only theologically uninformed, but may increase the suffering that someone is already undergoing. Not everything has an ultimate cause. Sometimes stuff just happens.

And what about Publius's sick father? The friend who recovered from COVID-19? Biblical texts suggest that healing may occur naturally, through the actions of ourselves or others, like physicians, and on occasion, through divine action. With respect to the last, remember that miracles always have a theological purpose, and we should use the term cautiously. I've heard many stories, mostly in missionary contexts, of people recovering unexpectedly from various afflictions following prayer. Divine or faith healing, a type of miracle, does occur and is usually associated with advancing the kingdom of God.[88] This makes sense given what we know about God's overall aim. He works from within creation, and his presence and action are strongest within the community of Christ.[89] Therefore, although we may not know details, it is likely that the indwelling Holy Spirit primarily works through people to bring about healing in ourselves and others. This reinforces the commands to pray and care for those who are ill.

In sum, events in the world are typically caused by an interaction between divine, demonic, human, and natural factors. Not all of these are involved in everything. What happens is determined partly by our own choices, the choices of others, possible actions of spiritual beings, possible direct divine intervention, indirect divine guidance (an intuition to act), and random factors (like viral mutations). We are unlikely to know the degree of involvement of each of these. They all cause things to happen *sometimes* but not *always*.

God desires healing and salvation for all. His Spirit indwells and flows through creation continuously to renew and restore order and holiness. Illness is contrary to his will but, because he respects the freedom of both humans and natural processes, sometimes it happens. He works from within the world, primarily through humans, to bring about healing, light, and love.

CONCLUSION

A well-known children's song refers to God's care and sovereignty: "He's got the whole world in his hands." The Bible and Christian theology affirm this concept, but it needs some clarification. God holds creation in his hands like a sparrow or a chick, lovingly and loosely, tenderly and tentatively. And the world is alive. It wriggles and squiggles in his hands. Parts leap away from his gracious grip. Slimy bits slide through his fingers. Aspects of creation refuse to be held in love.

We can be confident that, although the world itself is always in flux, God is steadfast. Although much in the world cannot be known, God can. Although experiential reality is elusive at times, we can seek the true reality of God's kingdom. Although we may not know the precise ways in which he acts, we can be assured of God's loving care for creation. God created the world with randomness and risk, and takes risks himself in letting it be.

Although affliction is inevitable in a free and complex creation, God does not desire it, and enacts healing in general, cooperative, and occasionally miraculous manners.

We can affirm that the Holy Spirit is present and active in the world, working from within creation and especially within humans, while respecting the integrity and freedom of creation. He acts in various ways and does not need to micromanage. He is especially active in the church, persuading Christians towards loving obedience. God's action is limited by his nature and involves more care than control.

We need to exercise our divinely appointed responsibility in working with the Lord to care for creation. Sometimes things happen because of divine influence, but sometimes they happen for other reasons, or no particular reason. It is difficult to evaluate cause and effect, especially in regard to the triune God, but we can be alert for divine involvement in events that fit with what we know about God's sovereignty, his love and limits, and his concerns for the world and his kingdom. We need to be careful in the type of questions we ask, and remember Aristotle's levels of causality. If we ask a question about the material nature of a thing, then science, not theology, is better equipped to address this. If we are asking about ultimate, divine causation, then we need to consider how it might relate to other levels—this is where knowing about the various interacting factors that cause things to happen is helpful. I believe that it is important to integrate our Christian faith with all areas of life, exercising the grace and gifts we've been given. I also suggest we express our thoughts using tentative and flexible language, and multiple metaphors.

God cannot be put in a box. We need to accept mystery and uncertainty and be very cautious in our conclusions about his action in the world. God can and will achieve his overall aims for all creation, but the exact manner in which this is accomplished is affected by many factors, especially human disobedience. His Spirit hovers over the world, inviting all to participate in the divine, inspiring and guiding. The breath of God, his flame of love, indwells creation, acting through it to restore its original shine and reconcile it to its maker. He shines through all things bright and beautiful.

But the path of the righteous is like the light of dawn,
which shines brighter and brighter until full day.

PROV 4:8

ENDNOTES

1. Alfred B. Smith, "I Know Who Holds the Future," public domain.
2. Kirkpatrick, *Mystery and Agency*, 1–6.
3. Redman, "10,000 Reasons."
4. Pinnock, *Most Moved Mover*, 56–8.
5. Bunch, "Theodicy," 193. Moltmann similarly points out that a god whose primary action is to control things is not worth following and does not describe the God who suffered and died on the cross (*Crucified God*, esp. 222–27).
6. This view, sometimes called traditional or classic, is associated with Augustine, Calvin, and Reformed theology.
7. This view is associated with Wesley, Arminius, and the contemporary open and relational theology movement.
8. As Pinnock states, "His sovereignty is partly unilateral and partly bilateral" (*Most Moved Mover*, 53). See also Fringer and Lane, *Theology of Luck*, 29; Young, *Lies We Believe*; Bowler, *Everything Happens*.
9. As White implies (*Fall of A Sparrow*). See critique in Saunders, *Divine Action*, 30–35.
10. Boyd, *Satan and Problem of Evil*, 153, see also 146–58. He argues that an omni-controlling view of God actually denies divine sovereignty. Boyd proposes and defends six theses of his trinitarian warfare theodicy: love must be freely chosen, freedom implies/requires risk, risk entails moral responsibility, moral responsibility is proportionate to the potential to influence others, the power to influence is irrevocable, and the power to influence is finite.
11. Grenz, *Community of God*, 106–8.
12. Fringer and Lane, *Theology of Luck*, 30. They further suggest that when we experience evil and suffering, most of the time it is simply back luck, unrelated to being fair or unfair, right or wrong, good or bad (44).
13. Ewart and Marks, "Mono-theism theorem"; Bartholomew, *God of Chance*, 145–55; Oord, *Uncontrolling Love*, 170–80.
14. Polkinghorne, "Credibility of the Miraculous," 754.
15. Koren and O'Keefe, *Bruce Almighty*.
16. The primary division here is between libertarian freedom (typically Molinists, traditional freewill theists, and open theists) and compatibilistic freedom (typically traditional Augustinian-Calvinists). E.g., Fischer et al., *Four Views on Free Will*; Balaguer, *Free Will*.
17. E.g., Hasker, *Metaphysics*, 29–56; Oord, *Uncontrolling Love*, 51–79.
18. Boyd, *Satan and Problem of Evil*, 115.
19. Jesuit Joseph Bracken envisions nested areas of responsibility. All creation exists "within the all-encompassing divine field of activity" but, because the created order has some autonomy, everything and everyone also "exists within their own limited field of activity" (*Does God Roll Dice?* 58); also 48–58.
20. Warren, "I Do Not Do What I Want." See also Boyd, *Satan and Problem of Evil*, 339–357.
21. Variations are that God intentionally exercises self-restraint, is unable to exercise anything but persuasive power, or is by nature essentially kenotic. E.g., Oord, *Uncontrolling Love*, 81–186.
22. Moltmann, *God in Creation*, 87–90, 119, 140–57.
23. Terry Wright says, "God's sovereign action within creation is to remain faithful to his promise that the world in its entirety shall be the place of God's presence" (*Providence Made Flesh*, 167). See also Murphy, *Divine Action*, 38.

24. E.g., Wiles, *God's Action,* 60–70; Waltke, *Will of God,* 60–80; Polkinghorne advises understanding providence in the space "between a facile optimism and a fatalistic pessimism" (*Science and Providence,* 52). Fales believes "we know as yet too little about causation . . . to come to reasonable definitive conclusions about the nature or even the possibility, of divine intervention in the physical order" (*Divine Intervention,* 154). I think he is overly skeptical

25. Oord, *Uncontrolling Love,* 16, 17.

26. Terrance Thiessen describes ten and adds one of his own (*Providence and Prayer*); Barbour lists eight (*Religion and Science,* 305–28); Oord counts seven models (*Uncontrolling Love*); and Gundry and Jowers include four (*Divine Providence*).

27. Also known as the Augustinian-Calvinistic view; both these classic theologians thought that God secretly guided their lives. Boyd refers to it as a blueprint model (*Satan and Problem of Evil,* 11–14). Contemporary works supporting this view include Sproul, *Not a Chance*; Highfield, *Faithful Creator.*

28. Piper, *Christ and Coronavirus,* 37.

29. A well-known variation, Molinism, relies on divine foreknowledge to say that because God knows all future decisions and actions, he is in control of all things, even though human choices are free. God has *middle knowledge,* which enables him to control events in the world, without predetermining the actions of free beings. This view has more relevance to divine omniscience than divine action. E.g., Craig, *Only Wise God.* For critiques see Walls and Dongell, *I Am Not a Calvinist*; Oord, *Uncontrolling Love.*

30. Fringer and Lane argue that God is not magical but mysterious (*Theology of Luck,* 107–21). They criticize Christians for blindly deferring to God, and suggest we "embrace the dynamic God who has conferred authority on his people through a yielding of power" (112).

31. Bartholomew, *God of Chance,* 121.

32. Thiessen makes this point (*Prayer and Providence,* 14–20). Historian Herbert Butterfield acknowledges human free will, laws of nature, and divine providence as factors to be considered in causation; later he states the only possible explanations are divine intervention or blind chance ("God in History," 195–7).

33. Cohoe, "God, Causality," 27.

34. E.g., Gruning, *How in the World,* 23–33. Wright similarly states, "if God causes everything to happen, then, essentially, the only thing that happens is God" ("Reconsidering Concursus," 210).

35. Also known as the nontraditional, Arminian, or Wesleyan view, with open theism being a contemporary variation. This last emphasizes divine responsivity and has been criticized for focusing on God's inaction rather than his action. E.g., Pinnock et al., *Openness of God*; Boyd, *God of the Possible*; Oord, *Uncontrolling Love,* 81–105.

36. Oord, *Uncontrolling Love,* 220; see also 151–60.

37. E.g., Jensen, *Divine Providence,* 2.

38. Many scholars suggest avoiding these terms, as they imply a false dichotomy; e.g., Gruning, *How in the World,* 1–9. Peter Harrison notes that prior to Aquinas, there was no natural/supernatural distinction; this developed partly as a result of the formal evaluation of miraculous events ("Introduction").

39. Orthodox theologian Christopher Knight calls this pansacramentalism (*God of Nature*; esp. 86–95, 134–38).

40. Wright, *Providence Made Flesh,* esp. 105–15.

41. Pinnock, *Flame of Love,* 188, 36–41, 185–205.

42. Welker, *God the Spirit,* 338.

43. Bartholomew, *God, Chance, Purpose* 206. God is ultimately responsible but not personally directing every atom to some predetermined end (139). "God's purposes are

achieved as we align our actions with his will and, perhaps, also by his direct action" (242).

44. Pinnock, *Flame of Love*, 73, 116. Welker argues that the "face of God" represents concentrated divine presence (*God the Spirit*, 152). See also Pannenberg, *Systematic Theology 1*, 383–412; Wright, *Providence made Flesh*, 230.

45. The first view is known as deism. The second is associated with Process theology. E.g., Barbour, *Religion and Science*, 281–304; Gruning, *How in the World*, 35–49; Thiessen, *Providence and Prayer*, 52–68.

46. E.g., Levison. *Inspired*.

47. Pollard, *Chance and Providence*, 118; further, the majority of "miracles" recorded in Scripture: "are the result of an extraordinary and extremely improbable combination of chance and accidents. They do not, on close analysis, involve . . . a violation of the laws of nature" (83).

48. There is often a threefold division: conservation (sustaining the world from moment to moment), cooperation (accompanying creation in its activity) and governance (moving creation to a particular end). E.g., Grenz, *Community of God*, 112–23; referencing Loius Berkhof and August Hopkins Strong. See also Barth, *CD* III/3.

49. E.g., Moltmann, *God in Creation*, 209; Polkinghorne, *Science and Providence*, 47–9.

50. Farrer, *Science of God?* 87–8.

51. E.g., Polkinghorne, *Exploring Reality*, 136–46; *Science and Providence*, 76–9; Du Toit, "Human Freedom."

52. Originated by Hume. E.g., Fales, *Divine Intervention*, 22–39; Loikkanen, "Does Divine Action?; Oord, *Uncontrolling Love*, 187–216.

53. Twelftree, *Miracle Worker*, 24–7, 350; Eve, *Healer from Nazareth*, xiii–xxi.

54. E.g., Worthing, "Divine Action"; Duffin, *Medical Miracles*; Oord, *Uncontrolling Love*, 187–216. Polkinghorne classifies miracles as significant coincidences (e.g., nature miracles), enhanced human powers (e.g., psychosomatic healing), and radically "unnatural" events (e.g., the Resurrection). Polkinghorne, *Science and Providence*, 57–60; "Credibility of the Miraculous," 752–3.

55. Polkinghorne, *Exploring Reality*, 34–7. Fretheim states, "the looseness of the causal weave allows God to be at work in the system in some ways without violating . . . it" (*Creation Untamed*, 53).

56. Bartholomew summarizes: "God acts from within by upholding and directing rather than acting on creation from outside" (*God, Chance, Purpose*, 154).

57. Moltmann, *God in Creation*, 14. The world is open to God's presence and influence—God allows his creation to influence him and creation in turn is influenced by the indwelling Spirit. There is a natural exchange of energy between the two.

58. Knight, *God of Nature*; esp. 86–95, 134–38. See also Warren, *Cleansing the Cosmos*.

59. Torrance, *Divine and Contingent Order*, 116–22. See also *Christian Frame of Mind*, 30–48.

60. Much literature has arisen from the Divine Action Project, co-sponsored by the Vatican Observatory and the Center for Theology and the Natural Sciences; six volumes on scientific perspectives on divine action were published in 1990–2003. See also Saunders, *Divine Action*.

61. E.g., Polkinghorne, *Quarks, Chaos*, 89; see also Loikkanen, "Does Divine Action?"

62. E.g., Moltmann, *God in Creation*, 10; Moltmann, *Spirit of Life*; Pinnock, *Flame of Love*.

63. Reichard, "Beyond Causation," 122. Austin Farrer famously coined the term *double agency* (*Faith and Speculation*, esp. 104–5). See also Grenz *Community of God*, 112–23.

64. This is the Thomistic idea of a primary cause working through a secondary one,

much as a woodsman uses an axe; see discussion and critique in Wright, *Providence Made Flesh*, 1–112. Another variation, *permissive concursus*, claims that human free will is permitted; this view is still ultimately deterministic. Reichard, "Causality to Relationality."

65. Reichard, "Beyond Causation," 118.

66. Vincent Brümmer notes that even good human actions do not necessarily reflect cooperation with God ("Farrer, Wiles," 5–10).

67. Wright, "Reconsidering Concursus," 214. See also Wiles, *God's Action*, 14–25, 95–108; Tracy; "Divine Action, Created Causes"; Tracy, "God and Creatures Acting."

68. Reichard, "Beyond Causation," 133.

69. E.g., Cohoe, "God, Causality"; Smith and Yip, "Partnership with God."

70. Barth, pointing to the example of Christ, argues that God does not use coercive power (*CD* III/3: 90–93). See also Grenz, *Community of God*, 112–23.

71. McDonald, *Princess and the Goblin*.

72. E.g., Langford, *Providence*, 68–74.

73. Moltmann suggests four clusters of metaphors for the Holy Spirit: personal (mother), formative (energy), movement (wind, fire), and mystical (light). Moltmann, *Spirit of Life*, 268–300.

74. Bartholomew suggests this analogy (*God, Chance, Purpose*, 293).

75. Langford, *Providence*, 56–74.

76. E.g., Langford, *Providence*, 143–5; Moltmann, *God in Creation*, 303–12; Murphy and Ellis; *Moral Nature*, 53–9.

77. E.g., Wiles *God's Action*, 27–28.

78. Dorothy Sayers notes that a writer's pen can have autonomy (*Mind of the Maker*, esp. 111–22, 169–206).

79. Watts, "Cognitive Neuroscience."

80. Pinnock, *Flame of Love*, 56. See also Moltmann, *God in Creation*, 304–10.

81. E.g., Watts, "Cognitive Neuroscience."

82. Reichard, "Beyond Causation," 131.

83. Boyd, *Satan and Problem of Evil*, 387, 282–4. He believes that evil spirits can influence elements of nature, and further notes that the mystery of evil is "*not about God's character or plan . . . it is rather a mystery about the complexity of creation* (215–16). Because there are multiple causes for events, it is hard to know where to assign responsibility (386–93).

84. Hart, *Doors of the Sea*, 49. He points to the myriad "gods" worshiped in Asian nations, many of whom are thought to control the sea, and notes that evil is a corruption of creation.

85. E.g., Yong, *Spirit of Creation*, esp. 88–101; Clayton, "Natural Law"; Ellis, *How can Physics*.

86. Barth, *CD* IV/4: 366.

87. Well-known charismatic Francis MacNutt claims that illness could come from the human spirit, emotions, body, or evil spirits, although he does not discuss possible interaction between these (*Healing*, 248–61).

88. It is often discussed within charismatic Christianity. E.g., Williams, *Spirit Cure*, esp. 89–95; Brown, *Charismatic Healing*.

89. Amos Yong argues that divine healing is specifically related to the presence of the Holy Spirit in the church (*Spirit of Creation*, 72–132).

PART 2

All Things Bright and Beautiful, All Creatures Great and Small

WE HAVE CONCLUDED THAT the Creator God is sovereign but not omni-controlling. I do not believe he caused the COVID-19 pandemic. In order to understand how this happened, we need to look at the nature of the created world. A world filled with large and small creatures, concrete and abstract concepts, order and disorder, chaos and complexity. A world with paradoxes and randomness, in which cause-and-effect relations are often obscure. A wonderful world that delights and surprises us.

In this section we first review some statistical concepts that can help us understand and evaluate causation: probability, predictability, and unpredictability. Numbers are useful for comprehending God's world. Statistics helps relate the large and small, the group and the individual. Chapter 5 considers what science is and what we can learn about creation through its methods and findings. We examine cause-and-effect relations in many different levels and layers of our world; not only in creatures but in all aspects of creation, including unseen ones. We ask: What are possible explanations for the pandemic? Does science provide all the answers for how and why things happen? Are scientific and Christian views compatible? How can science inform Christian understanding?

4

What Does Mathematics Say about How to Understand Causation?

During the Covid-19 pandemic we were inundated with numerical facts and figures. Daily news reports detailed statistics about new cases, deaths, and disease transmission. We saw graphs and learned about "flattening the curve." We discovered that, although it is almost impossible to predict which individuals may get the disease, we could generally tell trends at a large societal level. Sadly, residents of long-term care facilities died more commonly, but we couldn't tell which particular individuals would die. We also became savvy about testing: if one city reported 20 positive cases on one day, we wanted to know how many people were tested on that day—if only 25 were tested, not 100, the concern is much greater. In our quest to understand how and why things happen, it is essential that we have some basic (and I mean basic) knowledge of the mathematical concepts that describe cause-and-effect relations in the world.

WHAT ARE SOME IMPORTANT STATISTICAL CONCEPTS?

Fourteen generations, 127 years, 720 shekels, 3 tenths of a measure: numbers have been around almost as long as humans have. We are surrounded by them in our daily lives: costs, rates, sizes, frequencies, probabilities, risks.

Even more so these days with easy internet access. But numbers are often a source of confusion and can lead us to misconstrue causation. Statistical methods are important for understanding both individual occurrences and societal events, because they help provide perspective and can inform our response to events.

Statistics is a science that deals with the collection, analysis, and interpretation of numerical facts. It can involve simple descriptions or observations, such as the exact number of people in a city who test positive for Covid-19 on a particular day. But it can also be inferential—drawing conclusions about a large group from a smaller but representative sample of the group, both at one point in time and over time. Pandemic patterns that were observed in one country were helpful in predicting trends in similar countries; patterns over a few days helped us plan for longer term trends. By using mathematical theories of probability, statistics can impose order and regularity on individual unrelated elements. It allows us to estimate the percentage of people who test positive for Covid-19 that will develop symptoms of the disease. Observations can be used to make predictions or develop theories to explain the data. Statistics is sometimes known as a theory of ignorance because it is applied when we lack knowledge, especially about causation. It attempts to measure uncertainty.

I suspect many people have played with coin flips. A toss may show *heads* five times in a row, but after a hundred or more tosses, *heads* and *tails* will be equal. In other words, our evaluation of coin toss outcomes is more exact with more measurements. Similarly, we can more accurately research if God heals people through prayer if we examine more than one reported case. An essential aspect of statistical analysis is sample size. In general, the more information we have, the more accurate our knowledge is. Numbers can be considered at one point in time or over a period of time. This concept is referred to as the *law of large numbers* and is important for judging cause-and-effect relations.

Other helpful terms (remember high school mathematics?) describe a set of data, or collection of measurements.[1] *Frequency* is simply the number of times an item occurs in a data set. You may note informally that your pastor preaches from the Gospels more often than Leviticus. Frequency relates to *average*, or what is most common. This is obtained by dividing the total measurement by the number of instances measured. In 52 weeks, your pastor may preach from the Gospels 23 times. This can also be described in terms of relative frequency or *percentage*, expressed as a fraction of one hundred. In a year your pastor preaches from the Gospels 44 percent of the time (23 divided by 52). The term *rate* also expresses relative frequencies. The birth rate in Canada in 2018 was 10.1 live births per 1000 population.[2]

These perspectives on events are helpful in figuring out cause-and-effect relations because, if we are aware of typical patterns, we are more likely to notice atypical ones. Exceptions and outliers can be informative, but we need to be very careful in making conclusions from rare cases. And remember, the larger the sample size, the higher the likelihood of unusual events. In some ways the COVID-19 pandemic was expected simply because there had not been a pandemic in a hundred years. Mathematicians Mosteller and Diaconis summarize: "There are 7.6 billion people on Planet Earth. Strange things are bound to happen once in a while."[3]

Public health officials urged people to "flatten the curve." Disease outbreaks initially follow a sharp upward slope as the infection spreads, but this levels out as it runs its course and people take action to prevent transmission. Collections of measurements can be repeated over time to observe patterns. With large amounts of data, we can find a line of best fit. This allows us to view averages, outliers, potential error, and to make tentative predictions about future trends. We use statistical measures in everyday life, usually without awareness: we research typical prices before we buy something; we look in the middle of a clothes rack when shopping for something that is an average size.

You may note that when your pastor preaches exceptionally well, her next sermon is likely to be mediocre. This important and commonly misunderstood statistical concept is *regression to the mean*: if we measure something or observe an event that is unlikely, or extreme, it will be closer to the average the next time we measure it. The first measurement is simply a relatively rare exception, and not particularly meaningful. In a coin toss, even if we throw five *heads* in a row, eventually *head-tail* outcomes are equal. Recall my cold virus story. If you followed me around for twenty years, that would be creepy. But you would notice that I seldom have laryngitis when presenting at conferences.

Initial reports indicated that fewer people died from COVID-19 in Africa and India. However, these nations include many rural areas where death certificates are not provided; therefore, we cannot be sure of exact numbers of coronavirus-related deaths. Conclusions from statistical data only relate to the exact *contents* of the data. There may be other important factors that are hidden or neglected. It was once thought that people afflicted with lice were in good health, but the reality was that unwell people usually had fevers, which act as a deterrent to lice.[4] I suspect, somewhat cynically, that Christians who claim that God always answers prayer favorably do not hear reports from the pulpit about those whose prayers were not answered. In other words, they base their conclusions on incomplete data.

Statistical data is notoriously misunderstood and misinterpreted, as in this humorous statement attributed to George Burns: "If you live to be one hundred, you've got it made. Very few people die past that age." Having some understanding of statistics can provide comfort. A friend once expressed discouragement when his pastor praised the work of two small groups in his church that were ministering to the homeless. Although my friend was not interested in that type of ministry, he felt his group was failing. I reassured him, noting that the sample size of those being praised was two. Since the church had 52 small groups, there were 50 that were not involved in praiseworthy ministry; therefore, he should not feel bad. Furthermore, those exceptional groups were likely to return to average over time.

Probability

Many of the disciples were fisherman. They knew that their catches would vary from day to day. They knew that having a full net after hours of nothing was improbable, or outside the realm of chance, and they marveled at Jesus's intervention (John 21:1–6). We deal with probabilities every day. There is an almost 100 percent chance that the sun will rise tomorrow, and close to a 0 percent chance that an asteroid will obliterate the earth. Forecasters may tell us there is a 45 percent chance of rain today, and political analysts may state that there is a high chance a particular candidate will be elected. Probabilities help us plan our days and add a sense of security to our lives.

Because certain knowledge is nigh impossible, it is in fact better to think in terms of *probability*. This term is sometimes expressed as chance, which is confusing because chance also implies randomness. Probability is not chance but a precise measurement: a basic ratio of the number of desired events divided by the number of possible events. It relates to frequencies as defined above, and is usually expressed as a number between 0 and 1, or a percentage. Probabilities may refer to personal belief or intent (I probably will come to your party next week) but, for our purposes, I am using it in reference to mathematics—hypotheses in relation to the natural, observable world.[5] Probabilities are often surprising, as in the well-known birthday problem: If there are 41 people in a room, there is a 90 percent probability that two of them will share a birthday (date and month, not year). This is easier to grasp if you consider that there are 820 pairs of people in the room.

The probability of anyone having a cold on any given day is about 8 percent. But if I also feel mildly unwell, with a sore throat and runny nose, and was in close contact with someone who was sick, this probability is much higher—other related variables change our calculations. Further, the majority of colds get better within a week, regardless of treatment or lack thereof. The concept in probability theory that describes the usual occurrence of something before a change is known as *base rate*, or prior probability. Base rates are important information to have because we cannot evaluate causation in specific situations without knowing the probability of the situation in general, such as common colds. For a more mundane example, the reason that casinos always profit is that they are rigged to win about 51 percent of the time.

Probabilities are a way of expressing ignorance, taming unpredictability, or quantifying uncertainty. They can predict but never with complete accuracy. They allow us to make decisions about individual occurrences based on knowledge of large numbers, or the behavior of groups. Automobile manufacturers know the typical life-span of an engine and offer guarantees based on this information. Insurance companies base their policies on data related to societal behavior. Note that probabilities only provide information on a group, not the individuals that make up that group. We can know human life expectancy in a particular location and time period, but we cannot know how long a particular individual will live (perhaps a good thing).

Let's consider birth: when a woman has four sons in a row, her fifth child is equally likely to be a boy or a girl, despite any hopes she may have. An important issue is the relations between events that are measured, or whether probabilities are independent or dependent. In a coin toss, the outcome of each event is independent of previous ones. In this case, they can be multiplied; the probability that a coin lands *tails* is 50 percent, and the probability that it lands *tails* twice in a row is 25 percent (0.5 x 0.5). Note that the probability is still 50 percent for each subsequent toss.

However, in many events involving various factors, the calculation is more complicated. What we do on one occasion may depend on what we did on a previous one, or it may depend on other things. If I once saw many snakes on one trail, I likely will choose a different one. My previous experience causes my current choice. If it is raining, I likely will not go cycling. This is a little like the necessary and sufficient causes we discussed before. The probability of me going cycling depends on my desire to do so, a necessary cause, but also on weather conditions; therefore, not a sufficient cause. We assume that people base their decisions on multiple factors, and learn from mistakes. Our probability calculations improve as we acquire more knowledge.

Statistical probabilities are very helpful in understanding cause and effect, and are applied in most areas of life, especially when the known causes are not perfectly predictive of the effect. However, we need to take care with our conclusions, remembering that they depend on what questions are posed and what variables are measured. Sometimes we pay more attention to occurrences with higher probabilities, and sometimes to rare events. The latter can sometimes clump together—shark attacks, or (my personal peeve) receiving three party invitations one weekend and none the next. This is not all that surprising, given the law of large numbers. We should not see too much meaning in rare events but neither should we reject them.[6] Low-probability events can be meaningful: credit card companies will notice if your card is used in places unusual for you and alert you to possible fraud. In addition, some things are not impossible but just highly improbable, as in this limerick:

> There was once a hairy baboon,
> who always breathed down his bassoon,
> for he said "it appears,
> in a billion years,
> I shall certainly hit on a tune."[7]

"Fortune tellers" take advantage of probability theory as well as people's ignorance of it. When they announce to a crowd, "someone here has an illness that will be healed soon," this has a high likelihood of being true, given the high base rate of any type of illness, the subjective nature of healing, and the high rate of spontaneous remission for many conditios. Note also that knowledge of probability does not eliminate the concept of randomness. Some things cannot be predicted but statistics can use individual random events to predict larger-scale patterns.

Randomness

If probability is challenging to understand, its relative, randomness, is even more so. The novel coronavirus, like many viruses, developed through random mutations, tiny changes in the organism's DNA. Randomness refers to states that lack principles of organization and are unpredictable. Recall that in biblical cultures, randomness was an accepted part of life. Many people today throw dice when playing games, wear "lucky" shirts or even open their Bible at random to receive a divine message. We may marvel at coincidences, such as someone phoning when we were thinking about them, someone winning the lottery three times, or our symptoms improving when we make an appointment to see a doctor. We may despair that the other line always moves faster, and machines break the day their warranty expires. Conversely, we may claim coincidences do not exist, believing that everything happens for a reason, or using the term "Godincidence." Random, unexpected occurrences are common and often a source of delight. But we do not always recognize them for what they are and may falsely believe that there is a specific cause and reason behind them.

Coincidences happen when events or circumstances occur together without having any apparent causal connection. They are low-probability events, but the term is applied when the event is especially meaningful, and when a cause is not obvious. Accidents are a type of coincidence, although usually have a negative, unhappy outcome. Both of these types of events occur when two or more different causes or causal chains (remember those?) happen to overlap, intersect, or coincide. So, coincidences are not really mysterious at all.

In a coin toss, the outcome—*heads/tails*—is caused by the interaction of undetectable friction in the air, dust particles on the coin, the speed and spin of the toss, and multiple other factors that are impossible to know. Randomness, aside from being unpredictable, can be defined in terms of lacking a discernible cause.[8] This means that there either *is* no cause or else we are unable to *detect* a cause. Philosophers and scientists describe two types of randomness. The first is *actual* (*ontological* in philosophical terms) randomness. It is sometimes called *pure chance* and claims that randomness is inherent in some aspects of reality. This occurs at the quantum level, the prototypical example being radioactive decay, in which two outcomes have equal probability and the process is completely unpredictable.

The second type of randomness is labeled *apparent* (*epistemological* in philosophical terms) and is common. In this type, randomness is only perceptual, due to our lack of knowledge, much of which is unobtainable. Classic examples include coin flips, the roll of a dice, the weather, and many illnesses, all of which depend on so many causative factors interacting over space and time that detection is impossible. Causation is unpredictable; therefore, the processes appear random. In fact, the distinction between actual and apparent randomness is more theoretical than practical. In real life they appear the same. Computerized pseudorandom number generators yield the same effects as truly random processes. And, you guessed it, the outcomes of such processes are best described in terms of probability.

This past summer I randomly scattered a cup of wildflower seeds in my garden. Given how little work I did, I was quite happy that five flowers grew. Random processes are used in many aspects of life. A common scientific method is *sampling theory*. In a simple random selection, each possible sample has an equal chance of being selected, which eliminates bias and allows fair representation. From this method, assuming a large enough sample size, we can extrapolate conclusions to large populations. In agriculture, cheap random scattering of seeds produces better outcomes than orderly processes. Spray paint uses a random scattering method to evenly coat a large surface. Most games rely on chance to ensure fairness, whether it's rolling dice, dealing cards, or picking tiles. Some are entirely dependent on random processes; others incorporate skill as well. Chance can reduce bias and provide equal opportunity, so less skillful players can win too. An element of uncertainty can add surprise, excitement, and enjoyment to games. Indeed, games are said to imitate life.

Adventurers climb mountains, walk tightropes, and play slot machines. Early explorers ventured into unknown, unpredictable territories. People sometimes seek out randomness and the risk it entails.[9] As a physician, I don't recommend dangerous behavior (!), but we all benefit from some degree of unpredictability in our lives. It allows flexibility, alleviates boredom, and challenges personal growth. If life is too precise and orderly, we may stagnate—like Burundian's fictitious donkey, who died from indecision when faced with two identical bales of hay.

However, randomness can cause shock and fear (airplane crashes, disease), or amusement (winning games, meeting someone when we were thinking of them). It affects us at an emotional level. We may ignore rare events or give them too much meaning. Coincidences—in large populations over long periods of time—are relatively common but, because they are unexpected, we react personally. Randomness can cause us to feel we lack control over our lives. I think it's fair to say that few people experienced no anxiety at all during the COVID-19 pandemic. This fear and anxiety can lead to and/or influence other beliefs and theories, such as karma, fate, conspiracies, and divine control. Like it or not, random processes are a part of life: politics (voting methods), economics (the stock market), the arts (Mozart apparently composed music according to the roll of dice), and medicine.

MEDICINE AND PROBABILITY

Medical students are often teased for "developing" symptoms of each new disease they study. Of course, most of the time, their condition can be explained by something much more mundane, like a common cold. We are taught to "look for horses, not zebras." It is exciting to diagnose a rare condition, but we need to remember base rates and consider common causes before we think about those that are less common. The field of epidemiology studies the occurrence of diseases in large populations, using statistical methods to document how common a disease is. Epidemiologists also attempt to detect the sources and causes of diseases. The 2020 pandemic made these ideas familiar to us.

Medical science uses many types of diagrams and models to help us understand diseases. Epidemiologist Kenneth Rothman pioneered the concept of causal pies.[10] These diagrams document the causative factors for a disease, with each represented according to how large its contribution is. For most conditions, not all factors are needed for a disease to develop and sometimes the interaction of two or more causes is needed—recall the philosophical concepts of necessary and sufficient causes. Whether someone gets ill from the coronavirus depends on them having been exposed to someone with the virus, even if indirectly by touching something the other person recently touched. Exposure is a necessary but not sufficient cause because some people contract the virus but do not get ill from it. We also know that people who develop serious symptoms tend to have underlying health issues like smoking, advanced age, or lung disease—these are causes that are neither necessary nor sufficient, but contributory.[11] Simply put, there is no simple causal diagram for understanding diseases.

We know that adults in North America will get about three colds per year, by studying multiple individuals over time. However, this knowledge cannot be applied in the reverse direction. Some individuals may get ten colds one particular year, others, none. How many times one specific person gets sick is random and unpredictable. Remember, probability tames unpredictability, at least when we have large numbers available. Random events at small or individual levels can yield patterns and predictability in aggregate or groups. However, probability theory is limited with respect to prediction.

Probabilities in medicine are helpful for understanding the results of laboratory tests. Contingency tables (Table 4.1) are used to evaluate how accurate a test is.[12] In this example, someone could have COVID-19 and have a positive (quadrant a) or negative (quadrant c) swab result; they could be disease free and have a positive (b) or negative (d) result. A good test would minimize false negatives, which miss disease, as well as false positives, which create anxiety and prompt further testing. The coronavirus test is still new but appears to have a very low false positive rate and about a 25 percent false negative rate. It's possible that someone may have only recently acquired the virus and therefore test negative. Contingency tables can be helpful in recognizing sources of errors, such as only paying attention to one quadrant of the table or not considering the total numbers. They have many applications. Overall, probability theory is immensely useful for understanding disease causation.

Table 4.1: Contingency Table

	Covid-19	Healthy
Positive Swab	(a) True positive (Accurate)	(b) False Positive
Negative Swab	(c) False Negative	(d) True Negative (Accurate)

RANDOMNESS, PROBABILITY, AND CHRISTIANITY

I confess that at times of desperation I have played "Bible roulette": Ask God a question and open the Bible randomly, expecting to find the answer on that page. Aside from this practice not actually being advocated in Scripture, is it really random? It is much more likely that the Bible will open closer to the middle than either end. It is also possible that we may subconsciously open to a place that will give us an answer we want.

However, when things happen in our favor or if we learn a spiritual lesson through an event, many of us are eager to deny any role to circumstance or chance: "God made this happen!" Certainly, God can work through circumstances, but we can evaluate cause and effect better when we have background information, such as how often a Bible will open to a certain section when opened at random. Occurrences that lack organization and a discernable cause are common and can be useful in God's good creation. Predictability and unpredictability, certainty and probability, order and disorder, coexist in our beautiful world. A world that is filled with numbers both great and small.

Recall that biblical texts, especially with respect to divine predictions, refer more often to groups than individuals. Probability theory helps quantify some aspects of randomness as well as providing perspective for understanding the connections between individual happenings and the big picture. Consider divine election: God chooses the people of Israel (Deut 7:6; Ps 33:12) and followers of Christ (1 Pet 2:9).[13] Individuals make up these groups, but they are not necessarily chosen as individuals. It is also possible that God exhibits foreknowledge in the same way that insurance and advertising agencies operate, by predicting group but not individual behavior.[14] Although individual actions may be arbitrary and senseless at times, they usually can be predicted when there are either enough similar people in a group, or enough instances of similar behavior in an individual (there's that law of large numbers again). It also seems likely that, since God created the world with randomness, he uses probability and predictability tools as ways to subtly direct randomness.[15] We cannot know for certain but, by increasing our understanding of the world he has gifted us, we can learn more about God.

To reiterate, it takes a bigger God to allow risk, rather than one who controls absolutely everything. Freedom means that God risks things happening against his will. People and planets may act in ways that neither God nor humans like. For us it means that life can be unpredictable and uncertain at times. God will ensure that his kingdom will come and his will be done overall, but this does not mean that the outcome of every event is guaranteed. I dislike the comparison, but recall that casinos are programmed to win 51 percent of the time. Similarly, we can be confident that God's overall plan will be accomplished, although I suspect he has greater than 51 percent confidence in the outcome. However, this may not be evident in our daily lives. This is where the tools of probability can be helpful. In the long run and in the big picture, life is more predictable. In addition, using terms that suggest probability—*maybe, most likely, perhaps*—protects us from overconfidence and potential embarrassment.

Yet many people are uncomfortable with the concepts of uncertainty and chance. This is understandable because we feel anxious when life appears arbitrary. Christians in particular may associate chance with purposelessness, meaninglessness, and atheism. They find the notions of unpredictability and randomness incompatible with, or even threatening to, their faith. Many consider "blind chance" to be in opposition to a loving God who cares for his creation. An interesting recent study showed that most Christians react negatively to the concept of luck as a real factor in life.[16] However, I believe these reactions are based on misunderstandings. The *Lord* is completely trustworthy, but *life* is often uncertain.

Theologies that view God as omni-causal or deterministic usually deny the existence of randomness. Reformed scholar R. C. Sproul believes that the "mere existence of chance is enough to rip God from his cosmic throne. Chance does not need to rule . . . [it is] a humble servant."[17] Note that he personifies chance and seems to pit God against chance. But chance is not a servant, nor any type of personal being. Randomness merely describes patterns of behavior in the created world. In fact, personifying chance risks diminishing the sovereignty of God.

Others appear to confuse divine control with divine care. John Calvin writes, "There is nothing cheaper than a sparrow . . . and yet God's eye is upon it, and nothing happens to it by chance. Will he then who looks after sparrows neglect to watch over the lives of men?"[18] Just because God watches over a sparrow—and by extension all of creation—does not mean that random events like a gust of wind cannot effect elements of creation. Calvin is referencing Matthew 10:29–31, which also mentions God counting the number of hairs on our heads. But counting is not the same as causing.[19] As we saw in the previous chapter, God deeply cares for his creation and is present to it, but cause and effect within the world are complex and God does not control every little thing.

I believe that randomness is not only compatible with, but beneficial to a Christian understanding of how and why things happen. Chance is not contrary to rationality because it can be understood at a mathematical level. William Pollard, in his classic work *Chance and Providence*, states that "the key to . . . providence in the form in which we as Christians perceive it, is to be found in the appearance of chance and accident in history."[20] Freedom within creation leads to variability and unpredictability; this fits with a view of a God who desires a reciprocal relationship with the world. He wants us to depend on him regardless of the random circumstances that may affect us.

Fringer and Lane propose a "theology of luck" in contrast to a theology of fate, or determinism.[21] God is neither absent nor all-controlling. It's neither all up to us nor all up to God. Instead, the one who created randomness values relationship, and wants to work with us in the ups and downs of life. There is not necessarily an overarching reason for every occurrence in life, although there may be specific causes and effects. Sometimes things happen that are not caused either by human choice or by God's plan.[22] If we passively wait for divine direction, we may miss out on chance opportunities to be God's coworkers. This may lead to a lukewarm faith. By contrast, belief in a divine dictator may lead us to subconsciously try to manipulate God: If I go to church regularly, maybe God will reward me with a new job. Instead, we are called to live our lives faithfully amidst often chaotic circumstances. We cannot always trust the world but can always trust a loving, sovereign God.

We will discover in more detail in chapter 5 that things happen in the world as a result of numerous factors interacting in various ways. As we saw, randomness in creation is beneficial. We need to recognize the web-like character of causation in the world. Bartholomew points out that if we portray God as a micro-manager, we may strangle him "in the complexity of his own creation."[23] Divine sovereignty is not affected by random events in the world and divine providence is "seen in the rich potential with which the creation is endowed."[24] Because most knowledge is uncertain and there are elements of randomness in the world, we should rely on probability to add precision to our beliefs. However, this should not be applied absurdly, such as saying we believe in God with 95 percent certainty.[25] Divine action may be indistinguishable from chance; it is possible that God may choose a child's gender, but the overall gender ratio is still 50 percent. As we saw, God works within the created order. Discerning divine action is understandably difficult but may be aided by viewing events in the context of God's overall salvific plan for creation as well as by learning some statistical concepts.

Remember, randomness does not equal disorder or purposelessness and does not negate God's love for us. Life is more complex than we would like it to be, but the complexity of the world is cause for rejoicing not resignation. Christians can trust in a sovereign God who cares deeply for creation, and, in fact, some degree of uncertainty can encourage our faith. And faith is "the conviction of things not seen" (Heb 11:1). If life was predictable, we could become complacent. God is the one who made all the large and small things that affect us in ways we don't always like. But we can trust that he walks with us through random, changeable events in life.

CONCLUSION

Consider this on-the-spot prayer: "Hail Mary, full of grace, help me find a parking space." Ignoring any theological concerns with this, I challenge you to keep a record for a month of every incident of parking space success and lack thereof. Given the law of large numbers and the fact that traffic and parking patterns are random, it is likely that good and bad results will be roughly equal. This does not mean that God doesn't care, just that we need to be cautious in attributing statistical successes to God. Remember, he is more concerned with character than circumstance—perhaps when parking is limited, we should pray for patience instead.

We all definitely need patience when dealing with large-scale arbitrary events like pandemics. But mathematical tools, although imperfect, can help us grasp them better and fulfill God's calling to care for his world. Statistics can provide some order and predictability to life by considering large amounts of data. It is especially useful when we realize that many occurrences in life follow random patterns, and not simple linear cause-and-effect patterns. Understanding some aspects of statistics is important because much of it is counterintuitive. Probability theory is a tool for taming unpredictability by organizing multiple pieces of information. Indeed, much of the world is better described in terms of probability rather than certainty. It is particularly helpful in the field of epidemiology, such as understanding aspects of COVID-19.

Randomness is not an enemy of God. It describes events in his wise and wonderful world that do not have an obvious cause and are unpredictable. Randomness in life can sometimes cause confusion and discomfort, but this can lead us to a closer relationship with our Creator. Knowing that not many things can be known with certainty can keep us humble and remind us to put our faith in God, not necessarily to control our circumstances, but to guide us in dealing with challenges in life. We need to recognize that creation contains much that is uncertain. We need to avoid false dichotomies and know that God can both create and use randomness. We need to be wise and discerning in our application of statistical knowledge. We need to accept our moral responsibility to work with God through the uncertainties of life, and recognize when norms and averages do not represent his calling for his followers. We can delight in our wonderfully complex world, a world filled with bright and beautiful, great and small things.

. . . under the sun the race is not to the swift, . . . nor riches to the intelligent, nor favor to the skillful. . . but time and chance happen to them all.

ECCL 9:11

ENDNOTES

1. E.g., Deviant, "Statisticshowto"; Bluman, *Elementary Statistics*; Huff, *How to Lie*. Statistical concepts date to about 500 BCE, but their contemporary form is usually attributed to John Graunt who studied mortality patterns in 1662 and was able to better predict life expectancies.

2. Statistics Canada, "Crude Birth Rate."

3. Diaconis and Mosteller, "Studying Coincidences." David Hand demystifies miracles on this basis, saying we should expect one every month (*Improbability Principle*).

4. E.g., Mazure, *Fluke*, 120–25. Another example involves flipping two coins 100 times but only recording combinations with *heads*; we are surprised at the results because we forget that we have censored *tail-tail* outcomes. This is known as a *collider bias*—a variable is affected by two or more other variables. E.g., Pearl and Mackenzie, *Book of Why*, 167–88.

5. E.g., Coles, *Cosmos to Chaos*; Rosenthal, *Struck by Lightning*.

6. E.g., Taleb, *Black Swan*, 38–50, 76–80; 343–57.

7. Attributed to Leo Moser; Mientka, "Professor Leo Moser."

8. Bunch describes randomness as the "confluence of deterministic causal streams that lead to an unpredictable outcome" ("Theodicy," 196). See also Eagle, "Randomness"; Mazur, *Fluke*; Taleb, *Fooled by Randomness*.

9. E.g., Gregersen, "Risk and Religion."

10. Rothman, *Epidemiology*. See also Gorman and Gorman, *Denying to the Grave*, 143–71.

11. Rothan and Byrareddy, "Epidemiology of COVID-19."

12. Screening tests for cancer are not perfect, which is why some people opt out of screening. E.g., Ehrenreich, *Natural Causes*, 32–50. See also Pearl and Mackenzie, *Book of Why*, 104–108.

13. Pinnock emphasizes that the purpose of election is for the "chosen" people to be a vehicle of salvation for all people ("Divine Election"). See also Boyd, *Satan and*

Problem of Evil, 117–21. Wiles notes that Old Testament prophecies point to wider patterns of fulfilment, rather than to individual circumstances (*God's Action*, 54–69).

14. God can foreknow behavior based on his knowledge of a person's character or typical behavior (e.g., Judas's betrayal, Peter's denial). Boyd, *God of the Possible*, 33–48.

15. Paul Ewart notes that random processes may carry information and meaning; God can operate through such processes ("Necessity of Chance"). Christian Barrigar suggests that God likely has access to predictability tools that we cannot comprehend. Further, "The universe constitutes a massive 'multidimensional probability space,' created by God to provide the conditions for an equally-massive directed random walk" (*Freedom*, 47).

16. Stevens, "Grounded Theology."

17. Sproul, *Not a Chance*, 3; see also Poythress, *Chance and Sovereignty*. Bruce Waltke states that providence often appears as chance but "nothing happens to Christians by chance." However, he inconsistently claims that God does not intervene when we seek his will (i.e., for us to mature in Christ) and we should not read too much into circumstance (*Will of God*). At a popular level, Rick Warren claims that "because God is sovereignly in control, accidents are just incidents in God's good plan for you" (*Purpose Driven Life*, 195).

18. Haroutunian, *Calvin: Commentaries*, 265.

19. Van Inwagen, "Place of Chance."

20. Pollard, *Chance and Providence*, 66. See also Bradley, "Randomness and God's Nature."

21. This "shapes a worldview that makes it possible to move from fate [which they equate with a deterministic view of providence]—through chaos—to faith." Fringer and Lane, *Theology of Luck*, 62. Boyd similarly observes that life appears arbitrary because it "embodies an element of chance," which is "a beautiful mystery" (*Satan and Problem of Evil*, 387, 386–93).

22. Fringer and Lane express concern that inconsistent and unhealthy views of God lead to inconsistent and unhealthy followers (*Theology of Luck*, 11–12, 125–30).

23. Bartholomew, *God, Chance, Purpose*, 129; 156–72. See also Bartholomew, *God of Chance*.

24. Bartholomew, *God, Chance, Purpose*, 242; furthermore, "the true location of the design is in the mind of the creator of the algorithm who could not—and did not need to—see the details of the path which the process would follow" (171). Bartholomew perhaps minimizes divine immanence; see critique in Peacocke, *God and New Biology*.

25. Bartholomew, *Uncertain Belief*, 18–23. He notes that we have only fragile bits and pieces of information, and suggests that we may be able to discern God's action if it is rare.

5

What Does Science Say about Causation in the World?

I AM FORTUNATE TO have a home that backs onto conservation land. As I write, the scene out the window is delightfully distracting. Leaves float gently to the ground, squirrels chase each other across the lawn, bunnies eat my weeds (but not enough), and I occasionally abandon my work to ogle at newborn fawns. We likely all have enjoyed and marveled at many aspects of creation—all creatures great and small. We have also at times, such as during the COVID-19 pandemic, been wary and weary about some aspects of the world. But unless unusual events occur, we seldom think about how and why things happen. We also don't usually think about the nature of our interaction with creation. Yet we are called not only to worship the Lord as revealed in the world, albeit tainted by sin, but also to care for his creation. As responsible Christians, we can better appreciate God's world by examining scientific observations of this world. This in turn can help us discern cause-and-effect relations.

We have learned from our examination of causation in the Bible and theology that God, as creator, is the indirect cause of everything. However, we have also seen that he gifts humans with the ability to make things happen, and that sometimes things happen just because that's the way the world is. Now we consider the nature of nature. We will look at how those who study the natural world explain how and why things happen. Not surprisingly, the nature of cause and effect in nature is complicated. There are elements of order and regularity, as well as elements of randomness. There are unseen factors that exert causal influence. We continually benefit from new scientific discoveries and technologies. Because we inhabit the same world as biblical authors, we expect to see some patterns similar to what we saw in our discussion on Christian views on causation. In addition, because the creation reflects its Creator, by better understanding the nature of how and why things happen in our wonderful world, we can perhaps come to know our Creator better.

WHAT IS SCIENCE?

Many people have fond memories of grade-school experiments: science can be fun. Science uses specific methods to understand the world, focusing on *how* things happen not *why*. It is an intellectual and practical activity, not a philosophy or a religion, as some people may think.[1] Recalling Aristotle's four levels of causes, science focuses on the first three: material, the nature of things; formal, how things interrelate; and efficient, or how things can be changed. Science is an important tool for Christians to use to understand God's creation. I believe that integrating faith and life is essential; therefore, Christian belief is relevant for all types of knowledge and levels of causation. Scientists *discover* more commonly than they invent, although many discoveries lead to new or improved technology. Newton did not invent gravity, he simply described it more precisely, allowing us to better conceptualize and interact with it.

Science can also be viewed as a body of knowledge acquired through scientific methods. It includes branches and sub-branches that study various aspects of creation, both abstract and concrete, living and nonliving, small and large. Many Christians with careers in the sciences integrate their faith and work in various areas: bioethics, climate change, geological time, responsible engineering, physics and divine action, the nature of personhood and sexuality, and mathematics and beauty.[2] They all seek to glorify God by understanding his creation. A Christian approach to science is unique in that we are motivated to be faithful to biblical teachings, we consider ethical issues, and we have the indwelling Spirit who offers insight and guidance. A recent example of how science and faith interrelate is the declaration I mentioned earlier: "Love Your Neighbor, Wear a Mask: A Christian Statement on Science for Pandemic Times."

The Scientific Method

A story told in the first chapter of Daniel is similar to scientific experiments. Daniel and his friends decline royal food for religious reasons and eat vegetables only. They suggest that the officials compare their health with that of similar young men who eat meat and wine. Ten days later, Daniel and his friends are healthier and better nourished than the others.[3] Note the "test" of causation implicit here; we can conclude that God's people are healthier because they refused pagan food and ate vegetables instead.

The scientific method is a procedure to investigate something new, involving rigorous, systematic observation, measurement, and experiment. This process leads to new hypotheses and explanations that can then be further tested. Put simply, one may start with a question, make an educated guess as to the answer, devise a way to test this conjecture, analyze the results (usually using statistics), and formulate an answer. The process is frequently circular, because experimental results lead to new questions. Note that this method is *deductive*, rather than inductive. This means that it starts with broad ideas and tests them with precisely designed experiments. The scientific method, because of its need to be specific and focused, generally assumes that models of causation are simple—linear, chain, or circle.

A COVID-19 trial involved giving the drug hydroxychloroquine to half a group of hospitalized patients while the other half received standard care: results after two weeks showed no difference in the patients' symptoms.[4] Researchers concluded that this drug is not effective against the novel coronavirus. The so-called gold standard in medical research is the randomized controlled trial (RCT). This involves comparing two similar groups; individuals are randomly assigned to receive a treatment (the test group) or not (the control group). The researchers, who do not know whether individuals have received an intervention or not, then measure the outcome that is being investigated and draw conclusions accordingly. Clinical practice that follows advice generated by RCTs is called *evidence-based medicine*. Most physicians base their decisions about testing and treatment on guidelines developed from scientific studies. Physical distancing is not some random political ploy but is based on research on how infections are transmitted between people. Although the scientific method is not perfect, it is helpful for us to understand how scientists and physicians arrive at conclusions. It shows how knowledge of cause-and-effect relations can impact our behavior.

Ideally, the scientific community reviews new discoveries and, when possible, repeats experiments to verify results. Fellow experts can point out potential errors. Scientists develop theories, concepts, and models that interact with what they have found. They look for areas of agreement and disagreement with other research findings, and consider all possible explanations when making conclusions.[5] Scientists often design experiments to disprove something, thus setting a high standard. Sometimes new scientific findings lead to what Thomas Kuhn famously labelled paradigm shifts—slow progress is followed by leaps of discovery.[6] A classic example is when people realized that the earth was round and not flat.

During the 2020 pandemic, advice about wearing masks changed. This is not because scientists are all incompetent, but because they revise recommendations when they find new evidence. Many predictions made by health scientists, such as the infection spreading less rapidly when people stay home, have proved true. The scientific method, and its applications in social sciences, has been immensely successful. When done with integrity, it leads to new discoveries and technologies, and new understandings of the world.[7]

The Limits of Science

However, science is imperfect. Its limitations are both practical and theoretical, and we need to be aware of these when we rely on scientific methods for learning how and why things happen in our wonderful world. First, no matter how rigorous the study, scientific findings are always provisional. Recall that knowledge is often elusive and constantly changing. A well-known example is Pasteur's germ theory of disease, which led to the practice of frequent hand washing and a consequent decrease in infectious diseases. When I was in medical school, peptic ulcer disease was thought to be related to stress and acidic foods; now it is known to be caused by a bacterial infection. As we have all experienced with COVID-19, we can only base scientific conclusions on current knowledge.

Second, there are limits to the methods of science. Realistically, resources are costly and imperfect: even the fastest computer in the world cannot compute or solve the problem of infinity and nothingness. Much research is impractical: try counting leaves on the ground in the fall—the number will change faster than you can count. Measurement errors are common, although scientists try and minimize them. When I give infants their routine immunizations, I confess that sometimes not every drop ends up where it is supposed to. Fortunately, vaccines are made with a little more substance than needed, because everyone knows that babies squirm. The fields of mathematics and science have some famous unproveable assumptions and paradoxes, such as Gödel's theorem.[8] Science only offers partial pictures of reality, and makes conclusions using the language of probability rather than certainty. Given what we've learned in the last few chapters, this is a good thing.

Third, human mind-brains have inherent limits. Try thinking of nothing again (sorry). Some concepts, such as infinity and four-dimensional space, are very difficult to grasp. Scientists also make mistakes: remember the unnecessary fears about Y2K.[9] Furthermore, our own worldviews, personal expectations, gender, and culture influence the way we design experiments, measure observations, and interpret results. Our interaction with creation affects what we find. Nature is not *just there* for us to look at. It requires us to interpret and understand, noting cause-and-effect patterns. What we discover depends on what we look for. If we only ask what shape a leaf is, we may not note its color.[10] Recall the importance of asking the right questions and being aware of the different types of knowledge and causation.

Fourth, there are intrinsic limitations in nature itself, much of which is unseen and ambiguous. Science only deals with what is observable and measurable. It can only describe scientific laws, not explain their origin. It cannot answer questions of ultimate meaning or final causation; it is not the only route to knowledge. Scientists sometimes have difficulty describing what they find; therefore, they rely on figurative language, using metaphors and models from things we are familiar with to help explain something new. Many of us have seen pictorial models that explain how the COVID-19 virus is transmitted. Because of the complexity of the universe, most scientists think that it cannot be understood through one theory, and more than one model is often needed to depict some aspects of nature.[11] There are also inherent paradoxes and ambiguities in the natural world. An interesting one that illustrates the complexity and circularity of causation is the Mobius strip (Figure 5.1).[12] This is formed by twisting a strip once, then connecting the ends. It represents an object with only one side, no end or beginning. You can trace your finger along it forever (maybe go to Paris instead).

Figure 5.1: Mobius Strip

Fifth, many scientific discoveries have little practical application. In medicine there is often a disconnect between science and clinical practice. A medication that works in the laboratory may not be effective in humans. Studies use specific research groups—college students are an easy target—and findings from one group may not apply to other groups or particular individuals. Physicians follow guidelines based on rigorous research. But this practice neglects both clinician experience, and patient values and meaning. In fact, the very nature of RCTs precludes study of phenomena like the placebo effect and the healing impact of the therapeutic relationship.[13]

Finally, science does not tell us how to apply results. It does not comment on how to employ technology responsibly, or how to handle moral and ethical dilemmas. Scientific findings can be misapplied or deliberately used for personal or political purposes.[14] Some people think that this happened in some countries during the COVID-19 pandemic. Science is an invaluable tool for studying creation, but we need to be aware of its limits and to recognize that knowledge is provisional and probabilistic. Christians may associate this with the virtue of humility.

WHAT IS THE NATURE OF NATURE?

We observe and engage with the physical world on many levels, from dust on furniture (that I mostly ignore) to craters on the moon. Some extremes of size can only be viewed with instruments, such as microscopes and telescopes. At one extreme, the novel coronavirus is approximately one-twentieth the diameter of a human hair. At the other, distant galaxies are barely detected by advanced instruments, and black holes can only be inferred from their effects on surrounding space. Humans mostly experience daily life at the midrange between microscopic and astronomic. But the extremes impact the middle and are worth knowing about.

Nature and its corresponding scientific specialties can be viewed in hierarchical fashion:

- small: subatomic particles and atoms—physics
- medium: molecules and cells—chemistry, biology
- large: plants and animals—botany, zoology, psychology
- extra-large: earth—geography and geology, stars and planets—astronomy[15]

This idea of larger fields building on findings from smaller areas can be helpful. Classical physics examines the building-blocks of reality and is often considered foundational to other areas of research. This fits with a simple bottom-up chain of causation model—changes at the subatomic level have effects on atoms, molecules, and all the way up the hierarchy.

However, we now know that the various fields interact. Human minds cannot be reduced to biological building blocks. Minds and energy fields can cause changes at chemical and physical levels. Most areas of science cannot be fully understood by studying an area smaller than them. A low-level factor can cause changes in levels above and a high one can cause changes at levels below: bottom-up and top-down causation. And, of course, different levels intertwine. Even space and time are best considered as one entity.[16] Needless to say, cause and effect in nature, like the Bible and theology, is complicated, complex, and difficult to identify.

The Small-Scale World: Randomness

The desk I am writing at is composed, deep down, mostly of empty space. It feels solid because of the electrons that dance within the atoms. Yes, this is freaky, but such is the nature of the unobservable, subatomic world. This micro-reality is mostly studied within the field of quantum mechanics—a division of physics that studies atoms, subatomic particles, and other physical systems that are governed by uncertainty and randomness. The term *quanta* refers to miniscule packets of energy.

At the subatomic level, what appears to be empty space is actually full of particles that interact in complex manners. Many of these only exist very briefly. Whereas classical, or Newtonian, physics describes matter as stable particles with mass and predictability, quantum physics examines aspects of reality that include both matter and energy. These miniscule aspects of the world exist as a sort of combination of particles and energy waves. They are continually created, annihilated, and transformed in ways that involve sudden jumps. This explains why their actions are completely random and inherently unpredictable. Even their existence is hard to define, as physicist Paul Davies notes: "Atoms . . . inhabit a shadowy world of half-existence"; quantum fields consist of "quivering patterns of invisible energy."[17]

Quantum theory has three major aspects.[18] First, cause and effect at this level can only be understood in terms of probability. It is not that we lack information, such as air currents that affect a coin toss, it is the very nature of this level of reality that is random and uncertain. As philosophers would say, it is *ontological*, not simply epistemological. The position and speed of subatomic particles cannot be known at the same time. Most of the time an electron is nowhere, without a unique location; it is like a point on a circle, with an equal likelihood of moving left or right. If you go looking for it, an electron jumps either left or right, and if you measure its speed, it is either fast or slow. This fifty-fifty state can be considered a wave.

Second, not only are subatomic particles elusive but their very reality is affected by the observer. Measuring quantum phenomena is theorized to cause the quantum wave function to collapse into its observed state, to "choose" left or right.[19] This mind-boggling phenomenon was famously illustrated by physicist Erwin Schrödinger. He posited a hypothetical cat in a box with a flask of poison connected to a radioactive source. Radioactive decay follows random patterns with a 50 percent probability of being active or not. If the source activates, the flask is broken, and the cat dies from the poison released. This poor cat exists in a 50 percent state of life or death, simultaneously alive and dead, until sometime peeks in the box, "causing" it to be one or the other. (Don't worry, no cats were harmed in this experiment.)

A third feature of quantum theory is known as *entanglement* or non-locality. If two subatomic particles have interacted but are then separated by any distance, they continue to react in response to measurements of each other. These particles appear to know what the other is doing. They can continue to influence each other and remain connected.[20] Recall that we often infer causation when events are related in time and space. But quantum effects defy contiguity; they can exert their action on things far away. When considered together, subatomic particles and forces can be described as a *quantum field*. Quantum entanglement and fields further point to the complex nature of cause-and-effect relations in the world.

Quantum computer programs are being used to discover treatments for the novel coronavirus. Quantum effects are common and have led to much technological development, especially in the field of electronics. Probability, as a feature of subatomic reality, is a helpful tool to boost certainty. However, the problem of how the possible becomes actual, or how the micro-world relates to the macro- remains. We *see* certainty, like my desk, but uncertainty (subatomic particles and empty space) underlies it. It can be difficult to know what is real, and the thing we observe may have little relation to its underlying quantum processes.[21]

The findings of quantum mechanics have been misapplied and exaggerated, providing much material for science-fiction writers. Nevertheless, they have enormous implications for our understanding of how and why things happen. Quantum theory suggests that uncertainty is inherent in the universe, and that causation can occur at a distance. The created world includes a level that is inherently random and unpredictable. At levels of reality governed by quantum processes, cause-and-effect relations simply *cannot* be known. Amazingly, the world still mostly functions with some degree of regularity and predictability. The subatomic world is an astounding aspect of creation that we are still learning about. It is no wonder that physicist Niels Bohr states, "those who are not shocked when they first come across quantum theory cannot possibly have understood it."[22]

The Everyday World: Order and Regularity

Fortunately for us, we live our daily lives with consistency and a strong degree of predictability. Despite irritations of weather and illness, we experience the world as generally orderly and reliable. We plan our lives with this assumption. The sun rises daily, apples fall from trees, and rocks fall faster than feathers. Water boils at $100°C$ and freezes at $0°C$ (at least in usual conditions). Many undesired events also have some regularity: we feel pain if we fall from trees, we lose consciousness if a large rock hits us on the head or if we drink excessive amounts of alcohol (please don't).

In scientific terms, these patterns are known as *laws of nature*, or regularities. They frequently correspond to mathematical formulae. Scientists may name and describe these laws but are simply observing what is already present, fundamental properties of certain aspects of nature.[23] In other words, God did not necessarily create the laws, but created the world to be orderly. Recall Aristotle's material category and the philosophical notion of disposition. Regularities in nature demonstrate intrinsic causation; they do not require intervention by an external agent. They can be considered self-causing. God created the world to be relatively self-sustaining and everyone benefits from the presence of his Spirit. Murphy and Ellis, with respect to regularities in creation, point out that our daily survival is not dependent on God moment by moment: "What we see in nature is that the impartial operation of the laws of physics, chemistry and biology offers to all persons alike the bounty of nature, irrespective of their beliefs or moral condition."[24]

Most, if not all, of us have suffered mishaps because of the law of gravity (sorry, no personal stories). In fact, many aspects of nature that we experience can be described using laws. A law is universal, applying to a particular phenomenon in all times and places. It allows us to generalize or make predictions about similar occurrences. Effects of a law are consistent with repeated experimental observations. Common examples are gravity, thermodynamics, Newton's laws of motion, Kepler's laws of planetary motion, and Maxwell's laws of electromagnetism. Note that laws have causal properties but are not directly observable. An apple falls from a tree and hits the ground because gravity causes it to fall downward, but we cannot *see* gravity.

There are many other awe-inspiring regularities and patterns in nature.[25] Gaze at the clouds or the forest. All around us we see symmetries, spirals, waves, branches, and stripes. Many patterns can be depicted mathematically. Sierpinski's triangle (Figure 5.2) demonstrates an infinite pattern formed by dividing a triangle into four other triangles and so on.[26] This is an example of a *fractal*, a mathematical concept that describes self-similar patterns that recur at progressively smaller levels. Fractals are found throughout nature in snowflakes, galaxies, coastlines, and blood vessels. The famous Fibonacci sequence (1, 1, 2, 3, 5, 8, 13, 21, 34 . . .), formed by adding two preceding numbers to find the next one, is also a mathematical formula that appears in nature. Pineapples and sunflowers have spirals of 8 and 13 in each direction.

Figure 5.2: Sierpinski's Triangle

Another form of regularity in nature is reproduction. Living things multiply as per God's command in Genesis. Reproduction involves laws of genetics, biochemistry, cell division, and cell development, among others. Coronaviruses use their outer spikes to invade human cells and turn them into virus-producing machines. The desire to reproduce appears to be innate in all living organisms, which makes a lot of sense given that species would die otherwise.

To a degree, humans are self-sustaining: we do not have to think to breathe, our hearts beat regularly, we create new cells daily as others die. People have taken advantage of mathematical and other principles in nature to create technology, which has its own order. We flick a switch and a light turns on. We press a pedal and our cars move. We are usually unaware of these processes, unless something goes wrong. Societies also recognize the importance of social order and regularity, and we all know the dangers when that breaks down.

Laws and patterns in nature fit simple models of causation, such as lines, chains, forks, and circles. However, to reiterate, life is typically more complicated, and causation is difficult to determine. The laws of nature are scientifically problematic. First, many natural processes have inbuilt redundancy. There are backup plans for when things go wrong. Many animals produce numerous offspring of which only a few survive—note that this moves us beyond simple cause-and-effect to probability explanations. Indeed, we live our lives assuming (usually subconsciously) that things may go wrong. We plan different routes when there's heavy traffic. We expect that there will be one bad apple in a bag. In other words, we assume a nonlinear causal model of the world. Furthermore, diverse biological pathways often produce the same effect. We can eat a large variety of food that has the same nutritional value. Different patterns of muscle contraction have similar outcomes.[27] Biological systems allow for genetic mutations, such as what happened with the novel coronavirus. Finally, death, although regrettable, is part of an intricate ecological cycle. Indeed, death frequently brings new life.[28] One could conclude that a degree of "error" and "backup plans" are part of God's design.

A second issue with the laws of nature is that they are easily affected by a variety of factors. Gravitational pull varies with air currents and friction. More obviously, human agents can manipulate and interfere with regularities in nature. We build airplanes that overcome gravity. We splice genes and clone animals. Humans also have responsibility to care for creation and to preserve some of its intrinsic causality. We can choose to eat nutritious food, avoid toxins, and exercise regularly in order to keep our biological systems functioning optimally. Scientists paradoxically use virus particles to manufacture vaccines that protect against the diseases that the same virus causes. In this way, the chain of causation sort of becomes a circle.

Finally, laws are not absolute and fixed, but are more like persistent regularities or idealized principles. In many fields of science, laws of nature have limited use. They typically only apply to one particular situation. Philosopher of science Nancy Cartwright describes the world as *dappled*. It is a patchwork of differing cause-and-effect relations. There is order in the world, but it is diverse and piecemeal. She suggests the terms power, capacity, or disposition rather than law.[29] God has created all things great and small, and gifted the natural world with order, but in a wonderful, intricate fashion.

The Everyday World: Human Interaction

Even people who were fortunate enough to remain healthy suffered during the 2020 pandemic, mostly as a result of the need for physical distancing. This infection disrupted the order of our lives at many levels: churches, schools, grocery stores, workplaces. It also reminded us of the need to care for one another, such as by wearing a mask. What happens at an individual level affects us collectively, and vice versa. Earlier we discussed how statistics and epidemiology can help us understand relations between single occurrences and group trends. Now we turn to the social sciences to consider how and why things happen at societal levels.

In attempts to establish order and find meaning in life, people design rules, systems, and institutions: government, police forces, education, health care, marriage, religion, gender, work ethics.[30] Recall that the Bible talks more about groups—the nation of Israel, the community of Christ—than individuals. And these communities are given many rules and regulations to live by. Societal structures are essential for human functioning and flourishing. Let's consider some aspects that are relevant to causation.

First, societies can be fluid and it can be difficult to separate out groups from the individuals that comprise them. I have noted that teenagers become something quite different when they roam around in packs. Groups are more than the sum of their parts. Conversely, individuals are often defined by the societies of which they are a part. With respect to cause and effect, there is a two-way arrow, or circular causation, between individuals and groups: people are both causes of social changes and are affected by them. A doctor may advise physical distancing, but then have to treat the mental problems that may result. Recall web-like models of causation. Well, when multiple autonomous individuals relate to each other, the networks of various types of human interaction are endless. This is evident especially in our online contacts: it is no surprise the internet is described as a web. Given the multiplicity and complexity of human relationships, it is surprising that our social world has as much order as it has. Of course, without embarking on a tangent, there are many possible explanations for this, including social structures and the presence of God's Spirit in the world. And remember, although individual behavior may be unpredictable, group behavior is generally consistent.

Second, human freedom is limited. In particular, our choices are affected by the choices of other people. Among Christian youth, I have heard stories of men declaring to women, "God told me to marry you." Of course, this depends on God having told the woman the same thing. I've also heard many if-then statements: "If I hadn't gone on that mission trip, I wouldn't have met my wife," implying that God orchestrated the event. But what if the "wife" had decided not to go on that trip? Or the organizers canceled it? When considering cause and effect in life, we always need to remember the impact of the free choices of other people.

Third, and related, all of us are easily influenced by those in our social circles.[31] Being empathetic and compassionate towards others is laudable, and a Christian virtue. We sometimes see this in newsworthy events: inappropriate treatment of an individual may lead to a large group of people marching in protest. However, sometimes our desire to fit in with a group results in judgment errors. In Solomon Asch's famous study on conformity, people were asked to judge which of three lines was closest in length to the target line—the answer was always obvious.[32] Sneakily, the other seven participants in the group were stooges and deliberately chose the wrong line. A third of people always went along with the incorrect group response and three quarters conformed to the group decision at least once. In many life situations, our actions are caused by what a certain group desires, or what we think they desire. (This has been exacerbated in recent years by social media.) *Social identity theory* explains how our sense of self is dependent on our identification with a group. We have a need to belong and subconsciously divide the world into ingroups and outgroups. As you can imagine, this mentality easily leads to stereotyping.[33]

Finally, society in the abstract can be considered a cause. It is well known that urban growth is associated with an increase in crime and disease. But recall that causation is frequently ambiguous—how much garbage in the street does it take to affect health? Health care professionals have only recently been paying attention to social determinants of health, such as poverty and isolation. Once again, we see the complexity and circulatory of cause and effect; people develop societies but are in turn affected by them.

The Large-Scale World: Chaos-Complexity and Emergence

The COVID-19 pandemic has affected both the social world and the natural world. It is an example of a complex dynamic system. Whether and how it infects people depends on so many intermingling factors and processes that direct cause-and-effect relations are impossible to detect. Other common examples of inherently unpredictable systems include the weather, a pile of sand, insect colonies, interpersonal relationships, traffic, and the stock market. These follow web-like models of causation (recall Figure 1.2) in which many aspects interact with each other in many directions. The study of such systems and how order and structure can develop from them is called *chaos-complexity theory*.[34] It describes larger systems in life, in which there is still evidence of order, but not in any simple cause-and-effect manner.

Complex systems are characterized by extreme sensitivity to initial conditions, irregular patterns, and self-organization. With respect to the first, the classic example is the *butterfly effect*. Edward Lorenz, a meteorologist, suggested that a butterfly flapping its wings in Brazil can cause a tornado in Texas.[35] He used this theoretical example to illustrate how small events can produce large effects over time and space. Weather results from the interaction of many factors, such as collisions of millions of miniscule molecules of air and water—this is why it is frustratingly unpredictable. A small change at the beginning of a complex process can cause enormous changes at the end of it. I have experienced something similar when traveling: I am ten-minutes late and miss my bus to the airport; the next bus is scheduled an hour later, but it is thirty-minutes late and I miss my flight—the ten-minute delay turns into a two-day one. Although effects like this are not always desirable, sensitivity to initial conditions is often beneficial: random genetic mutations can, over time, increase the hardiness of some species of animals.

We've all likely experienced situations in which a small change has large effects—commonly described by the maxim, "the straw that broke the camel's back." Such nonlinear, irregular patterns develop in complex systems because of the number of factors involved. Interactions between components are erratic and typically follow exponential growth patterns. The more components in a system, the more possible connections, and the greater the degree of instability and uncertainty. Many events that appear to occur suddenly, such as water freezing, are actually the result of gradual processes. They may start slowly, but speed up toward the end of the process. A related aspect is positive feedback—this occurs when the end results of a process affect the beginning and accelerate the process. Many chemical reactions produce heat; heat increases the rate of these reactions and produces more heat, and so on.

The spread of many diseases follows exponential and chaotic patterns. Epidemiologists work hard to track epidemics but after a certain point, it is impossible. In chaotic systems, negligible effects are no longer negligible. Although we can observe outcomes, we can never know all the variables. Nonlinear systems may involve both random and orderly processes; they are flexible and open to new input and changes. Viruses, unfortunately for us, continually mutate. This is why the 'flu vaccine has to be modified every year.

In one classic experiment, 200 lightbulbs in a network were each programmed with simple rules (e.g., 23 turns on when 46 is on, and off when 91 is on). Within only fourteen iterations, they settled into a limited and stable pattern out of millions of possibilities. This illustrates the ability of complex structures to *self-organize*. Order can develop from chaos. Recall fractals: these repetitive, self-similar patterns also demonstrate self-organization. Most complex systems favor stability and balance. A marble in a bowl settles to a position of minimal energy, water on the top of a cliff will run to either valley. In the long term, most systems select the simplest set of possibilities. Some systems appear to follow simple laws. A school of fish forms a pattern if each fish follows the one in front and keeps pace with the one beside it.[36]

However, if there are too many, this order becomes chaotic. The school may then divide into two parts, thus restoring order.

A group of teenagers is seldom orderly, acting very differently from individual teens. A cake tastes like cake, not flour, eggs, and sugar. *Emergence* theory, which is related to chaos-complexity theory, tells us that many effects cannot be reduced to their component causes.[37] A group or substance emerges from other substances but develops properties that are different from its individual pieces. It is something new and different. A water molecule is not wet, but billions together are. The Mobius strip, we saw above, is also an example of an emergent phenomenon. It is quite different from a strip of paper. The term emergence includes both the process and its novel results. Such processes are common in the natural and social world, and are not amenable to formulaic analysis. Original components, causative agents, and/or antecedent events are usually difficult to detect, and different processes follow different patterns. Something new, whole, and stable arises from the merging of multiple factors.

The concept of emergence is especially relevant in philosophical discussions on the mind-brain problem, or the question of how a biological, material entity produces a psychological, abstract one. The mind somehow emerges from the brain, but is so much more. Neuroscientist Bill Newsome points out a paradox: "If mental processes are determined wholly by the motion of the atoms in my brain, I have no reason to suppose that my beliefs are true . . . and hence I have no reason for supposing my brain to be composed of atoms."[38] Mind and brain are not identical but almost impossible to separate. Emergent phenomena are common in both the sciences and the social sciences. Although perhaps a stretch of the theory, we could view the Trinity as something new that emerges from the Father, Son, and Holy Spirit, but is not separable into its components.

Theologian David Toolan poetically summarizes: "lawfulness . . . rides in fact on a wildly chancy underworld of vibrating, oscillating, aleatory clouds."[39] Most of life's systems exist in a chaotic web, yet nonetheless have some order. Research on complex dynamic systems tells us that most of what we experience in life is caused by diverse, different elements that relate in diverse, different ways. Order can develop from chaos (a flock of birds), and sometimes chaos results from initially orderly processes (a flock of birds in a hurricane). Sometimes completely new phenomena are caused by the intersection of other factors. These observations reflect the diversity and wonder of a creation that does not require constant divine intervention.

The Nonmaterial World

Missionary Heidi Baker tells how, after attending a service at the Toronto Blessing (a church associated with an outpouring of the Holy Spirit in the 1990s), her pneumonia was healed. On another occasion, after a long hospitalization for a serious infection, she checked herself out, flew to Toronto, preached at this church, and again was healed. Medical records confirmed her experience.[40] Although we may question such stories, divine healing, caused by nonphysical factors, is something we need to consider when asking how and why things happen.

Most religions believe that there is an unseen, nonmaterial world. Spiritual beings—God, the Holy Spirit, angels, demons—cause changes in the physical world. This is certainly evident in the Bible. Many people report a connection to the spirit world through prayer and meditation. Numerous anecdotes about spiritual experiences defy material explanations: Francis of Assisi developed stigmata, Teresa of Avila could levitate, many healings have occurred at sacred sites such as Medjugorje where visions of Mary were seen.[41]

In science, an area that is receiving increasing attention is mental causation, or the power of *mind over matter*. This relates to healing, as we will see, but it is often studied within the domain of *parapsychology*, a branch of psychology that investigates allegedly psychic phenomena. This subdiscipline considers experiences outside the realm of human capabilities as presently understood by conventional science.[42]

Parapsychology includes several domains; psychokinesis, or mental interaction with matter, is most relevant to our discussion on causation in the natural world. We may have heard amazing stories of people bending spoons merely by looking at them: most of this is stage magic, but there are some scientifically demonstrated effects of mental causation. Research on this uses small objects, because they are perhaps easier to influence than larger ones and can be measured. A typical study involves participants attempting to mentally manipulate the results of a toss of a die, so it rolls fours more than one-sixth of the time for example. A more sophisticated version involves people "willing" a random number generator (RNG) to produce more ones than zeros over a period of time. When hundreds of these studies are analyzed, a typical hit rate is 51.2 percent. Although this is small, it is significant, at least in scientific terms. Its real-life meaning is yet to be established.

The power of mind over biological systems has also been studied. In one well-known experiment, a self-proclaimed healer Oskar Estebany placed his hands over a group of seeds—they grew much faster than a similar control group. He also accelerated the healing of mice that had received skin grafts.[43] A new area of study, field consciousness, has demonstrated changes in RNGs in labs in various parts of the world during noteworthy events. When the verdict in O. J. Simpson's trial was announced, a sudden pattern in RNGs was noted (remember, being random, they usually have no pattern).[44] These observations suggest that humans are able to mentally cause changes in the observable world.

Many people are skeptical about the research (and there are charlatans around who are worthy of skepticism). However, there have been over 4000 well-designed parapsychology experiments worldwide over many decades. The phenomenon cannot be dismissed. One problem with this research is that it is "data without a theory." Scientists do not know how minds can change physical things, although many are willing to speculate.

Parapsychologist Dean Radin uses concepts from quantum physics in his theory of entangled minds. He proposes that all of reality is connected through invisible threads that extend beyond the boundaries of space-time. Human minds, with conscious attention and intention, are able to affect the material world by working through this medium of interconnection. Radin concludes, "psychic experiences are reframed not as mysterious 'powers of the mind' but as momentary glimpses of the entangled fabric of reality."[45] His theory is speculative, but it stretches our understanding of cause-and-effect relations.

Many scholars are interested in the interconnectedness of all aspects of reality. Attempts to find a theory of everything, such as superstrings that connect through undulating waves of energy, have limited success and are generally regarded as futile.[46] Nevertheless, scientists, psychologists, and philosophers speculate about the possibility of a unified reality or cosmic consciousness. Various theories have been proposed, such as Carl Jung's synchronicity and the collective unconscious,[47] David Bohm's implicate order,[48] and Ervin Laszlo's connectivity hypothesis.[49] These views are fascinating but inconclusive. However, it is noteworthy that many scholars take the existence and causative powers of nonmaterial realities seriously. Suffice it to say that the universe, with its multiple material and nonmaterial causes, is more complex than we can imagine.

WHAT CAUSES ILLNESS AND HEALING?

During the 2020 pandemic, people received more education about viruses and illness than they likely ever wanted. Pictures of the novel coronavirus appeared on our screens, symptoms were listed, and precautions advised.

Especially at the beginning of the pandemic, there was much misinformation and fearmongering. The World Health Organization listed some *Mythbusters* about the disease to correct and clarify what science has shown: consuming hot peppers, garlic, alcohol, or bleach does not prevent or cure COVID-19; mosquitos, houseflies, and mobile networks do not spread the virus.[50]

Recalling our discussion on why we ask why, most people are very interested in cause and effect when it comes to illness. When our health is threatened, our concern is personal. Illness can impact who we are, never mind how we function. It is not just biological, but psychological and sociological. This is as true today as it was in ancient times. As we saw, biblical authors did not clearly separate spiritual and physical affliction. They were not interested in scientific-type examinations, but recognized that illness is sometimes caused by natural factors, sometimes by personal ones. Not surprisingly, Christian wisdom lies in the background of much scientific knowledge of causes and treatments of illness. Similarly, science adds details that can inform Christians who are called to study and assist in the healing of creation.

Let's begin with some general comments about illness and healing.[51] First, it is important to recognize that many symptoms are in fact helpful. Like much self-causation in nature, our bodies are created to be self-sustaining and self-healing. Pain indicates a problem that needs attention, which is why pain killers are not always a good thing. Fever enhances the body's ability to eliminate infections. Inflammation is a result of an influx of physiological healing material. I remember treating a child with asthma once. His mom told him to stop breathing so fast, likely thinking he was anxious. However, his respiration rate was rapid because his body was automatically compensating for the lower oxygen intake caused by narrow air passages.

Second, there is a difference between *illness*, the subjective experience, and *disease*, the scientific term. With respect to the first, I am often amazed how conditions affect people in different ways. Even family members who have been inflicted with the same virus will have different symptoms—some a cough, some nasal congestion, some laryngitis. I have had patients with arthritis who can barely get out of bed; others with the same degree of disease who cheerfully, though slowly, walk everywhere. Not all medical conditions cause suffering: it can be challenging to get patients to take medication for high blood pressure because they feel fine. And of course, suffering associated with physical diseases is very different from that associated with mental illnesses. In addition, *healing* and *cure* may be connected but not always; someone with a chronic disease that is stable often feels well. Treatment does not necessarily eliminate a disease but may relieve suffering.

Finally, there is also variability and ambiguity with respect to diseases. The specific causes and biological abnormality of many conditions, such as chronic fatigue syndrome, are unknown. The numbers that lead to a diagnosis of high blood pressure or high cholesterol are determined by panels of experts and change periodically.[52] Some conditions, like female hysteria, were once considered an illness, but not anymore. Medicine is not an exact science; therefore, our understanding of causes and effects is not exact either.

Illness

Doc, why is my throat sore? What's causing this rash? Patients usually want instant explanations. *Cause* in medicine refers to events or conditions that have a *necessary* role in producing a disease. Learning the origins of diseases (in medical language, *etiology*) is important because clinicians typically base their treatment and prevention of diseases on known causes. If a throat swab shows a bacterial infection, we use an antibiotic to treat it. If stress at work leads to a headache, we counsel about stress reduction. Of course, sometimes a treatment is effective, such as acetaminophen for a headache, regardless of the cause.

Medical anthropologists distinguish between *personalistic* and *naturalistic* causation.[53] The first claims that supernatural beings cause illness; the second claims that impersonal factors, such as germs, cause illness. This is similar to how we classified causation in the Bible. Contemporary Western medicine is almost exclusively naturalistic and has been so for about 125 years. This so-called *biomedical,* or *body-as-machine,* model of disease focuses on underlying biological processes and treats physical aspects of disease. In medical school, I looked at healthy and diseased cells under a microscope to learn the difference. I also assisted in surgeries that removed or repaired diseased organs. I learned treatments (pharmaceutical or surgical) to correct abnormalities. This perspective is an example of a simple linear model of causation. It can be helpful in some areas, such as pharmaceutical trials.

However, recall that Covid-19 and many other conditions are caused by the interaction of many different things. Medical science, like other sciences, now views causation as complex and usually nonlinear. Each node of the causal web can be influenced by external and internal factors. Even genes are affected by the environment. And medicine increasingly recognizes that psychosocial and mental factors can affect health—*mind over matter*. Stress is well known to be associated with illness, although it is neither a necessary nor sufficient cause.[54] Epidemiologists, who study diseases at population levels, point to the interactions between host, agent, and environment in causing an illness. With COVID-19, the *host* is an infected person, with specific influencing factors such as age and prior health; the *agent* is the novel coronavirus; the *environment* includes things like contaminated surfaces and how the person was exposed to the virus. This is similar to some causal relations we discussed earlier: contiguity, temporality, and agency. Knowing the variety of causal components is particularly important in mental illness. Mood disorders usually result from a combination of genetic, biochemical, environmental, psychological, and spiritual factors.

I sometimes enjoy the looks on people's faces when I tell them how little physicians know. The exact cause of many illnesses is one of the areas that is often unknown, but we have some strategies that help. When we evaluate the origin of illnesses, we consider whether cause and effect are related in a strong, consistent manner, and whether the connection between them is biologically plausible.[55] The novel coronavirus is a necessary cause for the disease COVID-19 because of the number of causal associations and our knowledge of other illnesses caused by viruses—it makes sense biologically. Remember, however, that it is not a sufficient cause because infected people can be asymptomatic. Medical science is inexact; consequently, contemporary models of illness are multifactorial and probabilistic.[56] Such views include many different causes and are seldom absolute in their conclusions. Perhaps understandably, most people prefer certainty and simple explanations of illness. They frequently misinterpret *a* cause as *the* cause. But most of the time many interrelated causes produce illness.

As expected, medical science reinforces the idea that most causation is complex. Although medicine is primarily naturalistic, it is now recognizing that personalistic factors, humans, have a role in causing illness. Disease development usually involves an interaction between host, agent, and environment. Each of these has other associated variables. Whether we get ill or not depends on predisposing factors (stress, poor nutrition), precipitating factors (exposure to a virus), and a critical point at which these factors and others intersect.

Healing

Most people don't want to know this, but our bodies are bombarded by vicious infectious agents and rogue cells daily. It is truly amazing that humans function so well most of the time. Fortunately, our bodies are self-healing (an example of dispositional or intrinsic causation). Approximately 90 percent of ailments resolve spontaneously, especially when we take care of ourselves. Skin rashes, common colds, headaches, and muscle aches are familiar examples. Since many illnesses are self-limited, physicians often take a watch-and-see approach. Other times we merely encourage the body's natural healing abilities, such as aligning broken bones so that they reconnect properly. When more is required, physicians use treatments that work from the bottom up, such as antibiotics that kill bacteria, and genetic therapy, as well as those that work from the top down, such as stress management strategies, rest, and psychotherapy.[57]

I have encountered patients who are angry because I did not prescribe an antibiotic for their viral illness. Despite my efforts, they likely misunderstood that antibiotics are not effective against diseases caused by viruses. I suspect they also hoped for a quick fix. I have also had many patients who were happy that I found the correct cause and subsequent treatment of their condition. But of course, because of the complex nature of disease, a clear cause and clear treatment cannot always be found. My medical students are often quick to suggest drug treatments. However, top-down, or nonmaterial, therapies are just as important. Educating and reassuring patients about the nature of their illness can decrease their anxiety, which in turn can improve their condition. Education can also help people understand the reasons for treatments such as regular exercise, good nutrition, and adequate sleep. I remember one patient who developed prediabetes; he prevented it progressing into diabetes by cycling every day.

The *placebo effect* is an interesting nonmaterial factor in healing.[58] This describes a positive response, such as feeling better, when people are given a substance that has no scientifically proven effect, but that the patient *believes* to have an effect. People are given a fake treatment, such as a sugar pill, but not told what it is. This phenomenon is used in medical research, allowing scientists to compare results in subjects who took a new medication with results in those who took a sugar pill (recall RCTs). No one is sure exactly how the placebo effect causes symptom improvement, but it is an important factor to think about when we are evaluating cause-and-effect relations. In my psychotherapy practice, I sometimes observe people being healed through psychospiritual means. One patient who suffered from compulsive shoplifting was "cured" by reading a note she had written to remind herself that God viewed her as worthy. This illustrates how God operates in the world through our minds, reminding us of biblical truths and guiding us in the way, the truth, and the light.

Interestingly, contemporary medical practice recognizes the roles of meditation, prayer, and church attendance in health and healing, although exact cause-and-effect connections are unknown.[59] Recall that those who practice religion may also choose healthier lifestyles. Some specific research suggests that prayer aids recovery: one well-designed study in a cardiac-care unit showed that patients who were prayed for developed statistically-significant fewer complications from their surgeries;[60] and another demonstrated statistically-significant improvement in both vision and hearing following healing prayer.[61] Such research is interesting but leaves many questions. Remember, most healing processes involve multiple factors, including mental ones, such as the placebo effect. In other words, other interpretations for these studies are possible. I believe in the importance of prayer, but am not convinced that research on prayer can provide definitive conclusions about its causative powers. And, perhaps more importantly, I question whether such research is completely ethical or responsible. We should not give God a wish list like Santa Clause, but rather ask him to direct our prayers. I've also heard cynical questions about whether God signed a consent form to participate in the study.[62]

Fortunately for us, healing occurs quite frequently. It can occur naturally, through the restorative mechanisms within our minds and bodies, or through intentional intervention. Both physicians and the Great Physician can aid healing but, I suspect that most of the time, many different factors work in combination to restore health.

HOW ARE SCIENTIFIC AND CHRISTIAN PERSPECTIVES ON CAUSATION RELATED?

Early in my medical career, someone asked how I could be both a physician and a Christian. I was astounded because to me they go hand in hand. I remember being unnerved when studying embryology, knowing how many things can go wrong between conception and birth. In many ways, every newborn is a mini miracle. Even before studying theology, and intentionally integrating my faith and work, I was aware that as my knowledge grew, so did my faith. Given that scientists investigate the world that God created, it is not surprising to find compatibility and areas of fruitful dialogue between science and Christianity.

In our discussions on how God acts in the world we concluded that he works within it, guiding and sustaining, but not micromanaging. The Creator is deeply involved with his creation but does not need to create from scratch every day. He calls us to be coregents in caring for the world and restoring its shine. Aside from inspiring worship, nature can be seen to reflect God.

Recall pineapples, coastlines, and gravity: at the observable level of reality, we see regularities and patterns. These point to a God of rationality, who creates with purpose, and brings order out of chaos.[63] However, we also see elements of randomness and interconnection; chaos developing from order, and new phenomena emerging from old. This reflects a God who is creative and flexible, working within the variability of nature. When we ask how and why things happen, the answers vary. Sometimes it is the nature of things to act a certain way: gravity pulls things down. Sometimes free agents make things happen. Often many differing factors are involved. We saw this with the COVID-19 pandemic—natural factors like viral mutations, random or accidental factors like someone touching a contaminated surface, intentional factors like people refusing to wear a mask. Some occurrences that we don't like (falling from a tree) are merely side effects of good things (gravity).[64] Cause and effect in both natural and social worlds relate in a web-like manner. Remember, to best appreciate its teaching, we need to consider the whole Bible, not isolated verses. Likewise, in the created order, we need to think about all possibilities rather than trying to find isolated steps of causation. I suggested that we need multiple models to understand God's action in the world. Similarly, science requires multiple models to understand our dappled world.[65]

We usually appreciate the immense variety in our world, but we don't like it when things, like COVID-19, happen randomly, with no specific cause. Scientific conceptions of randomness can inspire Christian reflection. Recall that randomness can be actual or apparent. At the small-scale level, quantum theory shows that there is uncertainty built into processes at the subatomic level. At the large-scale level, chaos-complexity theory shows that randomness occurs simply because there are too many variables involved in most processes for us to be able to predict outcomes. Note that uncertainty is not the same as nihilism or atheism. Randomness represents freedom, not purposelessness. God has gifted the world with both reliability and independence; both order and disorder are needed. He designed a world with random occurrences because this allows for new things to develop.[66] This is an exciting, if sometimes scary, aspect of the world, but we can be assured that God is present within creation.

Christian scholars have used scientific theories as ways to understand how God acts in the world.[67] Some suggest that God works through the uncertainty of the subatomic world, causing the collapse of the wave function, for example. This allows him to intervene in random processes without interfering with natural causes.[68] However, I think that this view potentially limits God's action to one sphere. It is also deterministic, because it denies that randomness is truly random.[69] Others use chaos-complexity theory to explain divine action. God can act by altering one or more of the many variables in dynamic systems.[70] He still respects the freedom of natural processes and acts responsively toward the world. This view does not imply that God micromanages, although it may also limit areas of divine action.

A third set of theories uses variations on whole-part or top-down models, which emphasize general divine action. God acts holistically within creation in a noninterventional way. He uses parts of the created order but is not limited by them.[71] Such views are helpful but relatively nonspecific. Somewhat similarly, various scholars claim that the Holy Spirit is a force field through which God acts.[72] The universe is radically interconnected and God is "the great Energy Field in whom all creation lives and moves and has its being."[73] I think that force fields may work as an analogy for how God acts, but I think it is going too far to claim that they are actual mechanisms of divine action.[74] Yes, the Spirit indwells Christians and flows through the world, but this Spirit is also a personal being, not just an impersonal force. Scientific theories can certainly stimulate theological reflection; remember, our views on divine action should fit with our knowledge and experience of the world. However, we need to take care that we don't attempt to tame God. The wind blows where it wills. As I've suggested, many different models of God's action in the world are likely most helpful, even if they do require us to be flexible and accept ambiguity.

The concept of spiritual interconnectedness has some interesting similarities to theories about parapsychology. The few Christian scholars who have engaged with parapsychological research note that it provides strong evidence for a spiritual level of reality, and relates to phenomena such as divine healing and apparitions. It is possible that the spiritual gifts of healing that some people have are the same as psychic abilities. Roman Catholic John Heaney postulates that Jesus was gifted with psychokinesis and precognition, the ability to see into the future.[75] My concern with this view is that it uses contemporary science to interpret an ancient text and risks demythologizing Scripture. Lisa Schwebel similarly speculates that phenomena such as weeping Madonnas may be caused by psychokinetic after effects; "psychological infections" lingering after someone with psi abilities has been close.[76] It is also possible that evil spirits work through paranormal phenomena; interestingly, psychic abilities are sometimes observed more commonly in people with mental health problems—recall that demons prey on vulnerabilities.[77]

Psychic processes may indeed be a way that the Holy Spirit operates within humans, especially since these involve perception beyond the five senses.[78] They may also be a way that evil spirits cause affliction. However, we cannot be certain. Discerning whether psychic phenomena are natural, evil, or holy is challenging. We need to be careful not to domesticate

God—he is so much more than we can imagine. Even if he does use psychic phenomena, it is near impossible to distinguish this from genuine revelation and exceptional divine action. I think the connection between Christian theology and parapsychology has much potential for fruitful research. We also need proper perspective. I agree with Schwebel that we "ask not how did it happen but rather what was the significance of the event within the total life of faith."[79] Recalling the model of Jesus, we should not seek power but offer forgiveness, prayer, and praise.

To reiterate, I believe that science and faith should be integrated, as should our work and faith. Christian theology and scientific study can be mutually informative. Science can help us fulfill the divine command to care for creation; perhaps particularly applicable in healthcare. Although science does not consider final levels of causation, or questions of meaning and purpose, Christians can think about this level in relation to material and efficient levels. We can consider how God works through natural processes, without being too specific and confident. We can use scientific models to help us understand God's action. We can also consider how God walks with us through all the levels and complexities of life. And we can pray for guidance in comprehending his wise and wonderful world.

CONCLUSION

Sunsets and seas, chocolate and cheese, technology and tea—we appreciate these daily. God made all creatures great and small, and he is very much involved with his creatures. Beneath the surface of our everyday lives, myriad unseen causative forces are at work, organization and order arise, new emerges from old, and psychic and spiritual forces operate unseen. The universe is dynamic, interconnected, and multilayered; causality flows in all directions and is sometimes random. Almost everything we encounter in our daily existence has apparently limitless levels of causal complexity. Reality is flexible and intertwined, and humans are participants in creating reality. We can have some knowledge of causation, but it is best understood in probabilistic terms. This intricate and interconnected world that God has given us is cause for awe and worship. I believe that responsible Christians need to be aware of the nature of the world we live in and to respect the ways God has created and ordered it.

Despite its limits, science is a useful tool for us to understand how and why things happen, and in turn to help us cope with difficult things in life, such as pandemics. People mostly ask questions about causation when things go wrong, and usually prefer simple and definite answers. We forget that knowledge has limits and that there can be many different causes for one event. I suspect that many people are satisfied with mechanical-type explanations for things like electricity, but when it comes to health, which is more personal, they focus on questions of purpose and may not consider the scientific nature of cause and effect in medicine. We tend to separate and confuse categories. If people think that medicine and prayer conflict, they may refuse a vaccination against COVID-19. But God has put us in this world, and we are susceptible to all the causative forces that are part of it. It behooves us to be aware of them. We are also responsible for working with God to improve creation and inaugurate his kingdom. We live our lives in a delicate, sometimes scary, but delightful dance between order and disorder, between the known and the unknown. In our bright and beautiful, wise and wonderful world, God promises to be with those who seek him, and gives wisdom to those who ask.

I praise you, because I am fearfully and wonderfully made.
Wonderful are your works; that I know very well.

Ps 139:14

ENDNOTES

1. Science is not the same as *scientism*, which claims that science can explain everything in life. E.g., White, *Science Delusion*.

2. E.g., Haarsma and Hoezee, *Delight in Creation*.

3. Pearl and Mackenzie, *Book of Why*, 135–8; of course, this "study" does not consider confounding factors; e.g., Daniel and his friends may have been healthier to begin with.

4. Cavalcanti et al., "Hydroxychloroquine."

5. Theories generally need to be explanatory (fit with data), consistent, falsifiable, coherent, and applicable or relevant to real-life situations. E.g., Barbour, *Religion and Science*, 106–24.

6. Kuhn, *Scientific Revolutions*.

7. From Copernicus, Galileo, Newton, Darwin and beyond, our views of nature have changed from geocentric to heliocentric, from static to dynamic, and from mechanistic to ecological. E.g., Barbour, *Religion and Science*, 9–24.

8. Gödel's theorem notes that all logical systems contain assumptions and new axioms that cannot be proven; arithmetic cannot be used to verify itself. E.g., Rescher, *Limits of Science*; Yanofsky, *Outer Limits*; Ewart and Marks, "Mono-theism Theorem."

9. E.g., Livio, *Brilliant Blunders*.

10. Physicist Werner Heisenberg points out, "what we observe is not nature in itself but nature exposed to our method of questioning" (*Physics and Philosophy*, 58). See also Barbour, *Religion and Science*, 106–10.

11. Contemporary science refers more to models than laws. Cohen and Stewart, *Collapse of Chaos*, 19; Barbour, *Religion and Science*, 106–36. Physicist Lars English

concludes, "No single theory could explain, however indirectly or remotely, the myriad of phenomena we observe across the spectrum of human inquiry" (*No Theory*, 4).

12. Benbennick, *Mobius Strip*. Changed to grayscale. Douglas Hofstadter describes "strange loops," recursive flip-flops in art and music, such as Escher's drawings (*Strange Loop*). See also Ewart and Marks, "Mono-theism theorem."

13. E.g., Strauss and McAlister, "Evidence-Based Medicine"; Benedetti, *Placebo Effects*; Rankin, *Mind Over Medicine*; Ehrenreich, *Natural Causes*.

14. The overuse and misuse of measurement and mathematics has been discussed. E.g., Huff, *How to Lie*; O'Neill, *Weapons of Math Destruction*.

15. This view is attributed to Auguste Comte in the nineteenth century. Bhaskar developed the notion of stratified reality (*Realist Theory*, 165–80). See also Murphy and Ellis, *Moral Nature*, 19–45; Ellis, *How Can Physics*, 4–13.

16. As Einstein has famously shown, time is relative. This is a complex issue with multiple conundrums; theoretically, time may have a backwards arrow. E.g., Polkinghorne, *Exploring Reality*, 113–26; Fanthorpe, *Mysteries and Secrets*.

17. Davies, *Mind of God*, 85.

18. E.g., Polkinghorne, *Quantum Theory*; Barbour, *Religion and Science*, 166–77; Coles, *Cosmos to Chaos*, 121–35.

19. This is the most common explanation, known as the Copenhagen interpretation; another common view, the multiverse interpretation, is that both outcomes occur but split into different worlds.

20. Einstein, who was part of a team to propose this, allegedly called this effect "spooky action at a distance."

21. E.g., Becker, *What is Real?* Anderson, "More is Different."

22. Bohr, quoted in Heisenberg, *Physics and Beyond*, 206.

23. There has been philosophical discussion as to whether "laws of nature" are ontological or epistemological; whether God *created* them or humans *invented* them. I favor the view that they are ways of describing regularities within the created order. E.g., Cartwright and Ward, *Rethinking Order*; Psillos, *Causation and Explanation*, 137–282; Mumford and Anjum, *Causation*, 15–26; Saunders, *Divine Action*, 48–82.

24. Murphy and Ellis, *Moral Nature*, 210. They argue that there is freedom within the parameters of laws (206–20).

25. E.g., Ball, *Patterns in Nature*; Falconer, *Fractals*.

26. Sierpinski triangle, *Wikimedia Commons*, public domain.

27. Edelman and Gally, "Degeneracy and Complexity."

28. E.g., Wood, "Ecological Perspective."

29. Cartwright, *Dappled World*; Cartwright and Ward, *Rethinking Order*. Polkinghorne similarly describes the world as supple and subtle, with both fuzziness and regularity, clouds and clocks (*Science and Theology*, 42, 53).

30. Sociology studies human behavior in large groups such as institutions and cultures. E.g., Little, *Sociology*.

31. Social psychology studies individuals in relation to groups. E.g., Myers and Twinge, *Social Psychology*.

32. Asch, "Group Pressure."

33. E.g., Taijfel, "Intergroup Discrimination."

34. Although there are some differences, the terms *chaos theory*, *complexity theory*, and *chaos-complexity* theory are often used interchangeably. These theories evolved in diverse ways; their origins can be traced to Poincaré in the late nineteenth century. E.g., Cohen and Stewart, *Collapse of Chaos*; Stewart, *Does God Play Dice?*; Polkinghorne, *Exploring Reality*, 7–37; Coles, *Cosmos to Chaos*; Smith, *Chaos*; Russell, *Cosmology*; Toolan, *Home in the Cosmos*; Hoffman, *Life's Ratchet*.

35. The title of a paper Lorenz presented in 1972 was "Does the flap of a butterfly's wing in Brazil set off a tornado in Texas?" Gribbin, *Deep Simplicity*, 60.

36. A similar computer simulation describes three rules: avoidance (keep separate from each other), alignment (move in the average direction of the closest others), and attraction (or cohesion, move toward the average position of those closest). Fisher, *Perfect Swarm*, 26.

37. The origin of this concept is attributed to George Henry Lewes in 1875. Emergence can be classified as strong or weak, depending on how easily properties are reducible to lower substrates or how amenable they are to computer analysis. The strongest forms can be considered ontological, and the weakest forms, epistemological, are sometimes not considered emergent at all. Emergence is also classified as synchronic, occurring at one point in time, and diachronic, occurring over a period of time. E.g., English, *No Theory*; Wegner and Lüttge. *Emergence and Modularity*; Morowitz, *Emergence of Everything*; Cook, "Emergence."

38. Newsome, "Human Freedom and 'Emergence.'" See also Ellis, *How can Physics*.

39. Toolan, *At Home*, 181.

40. As related by Brown, *Testing Prayer*, 239–44.

41. E.g., Kydd, *Healing through Centuries*, Porterfield, *Healing in Christianity*, Duffin, *Medical Miracles*.

42. Although there have been anecdotal reports of bizarre psychic phenomena throughout history, parapsychology developed as a science in 1935. E.g., Irwin and Watt, *Parapsychology*; Radin, *Conscious Universe*; Radin, *Entangled Minds*; Powell, *ESP Enigma*; Baruss and Mossbridge, *Transcendent Mind*.

43. Grad, "Biological Effects."

44. E.g., Radin, "Exploring Relationships."

45. Radin, *Entangled Minds*, 264.

46. There is no level of reality that is "fundamental." E.g., Kauffman, *Reinventing the Sacred*, 3; English, *No Theory*.

47. Respectively, the tendency in nature for two systems to coincide without a specific cause-effect relation, and a deeper stratum of unknown material from which consciousness emerges, and which has an innate patterning power. Jung, *Synchronicity*.

48. He claims that all life forces are interrelated and multidimensional, and proposes a fifth force field which exists at a deeper level, pervades all space, and is equally powerful everywhere. The universe is divided into explicate order (what we experience) and implicate order (a deeper, hidden reality from which everything rises and returns to). Bohm, *Wholeness and Implicate Order*.

49. He proposes a model that unifies quantum, cosmos, life, and consciousness. Coherence in nature implies system-wide connectivity, which in turn implies the presence of an interconnecting medium or system-wide field. Any point in space-time has a quasi-instantaneous connection to every other point, and the coherence response of the plenum to particles is scale-invariant and universal. Laszlo, *Connectivity Hypothesis*.

50. World Health Organization, "COVID-19 advice."

51. E.g., Firth et al., *Oxford Textbook*; Rabins, *Why of Things*.

52. Aronowitz, *Making Sense of Illness*; Donovan and McDowell, *AFMC Primer*, chapter 1.

53. Attributed to George Foster, "Disease Etiologies."

54. Hans Selye did the pioneering research on this (*Stress of Life*).

55. Austin Bradford Hill developed these now classic nine criteria to evaluate causation: strength of association, consistency, specificity, temporality, biological gradient, plausibility, coherence, experiment, and analogy ("Environment and Disease"). Paul Thompson argues that causal claims need more than a scientific study—they need to be

supported by an underlying theory that explains, not just describes, observed phenomena ("Causality, Theories").

56. E.g., Rabins, *Why of Things*; Illari et al, "Causality;" Evans, "Notion of Cause."

57. E.g., Ellis, *How can Physics*, 133–240.

58. Benedetti, *Placebo Effects*; Rankin, *Mind over Medicine*; Ehrenreich, *Natural Causes*. The lesser known *nocebo* effect describes negative outcomes of beliefs, such as in the practice of voodoo.

59. E.g., Koenig et al., *Handbook*; Pargament, *Psychology of Religion*.

60. Byrd, "Positive Therapeutic Effects." A similar study found retroactive benefits on prayer on patients with sepsis. Leibovici, "Remote, Retroactive Intercessory Prayer."

61. Brown et al., "Proximal Intercessory Prayer."

62. Richard Sloan expresses concern about "trivializing the transcendent" (*Blind Faith*, 241–52).

63. One of the first discussions on this was by Henry Drummond (*Natural Law*). See also McGrath, *Science of God*, 66–71. Contemporary science favors a nondeterministic and complex view of causation. E.g., Kauffman, *Reinventing the Sacred*, 3; Cohen and Stewart, *Collapse of Chaos*, 221, 246; Illari et al., "Causality."

64. Bartholomew notes, "the highly interconnected character of the world may mean that one cannot have some desired outcome without having others which, so to speak, necessarily go along with it" (*Uncertain Belief*, 58).

65. As Ian Stewart notes, there are only approximations within a defined domain, the result being a "pluralistic patchwork of locally valid models" (*Does God Play Dice?* 376).

66. Polkinghorne summarizes: "Chance is the engine of novelty. Necessity is the preserver of fruitfulness" (*Quarks, Chaos*, 53. He further notes that "novelty emerges at the edge of chaos" (*Exploring Reality*, 144) and that there is an interplay of necessity and chance—the first relates to scientific law, the second allows the realization of possibilities inherent in flexible processes (*Science and Providence*, 46). Fellow scientist-theologian Arthur Peacocke similarly describes chance as "the search radar of God, sweeping through all possible targets of its probing" (*Creation*, 95).

67. E.g., Saunders, *Divine Action*; Barbour, *Religion and Science*, 312–22.

68. E.g., Robert Russell states: "We can view God as acting in particular quantum events to produce, indirectly, a specific event at the macroscopic level, one which we call an event of special providence . . . Quantum mechanics allows us to think of special divine action without God overriding or intervening in the structures of nature" ("God Who Acts," 89, 94). Pollard was one of the first to suggest that God may act through events at the submicroscopic level (*Chance and Providence*, 48–60). See also Saunders, *Divine Action*, 94–125.

69. E.g., Bartholomew, *God, Chance, Purpose*, 153–55.

70. Polkinghorne claims that God interacts with creation through "information input" into dynamic processes. There is "room for divine maneuver" without divine interference (*Quarks, Chaos*, 89; *Science and Providence*, 34–42, 62–79; *Exploring Reality*, 136–46). Boyd also uses chaos-complexity theory to support his view that because the world can be predictable, God does not have to be omni-controlling (*Satan and Problem of Evil*, 151–58; 218–19).

71. Arthur Peacocke thinks that some events "can be intentionally and specifically brought about by the interaction of God with the world in a top-down causative way that does not abrogate the scientifically observed relationships operating at the level of events in question" (*Theology for Scientific Age*, 182). Yong concurs with the concept of downward causation; the life-giving Spirit acts superveniently on humans (*Spirit of Creation*, 98–103, 120–60). Moltmann believes the Holy Spirit creates possibilities and interactions, individuates and integrates (*Spirit of Life*).

72. Torrance claims that "a continuous dynamic field structure in which particles are interlocked with one another . . . is the only way we can think of God's interaction with us in his revealing and saving acts in space and time in history" (*Space, Time,* 70–75). Wolfhart Pannenberg believes that everything is interconnected and force fields are how God acts in history (*Systematic Theology 2,* 104–11, 129).

73. Toolan, *At Home,* 200. Moltmann states: "God's Spirit is life's vibrating, vitalizing field of energy: we are in God, and God is in us" (*Spirit of Life,*161). Moltmann's views may conflate divine immanence and transcendence and are underdeveloped; see Lett, "Moltmann's Theology."

74. See similar critique in Worthing, *God, Creation,* 118–25. In his review, Saunders favors whole-parts models, although admits that we may never find the perfect theory (*Divine Action,* 213).

75. Heaney, *Sacred and Psychic,* 58–116.

76. Schwebel, *Apparitions, Healing.*

77. Marguerite Shuster, in her nuanced examination of evil powers, suggests this (*Power, Pathology, Paradox*).

78. As suggested by process theologian David Griffin (*Parapsychology, Philosophy*). Pentecostal Amos Yong, who argues that psi phenomena are emergent realities, insists that psychic phenomena are not identical to charismatic manifestations and cannot prove the existence of the Holy Spirit (*Spirit of Creation,* 196–225).

79. Schwebel, *Apparitions, Healings,* 175.

Part 3

All Things Wise and Wonderful

WE HAVE SEEN THAT our wonderful world is amazingly complex, especially with respect to cause-and-effect relations. Causation is seldom clear; therefore, we need much wisdom in order for us to properly evaluate how and why things happen. Sadly, this is not common. Humans are perhaps the most wonderful of all created things, but we are finite and flawed. Fortunately, we are able to learn and gain knowledge and wisdom.

In this section we first consider psychological research on how humans think and decide, including some explanations for the challenges we encounter and the many mistakes we make. We jump to conclusions and are easily swayed by our emotions and experience, as well as the views of other people. Our limits are cognitive as well as moral: Christian views on sin can help us understand the latter. Chapter 7 offers hope in the form of practical strategies that can assist our evaluations of causation. We can glean from both psychology and Christian spirituality. We ask: What mental processes do we use to judge how and why things happen? Are we accurate judges? How can we improve our judgment? How can we discern God's action in the world?

6

What Does Psychology Say about How We Understand Causation?

Theologian Austin Farrer tells a story about a sick man. His neighbors claim that his illness is caused by alcoholism. When they discover that he does not drink, they quickly redefine the illness as a trial sent by God. And then, when his illness prevents him from going on a trip that ends in disaster, they judge it to be a blessing of providence.[1] We quickly change our stories to suit our needs. I have heard similar justifications in Christian circles: "If I had gone on that mission trip then I would never have met my wife," "If I hadn't gotten sick, I would not have had the opportunity to witness to the guy in the bed beside me." Some Christians have suggested that God caused the Covid-19 pandemic to teach us to be kinder to each other and the environment. (Actually, this is something we are called to do with or without pandemics.) People like easy cause-effect explanations. Psychologists have studied and named our strategies for judging, and misjudging, causation—for a sneak preview, the above examples include hindsight biases, rationalization, and cognitive dissonance reduction.

We have already seen how complex and uncertain the world is and how easy it is to misinterpret statistics, misjudge causation, and misunderstand how God interacts with the world. Causation and curiosity about it are basic to daily life: babies learn that shaking a rattle causes a pleasing sound, teens sometimes fail to learn that drugs cause brain damage, adults know that regular exercise prevents disease. But there is often a mismatch between the way the world is, the way we perceive it, and the way we behave. Consequently, it is important that we learn not only how and why things happen in the world, but also some basics about how people judge cause and effect. Psychology is a helpful tool for studying a complex aspect of creation: human mind-brains.

Cognitive, or mental, processes include recognizing, reasoning, re-membering, imagining, thinking, judging, and planning. Because we don't fully know how mind and brain are related, I like to amalgamate the terms. The mind-brains that God has given us are capable of astonishing feats as well as abysmal failures. Some of our errors relate to the nature of knowl-edge, with its inherent paradoxes and nuances. Some relate to the way our cognitive processes operate. And some relate to our fears and anxieties about the complex and uncertain world we live in.

HOW DO OUR MIND-BRAINS WORK?

I am always amused by the behavior of toddlers: investigating how far the toilet paper unrolls, decorating the walls, throwing food across the room, taking one bite from each of five apples, poking the baby. Others may not find this funny. Children's mind-brains develop at a remarkable rate, mostly through interacting with the environment. Our style of learning changes as we age, but our mind-brains continually seek information.

Recall that we acquire knowledge, which then enables us to evaluate causation, through experience and education. We can sense and perceive something directly, or we can make a decision based on what we already know. To do this requires brains, minds, sensation, and perception.[2] The brain is the biological, physical part: a three-pound mass that squishes like jelly (eew). It contains billions of nerve cells that talk to each other via chemical and electrical signals. Sensation is also biological, resulting from stimulation of our various sense organs: eyes, ears, skin. The mind is the psychological, subjective part that deals with thoughts, feelings, and judg-ments. Paradoxically, it is what we use to study the brain. Finally, perception, also nonphysical, describes how we automatically interpret what we sense.

At the risk of oversimplifying, different parts of the brain have differ-ent functions. Lower, or basic, structures control functions that we need to survive, such as breathing. Upper/outer parts are responsible for abstract thought and social interactions. The left side of the brain specializes in lan-guage and logic. It processes information in an orderly, linear fashion. The right side specializes in emotions and creativity. It processes in a holistic, integrative manner. However, there is much overlap and interconnection between the parts. The amazing thing is that when there is damage to the brain, or a need for specialization, other parts of the brain can compensate. This is known as neuroplasticity. People born blind develop a larger "hearing" area in their brains. Musicians have larger "musical" areas.

Toddlers learn that making the baby cry makes daddy unhappy, and eventually they stop that behavior and poke the puppy instead. Amidst the fun and frustration, they are actually classifying the world into things that make noises when poked and things that don't. We understand our world either by engaging with it or by thinking about how we might act relative to it. Our mind-brains continually categorize and analogize, matching action, perception, and belief. This allow us to experience the world as consistent, stable, and predictable. Our neurocognitive systems function quickly and effortlessly, and we are seldom aware of how they operate. I shouldn't admit this, but sometimes when driving in familiar places, I arrive without having been much aware of the journey. My mind-brain and my car are in automatic mode.

However, there is not a simple one-to-one correspondence between what is actually there and what we perceive. Sometimes what we see depends on what we are looking for. Before COVID-19, people would associate a cough with a cold virus, or an irritation. Now a coronavirus infection is what comes to mind. Recall that scientific studies are blinded because researchers know that their expectations can influence their observations. What our mind-brains interpret depends on our beliefs, feelings, memories, and many other factors. There is a two-way interaction between the world and us.

Experts estimate that the unconscious mind-brain takes in more than a billion pieces of information per second but the conscious mind glimpses only 1 percent of what the brain receives. In short, most information is filtered out. However, this is necessary for us to function; we would be completely overwhelmed if we could not do this. We select and prioritize, and most of the time, we continually *interpret* the world rather than simply *see* or experience it. It could be argued that two realities exist simultaneously—an objective world in which we live, and a subjective world constructed by our mind-brains.

Consider a typical Sunday worship service: Before you arrive you likely have subconscious expectations—maybe last week's sermon was terrible, maybe you're looking forward to seeing a friend, maybe you're worried about a relative's health. You also arrive with sensations and feelings—maybe you didn't sleep well, maybe the kids are behaving badly. When you arrive, your friend may fail to greet you, there may be noisy chatter, the building may be cold. During the service, you will only be able to focus on a few things at a time. Which musical instrument is prominent? Which singer is loudest? Does the message relate to the Bible passage you read earlier? Many factors, aside from God's presence and your good intentions, influence your church experience. Our understanding of causation is similarly influenced.

HOW DO WE THINK AND DECIDE?

During the initial stage of the 2020 pandemic, toilet paper was a hot commodity, causing fights in grocery stores. We made jokes but also speculated about the thinking behind this behavior. Human decision making is not always comprehensible, but quite amazing. We use multiple mental skills simultaneously and often automatically. Psychologists have developed models to help understand how we process information and make decisions. A helpful one is *dual processing theory*. This model postulates two systems of cognitive processing. These have various names, but one of the simplest is System 1 and System 2 (Table 6.1).[3]

Table 6.1: Dual Cognitive Processes

System 1	System 2
Automatic	Deliberate
Rapid	Slow
Unconscious	Conscious
Experiential	Logical
Reflexive	Reflective
Emotional	Rational
Intuitive	Efficient
Creative	Goal Directed

System 1 operates automatically, processing pieces of information simultaneously. It considers the big picture and makes quick associations based on our experience and the first things we perceive. It distinguishes surprising from normal events and detects subliminal messages. It is instinctive and imaginative. Automatic processes enable us to turn towards a sound, run when we see a bear, swiftly recognize a familiar face in church, immediately know when someone is angry, and compute 2+2. Their benefits are obvious in chess experts and musicians, for example, who just *know* the right play.

System 2 operates at a conscious level, processing information relatively slowly, in a stepwise fashion. This is the process we commonly call *thinking*. It allows us to solve complicated mathematical problems, navigate our surroundings, attend to one person in a crowd, park in a difficult space, count the number of books in the Bible, and carefully read a book on causation. Most scientific knowledge is acquired through logic and reason. Indeed, rational causal judgments are much like a scientific experiment. We consider all the factors, consider if an association is causal or correlational, and consider evidence for and against our conclusions. Ironically, we use rational processes to study nonrational ones.

Most adults forget how much they struggled to learn a new skill, such as riding a bicycle. Some processes begin as logical but become automatic with practice: driving, reading. In contrast, processes that may appear ultrarational often have intuitive components: editing a book, practicing medicine. Systems 1 and 2 are intertwined. Intuition and other automatic processes are very helpful, and usually accurate, ways of perceiving the world. The "logical" brain in some ways acts as a backup for the "automatic" one, allowing for an efficient division of labor. We can solve 2+2 quickly but need concentrated effort to solve 25,391+8,184 (try it later). We quickly develop impressions and feelings—System 1. If these are approved by our rational processes—System 2, they develop into beliefs, attitudes, and intentions. Our beliefs then affect our System 1 judgments. I've had humbling experiences of immediately disliking someone, but changing my mind when I hear good things about them from other people.

Much of our daily functioning involves an interplay between the two processes, and these often conflict. We may experience this as a habit, such as overeating (System 1, automatic, emotional, easy), that we know is unhealthy (System 2, logical reasoning) but is difficult to overcome (System 2, conscious effort). Dual-processing theory is a helpful way to conceptualize how we think and decide. We are most familiar with System 2 processes but, because they are automatic, we are less familiar with System 1 processes. Let's examine some aspects of this system in more detail.

Intuition and Emotion

Once when driving in winter I had a weird feeling that I should change lanes. A minute later the car behind me, which didn't change lanes, spun out of control. I was relieved it didn't happen to me. Many of us have experienced hunches or gut feelings, and we marvel about our luck, divine guidance, or a mysterious sixth sense. But, in fact, System 1 processes are normal and are well documented in psychology.

Intuition is an aspect of fast, automatic processes and is indispensable to our daily lives, operating effortlessly with little information. It is a form of nonconceptual knowledge. A way of knowing that does not require logic and "thinking." Our brains make linkages based on our education and experience. When we encounter similar situations, we can easily access this knowledge. The toddler who previously touched a flame instinctively does not repeat this behavior. Intuition automatically fills in missing information, sees the big picture, and chooses a best plan among alternatives. Imagination is similar; it is associated with intuition and can be used to access it. Many of us have tried brainstorming—thinking outside the box to generate as many options as possible—to solve problems. Recall our discussion on considering other possibilities, or counterfactuals, when we evaluate causes and effects. This requires imagination. It is an example of how Systems 1 and 2 interact—we can use creative processes to help with rational judgment.

A toddler does not need to understand how fire works but quickly learns that touching it hurts. Intuitive processes can create instant causal associations. Some fascinating studies suggest that infants as young as three months have innate intuitive processes.[4] Researchers show babies geometrical objects that they soon tire of and look away. They next show babies solid objects that pass through each other, large objects unfeasible positioned on top of smaller ones, objects that move on their own, or balls that stop midair. Infants will stare for a long time at these displays. Even without direct experience, they recognize when an event is physically impossible. This research suggests that we have innate knowledge of normal cause-and-effect associations.

Psychological research has further documented the power of intuition. People quickly show surprise when a male voice says, "I believe I am pregnant."[5] In one study, participants rated teachers after viewing a ten-second video clip. Their ratings correlated accurately with end-term class evaluations of the same teachers.[6] In the Iowa Gambling Task, participants draw 100 cards from four different decks to win money. They are not told that decks A and B yield higher amounts, although they are given feedback after each draw. Most people learn to select cards from the winning decks after drawing 50 cards, but they can only explain their reasons after drawing 80 cards. It appears their intuitions are ahead of their thoughts.[7]

Watching an apple fall from a tree allegedly inspired Newton to develop the theory of gravity. I've heard many stories of scientific and medical discoveries occurring through intuitive processes. Clinical judgment, especially among experienced physicians, occurs largely through instinctive processes and overall impressions. Practitioners often cannot identify the specific fact that led to their diagnosis, but automatically integrate their academic knowledge with their knowledge of particular patients with unique clinical circumstances.[8] I teach first-year medical students that, even as beginners, they can judge whether someone has a serious problem or not. Later they learn the language of medicine, which allows them to explain this instinctive judgment. In general, intuitions are reliable in most circumstances. They are most accurate when we have "an environment that is sufficiently regular to be predictable."[9] In many situations we need to make quick decisions. When I was driving on the icy road, if I had rationally considered all possible reasons for my hunch before acting on it, I would have spun on the ice.

Intuitions relate to emotions, which are an essential aspect of being human. These are present, if not articulated, in infants likely even before birth. We may not always like them, but they allow us to relate to each other and to God in deep and meaningful manners. Feelings, like intuitions, are automatic processes. And they greatly affect the way we make judgments, including those about causation. When I have slept poorly, I tend to be irritable and quick to blame others for problems. So, if the traffic is backed up, I get annoyed at the slow driver in front of me, rather than recognizing that traffic issues typically have multiple causes.

It has long been known that emotions are connected to physical sensations, such as rapid breathing when we are afraid, or a red face when angry. Well, emotions are also related to our ability to make decisions. Neuroscientist Antonio Damasio noted that people with damage to the "emotional" parts of their brains had difficulty with decision making. He argues that emotions are essential to reasoning and rational judgment.[10] Emotions are a form of information processing; they make thoughts "real" and can override rational thinking.[11] Our beliefs can guide our actions, but emotions also shape beliefs and initiate actions. If a woman in a relationship is jealous, she may think that every woman her partner talks to is trying to steal him from her. Sometimes feelings or desires change or even create thoughts. And when there is a strong emotional connection, beliefs persist despite contradictory evidence. People who have been especially afraid during the COVID-19 pandemic stayed home even after restrictions were lifted (feelings affecting action), or adopted a comforting belief that the pandemic is a hoax or that God caused it for a good reason (feelings affecting thoughts).

Experimental psychology has demonstrated the connection between feeling and thinking. When people are told stories to make them sad or angry, and then asked to set a sale price on an object, they tend to set a price lower than the value of the object.[12] Judgments are affected by emotions, even when these are artificially induced. Physical feelings also affect belief. One study showed that people sitting in a warm room expressed more concern about climate change than those sitting in a cold room, even though both groups were given identical information.[13] Overall, intuitions and emotions are fundamental in shaping our beliefs, including those about how and why things happen. It is important for us to be aware of their influence on our evaluations of causation.

Pattern Recognition, Meaning Making, and Agency

If you can raed tihs, you msut be raelly smrat. Well, not really. You just have a fully functioning mind-brain. Recall that System 1 cognitive processes make quick associations and generalizations, noting the whole word and the context of the sentence rather than individual letters. We tend to approach information holistically and easily transfer knowledge from one situation to another. Toddlers can label most dogs as dogs even if they have only seen one dog. If we hear a bark, we will assume it was caused by a dog, even if we did not observe the scene. Pattern recognition enables us to recognize food as food, or the letter A in many different sizes, fonts, orientations, and colors.[14] Our marvelous mind-brains are designed for us to make sense of life. This of course extends to our understanding of how and why things happen. But, as we will see, even when things don't make sense, we work hard to *make* them make sense.

In a classic experiment, Albert Michotte demonstrated our preference for meaning with respect to the perception of causation.[15] He showed subjects an animation of two balls moving around and sometimes bumping into each other. When asked to describe what they saw, most people used words that attributed motivations and emotions to the inanimate objects ("the big ball gets mad and leaves"). A contemporaneous similar and equally-famous experiment involved participants viewing an animated film of geometric shapes moving in relation to each other. Again, the majority of people personified the objects, inventing stories such as two men fighting over a girl, who tries to run away because she's scared.[16] Our need to find meaningful cause-and-effect connections is powerful. We view the world through a causal lens.

Children also like to find meaning and purpose even when there is little evidence of it. In one study, grade-school children and adults were asked to explain various structures in the natural world. Compared with adults, children preferred purposeful accounts over physical ones ("rocks are pointy so that animals can scratch themselves"), even after they were given scientific education.[17] Surveys of adults have shown that the tendency to believe in fate and meaningful causes of personal events is strong, irrespective of religious belief.[18] Not only do we like to find meaning, but we also want to believe the world is fair and that everything happens for a reason.

Recall our discussions on agent causation. This is also important in how our mind-brains find meaning and understand how and why things happen. Infants easily distinguish between animate and inanimate objects and appear to recognize that only agents can create order and make things happen.[19] One study showed that six month olds prefer to watch humans interacting with other humans than with a ball on a stick.[20] Older children often ascribe agency to unseen entities, such as imaginary friends, Santa Claus, or God. Psychologist Justin Barrett coined the acronym HADD to describe a hypothetical innate *Hyper-sensitive Agency Detection Device*. He notes that children are seldom atheists, and suggests that we have a natural inclination toward religious belief because we are wired to notice and assume agent causation.[21] This may be true; however, Gilbert and colleagues argue that the *illusion* of external agency may explain the prevalence of belief in a God who orchestrates life events, regardless of whether God actually exists or not.[22] I would add that we can *believe* in God without assuming that everything is directly *caused* by him; although our agency-alert mechanisms may sometimes erroneously conclude this.

In sum, we like the world to make sense and subconsciously seek out personally meaningful explanations for how and why things happen. This natural human tendency enables us to easily adapt to human society and function well most of the time, but not always.

Judgment and Decision Making

The COVID-19 pandemic has forced many decisions at both public and personal levels: mandatory masks, school openings, border closings, quarantine, testing, treatment, financial compensation. Arguments arise, emotions elevate, and confusion abounds. Although we *think* we all make careful and logical decisions, this is not always the case.

So far, we have seen that we use both intuitive and rational processes to make cognitive assessments. Emotions, beliefs, and actions are intertwined, and we favor patterns, meaning, agent causation, and personal control. In particular, our understanding of cause-and-effect relations affects our decisions. If we think that masks cause difficulty breathing, we may not wear one. If we think that the novel coronavirus causes potentially serious illnesses, we may keep our distance from people who can transmit the virus to us. Our beliefs, especially when they have personal and emotional connections, are powerful and persistent. Changing a belief, such as with spiritual conversion, can be life changing.

Think about the last time you met a friend. In order to greet people we know, we need to visually identify them, access a memory of previously seeing them, access our knowledge of them (their name, where we met), and access our feelings about them. Making a judgment is complex, involving multiple levels of cognitive processing—perception, identification, association, emotion, intuition, memory, and logic.[23] Sometimes we are able to decide automatically and unconsciously, like stopping at a red light. Other times it is not easy to choose between possible options or solutions, such as what school to attend. Our judgments of how and why things happen is frequently automatic, dependent on our thoughts, feelings, and experience.

Precisely because they are automatic, we are usually unaware of most of the judgments we make, and especially *why* we make them. In one study, people were given morally and emotionally repulsive scenarios, such as eating part of a dead person. However, when asked, most could not logically explain why they thought it morally wrong.[24] We tend to favor our emotional decisions over rational ones, and often invent bizarre reasons to clarify our illogical choices. Recall my earlier examples of Christians who go to great lengths to justify their belief that God causes everything.

Sometimes when cycling on a trail I see a stick in the distance that looks remarkably like a snake. My heart races and my muscles tense. To be fair, sometimes the "stick" moves. What we think we see is not always the way things actually are. There is a two-way trail between us and the world that is strongly tied to our emotions. What we feel depends on our initial automatic evaluation of an event. This close connection between emotions and judgment has been explained through *appraisal theory*.[25] Our initial assessment determines our immediate actions, such as running when we see a bear in the wild. People may react differently to the same event because they interpret it differently. This theory is especially relevant in new or ambiguous situations, and involves assumptions about cause-and-effect relations.

We have discussed how some people think that COVID-19 was caused by God, the devil, or conspirators. In psychology, *attribution theory* describes how people assign meaning by answering *why* questions and explaining the causes of events and behaviors.[26] Attributions are related to appraisals, but are usually less immediate, more logical, and more permanent. Our beliefs about causation depend on our personalities, abilities, and motivations, our previous experience, our views on fate and luck, social norms, and the context and stability of the situation. Attributions can be internal or external. Most people take responsibility for their weight gain (internal), whereas few people believe that they are responsible for causing a hurricane, imputing some other factor (external). When students get a poor grade, some may blame themselves for not studying enough; others may attribute causation to external factors, such as the test being exceptionally difficult. Attributions can act to boost or diminish our self-esteem depending on how we explain our successes and failures. They help increase a sense of cognitive mastery over the world.

Recall that random events, like pandemics, are associated with unpalatable feelings of uncertainty and lack of control. Some people try to decrease their discomfort and "control" the situation by appraising it as punishment from God. Others may work hard to control the small areas that they can, such as mask-wearing and handwashing. Our beliefs regarding our ability to control an event affect how we appraise it. Psychologists have noted that people have either an internal or external *locus of control*.[27] With the first, they tend to assume responsibility for outcomes and events. With the second, they believe that most things are determined by external factors beyond their control. People make errors when they overgeneralize. Sometimes the reason we fail *really* is because the test was difficult, even if we tend to blame ourselves. People with an internal locus of control tend to be happier, more confident, and more successful than those with an external locus of control.

In sum, our decisions are affected by many factors including personality, perceptions, mood, memories, culture, context, expectations, social norms, and the number of options available. Yet we mostly manage to function quite well. Psychologist Gerald Clore concludes: "The genius of human thought is that despite its unconscious, automatic, emotional, and heuristic nature, we nevertheless generally arrive at rational, defensible conclusions."[28] However, the key word is generally; these processes can also easily result in poor and inaccurate decisions. Such errors can be quite informative.

WHAT ARE OUR COGNITIVE LIMITATIONS?

Some advice given by public health officials during the COVID-19 pandemic appeared overly simplistic: "stay home, stay safe," "smile, don't shake," "never touch your face, but always wash your hands," "facts, not fear." These were often paired with images. Recalling that our mind-brains are bombarded with information, simple slogans are helpful.

Mental short cuts, or heuristics, are an invention of System 1. They conserve brain energy, save time, and allow us to make quick decisions. But this efficiency comes at a cost and can result in significant biases and judgment errors. On occasion we sidestep short cuts and assume conscious control over the information we receive and process. This System 2 style thinking can mitigate errors but is inefficient and error prone. Recall that

Systems 1 and 2 are sometimes in conflict. Our automatic judgments may be logically wrong but effective for survival—running if we think we see a bear. Our rational mind-brain sometimes corrects our immediate conclusions—it's not a bear, just a dog. Remember that most of our judgments about how and why things happen are subconscious. As psychologist David Myers amusingly states, "what you know, but don't know you know, affects you more than you know."[29]

In the "competition" between our two types of cognitive processes, many experts believe that our intuitive, emotional, and experiential judgments are primary: intuition drives strategic reasoning, passion surpasses logic.[30] It is important that we are aware of the potential pitfalls in our judgments and know which process works best in which situation. Errors occur when we trust the "wrong" system and/or are unaware of the type of judgments we are making. We think we have made a careful evaluation, but instead are using quick and easy methods. There are many types of judgment errors; we will focus on those most relevant for our discussion on how and why things happen.[31]

Limits of Perception and Attention

First, our sensory abilities have limitations. It is quite humbling to be reminded that many animals are superior to humans in some ways. Certain animals can hear noises at higher frequencies than people can. Dogs have a better sense of smell than humans. Honeybees and birds have superior vision. Taste and touch are similarly limited.[32]

Second, because the brain interprets sensory information, we are subject to perceptual illusions. What you see is not always what is there. Travelers have all experienced the weird feeling that our train is moving, when it is actually the one next to us that is moving. A number of visual illusions result from the brain adding information in order to form a pattern (see Figures 6.1 and 6.2).[33] Interestingly, even when we are aware of the illusion, we can't not see it—I challenge you to try. Note that these errors are caused by brain functions that are usually helpful.

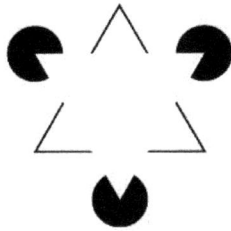

Figure 6.1: Kanizsa's Triangle: The brain fills in the shapes of two triangles

**Figure 6.2: Ponzo Illusion: The objects are the same size
but appear different because of the context**

One amusing study involved a researcher conversing with someone on the street. Midway through, a workman walks past carrying a board, and a similarly dressed person replaces the researcher. Most people don't notice the switch.[34] The term *change blindness* describes how we fail to notice large changes in our environment. A similar, now-famous experiment involves people watching a video of two teams bouncing balls to each other. They are told to count the number of tosses: almost no-one notices a person in a gorilla suit walking slowly through the scene (this is known as *inattentional blindness*).[35] Since we usually experience sensory and information overload, we have to choose what to attend to. Focus takes effort and energy: the more concentration required, the less we notice. We lack resources to attend to everything and consequently, we miss much information. This affects our ability to accurately judge causes and effects. Wise decisions require that our perception reflects reality, but this is not always true.

Thinking Too Much or Too Little

As a student I seldom did well on multiple-choice exams. Part of the problem was that I thought too much, analyzing every possible answer and why it may be the correct one. I've also had embarrassing occasions when I think too little . . . sorry, no examples.

Logical reasoning is tedious, energy inefficient, and not always accurate. In one study people were asked to choose the best piece of art or sample of jam. When they were told to explain their preference (engaging their rational brain), they frequently changed their minds and chose samples that were deemed inferior by experts.[36] Another study showed that people who were asked to list twelve instances of themselves behaving assertively rated themselves as less assertive than those who had only listed six. Apparently, the extra effort required to think of twelve examples made them believe they were not very assertive.[37] The problem of overthinking is common. Opera singers will "choke" when they have moments of self-doubt. Conversely, using intuitive processes often improves performance.[38] When we evaluate the cause of an event, at times we perhaps should avoid thinking too much.

However, our tendency to think too little, or rely too much on our automatic judgments, is far more common and problematic. Recall our previous discussions about the importance of statistics and probabilities in understanding processes in an unpredictable world. Well, it turns out our mind-brains don't do well with this.

First, we ignore the *law of large numbers*. When judging the sequence of boys and girls born in a hospital (which are independent events, only reaching the 50 percent approximation after a very large number), most people incorrectly conclude that the sequence BGBBGB is more likely than BBBGGG or GGGGGG.[39] Psychologists Amos Tversky and Daniel Kahneman titled an article "Belief in the Law of Small Numbers" to describe the observation that most people assume that the law of large numbers also applies to small numbers.[40] One study showed that people judge a disease that kills 1,200 out of 10,000 to be more dangerous than one that kills 24 out of every 100. The second one is actually twice as lethal—use your calculator if you must—but people are impressed by large numbers and forget about the denominator.[41] This somewhat relates to what we saw in the Bible about our tendency to generalize from the large to the small: just because God promises to fulfill his plans over time with many people does not mean he always has a specific plan for one individual.

Second, people tend to ignore the common phenomenon of *regression to the mean*. So, when a sports player performs exceedingly well, we are surprised when his next performance is abysmal.[42] A fictitious but possibly true statement, "Depressed children treated with an energy drink improve significantly over a three-month period," may lead us to incorrectly believe that this drink treats depression. But depressed children are rare, an extreme group; recall that all extreme groups move towards the average over time—regardless of what they drink.[43]

Third, we ignore *base rates* and misjudge probabilities. Consider Tversky and Kahneman's famous "Linda problem": [44]

> Linda is thirty-one years old, single, outspoken, and very bright. She majored in philosophy. As a student, she was deeply concerned with issues of discrimination and social justice, and also participated in anti-nuclear demonstrations. Which is more probable? 1. Linda is a bank teller. 2. Linda is a bank teller and is active in the feminist movement.

Most people choose the second option. But, statistically, the likelihood of two events occurring together is lower than the probability of either one occurring alone; sometimes less is more. We also tend to assume that things occur together more commonly than alone (known as the *conjunction fallacy*). And we make judgments based on preconceived ideas of what is typical (known as the *representative heuristic*). If we believe that sickness and sin are associated, we will judge our friend's illness to be caused by her sin. Our assumptions are sometimes true but not always. Being aware of common errors—ignoring numbers, statistical tendencies, and probabilities—can help us evaluate cause-and-effect relations more accurately.

Fourth, we have great difficulty understanding randomness.[45] We are surprised when a coin lands *tails* four times in a row, when someone wins the lottery, when a global pandemic occurs, when someone loses her voice at a theology conference, or when someone's cancer resolves. We forget that, with large enough numbers and large enough periods of time, strange things are bound to happen. Our problem with recognizing randomness relates to our neglect of sample size and probabilities, our failure to recognize when we have incomplete information, our discomfort with uncertainty, and our preference for patterns and meaning.

Finally, we think too little when we place too much weight on emotions. As we saw earlier, being tired, hungry, anxious, or sad affects our decision making. If we feel peace after choosing a course of action, we may assume that we made the right decision. Christians often think that this peace is a God-given affirmation of their judgment. This may be true; however, making any decision, right or wrong, always feels better than being undecided.

To reiterate, most of the time our cognitive processes serve us well. But, like most natural systems, these abilities have their downside. There is always a tradeoff between intuitive and rational processes. When we use the method that is not suited to the task, we will make errors.

Cognitive Laziness

Once, when I was travelling with friends, we drove down a street at night looking for a restaurant. Among many international varieties, we saw a bright-yellow sign: "PA KING." We discussed Chinese restaurants until someone drily pointed out that the R was missing. Because "thinking" takes effort, our mind-brains take shortcuts. This, of course, can lead to mistakes. Not all of these directly affect our judgments of how and why things happen, but they help us understand the general limitations of our cognitive processing skills.

Does the letter K occur more often as the first or the third letter of a word? It is more commonly a third letter, but most people think it occurs more frequently in the first position because instances of this are easier to recall.[46] We generally choose the easy path with visual tasks. Words that are written in bold, rhyme, or are easy to pronounce, are judged as more credible. By contrast, we are more accurate if a problem is presented in small, faint font, which forces us to concentrate and mobilize our rational thinking.[47]

We all know of people who refuse to fly after a publicized airplane accident. Because tragic events receive a lot of media coverage, they readily come to mind. People then incorrectly judge accidents to be more common than strokes, and tornadoes more often fatal than asthma.[48] We tend to favor information that is easily *available, retrievable, familiar, recent,* or *reinforced*. People can also be made to like something just by being exposed to it more often; familiarity feeds fondness. One study showed that people assume someone is famous simply because they recently heard his name.[49] Consider this familiar example: How many animals of each kind did Moses take into the ark?[50] Mental availability is especially relevant to bad outcomes. Rare events, such as terrorism, especially if accompanied by intense emotional images, cause an availability cascade, leading us to overestimate the probability of such events.[51]

Our judgments are also influenced by the vividness and personal relevance of events.[52] If we recently had two friends die of cancer, we will assume it is more common than it actually is. This relates to the phenomenon of *priming*. If we hear a name, then hear it again a few days later, we are primed to make an automatic association. In one study, participants completed the word fragment SO_P as *soup* if they had recently seen the word *eat*, but as *soap* if they had been exposed to the word *wash*.[53] (Just like my "parking" error.) Instead of logically estimating the frequency of an event or the numbers involved, we automatically note how easily instances come to mind. Christians may hear a sermon on forgiveness then read a devotional about the same topic the next day and conclude that God has a personal message for us. This is possible, but it could also be that we are primed to the word *forgiveness*. Try this for fun—ask someone to spell the word "shop," then ask what one does at a green light.

The phenomenon of *framing* also affects our judgments: people are more likely to buy meat labeled 85% fat-free than 15% fat. Experienced physicians make markedly different choices between two alternative treatments for lung cancer—surgery and radiation therapy—depending on whether the outcomes of these treatments are described in terms of mortality rates or in terms of survival rates.[54] We make mistakes because we are too cognitively lazy to think about statistics and how claims are worded—to the benefit of politicians and salespersons.

Consider this statement: "After spending a day exploring the beautiful sights in the crowded streets of New York, Jane discovered that her wallet was missing." In this study, subjects were given a surprise recall test, with cue words, after five minutes of distraction. People chose the word *pickpocket* more frequently than the word *sights*, even though it was not even in the story.[55] Our mind-brains make quick causal associations and we prefer stories that have explanations. Kahneman notes that our "associative machinery seeks causes."[56] Furthermore, things once connected, even if incorrectly, can become permanently so in our minds. An unfortunate example in medicine is the false belief that the MMR vaccine causes autism. Because the onset of this condition is around the same time that this immunization is given (recall temporal contiguity), the two become associated. The false belief is reinforced by our need for easy explanations, distrust of science, and conspiracy theories.[57] Our cognitive laziness also leads us to allow others to make decisions for us; potential errors are compounded by our susceptibility to social pressure and suggestion.

A story attributed to Cicero references a painting of worshipers who survived a shipwreck after praying. A nonbeliever rhetorically asks to see the pictures of those who prayed and then drowned.[58] Recall that statistical analyses need to consider hidden data. But we frequently neglect *silent evidence* or focus only on what is known or seen. We are "cognitive misers,"[59] making quick judgments and generalizations in order to avoid thinking. Seldom do we take the time to contemplate all possible explanations and counterfactuals. In a survey of airplane-crash survivors, 90 percent of people had studied where the exits were, prompting media advice for passengers to know where the exits are. But of course, as with Cicero's story, those who died were not interviewed.[60]

Cognitive ease is associated with good feelings, thus reinforcing our often-incorrect impression of correctness. In our laziness, we may unconsciously substitute a simpler question for the one that was asked. It is easier to answer the question "what is my mood right now" than "how happy am I with my life."[61] Judging problems with many layers and probabilities takes effort, whereas judging mood and beliefs is easy. In *Decision Making and the Will of God*, Gary Friesen points out that, because emotions are influenced by multiple factors (fatigue, the weather, our diet), if we make decisions based on feelings, they are only as reliable as our emotional state. Furthermore, the inner impressions that people use to discern divine guidance can also come from Satan, our past experiences, our own desires, or a television commercial.[62]

Some perceptions and causal assumptions made during the 2020 pandemic illustrate cognitive laziness. If someone coughs, we may assume they have the novel coronavirus infection because it is foremost in our minds; we forget about other causes of coughs. If a friend gets sick with Covid-19 after visiting a hair salon, we may avoid hair salons too, even though the friend may have contracted the virus in many other places. If we are uncertain and a few friends suggest that the pandemic was caused by malicious pharmaceutical companies, we may adopt this belief too. If we generally believe that God causes everything that happens, we assume this rare event was divinely designed. If we believe the end times are coming soon, we easily fit the pandemic into this readily available mental category. Our lazy mind-brains look for the easiest explanation.

Seeing Meaning Where There Is None

It is important to distinguish between different meanings of meaning. I do not think that *everything* happens for a reason, but this does not mean that everything is arbitrary and purposeless. There is a difference between ultimate meaning and the meaning of a cough or ice on a road. Christianity portrays an overarching picture of a God who so loves the world that he sends his son to reconcile sinful humanity to himself. This view shapes life in general, and provides purpose in terms of loving and obeying God and living righteous lives. However, this overall meaning is very different from assuming that every little occurrence in our daily lives happens for a reason. It is this last that I am addressing.

We like to know why. We ask questions about cause and effect, and seek explanations. We like stories, we like the world to make sense, we like to feel in control. If something has meaning and purpose, we feel in control. But, we sometimes we go too far in our search for meaning and causal explanations. Remember, there is often a mismatch between what we see and what is actually there; the mind-brain's automatic processes often override actual input.

Think about which of the following sort of statements you have heard more often: "Ann developed cancer because God wanted to teach her the meaning of suffering so she could be a better nurse" or "Ann's cancer was caused by a random change in one cell." The first is a much better story. Regardless of its truth, it gives us an explanation and relieves our fears about the sometimes random and scary world we live in. In one study, Kahneman and Tversky found that participants deemed "a massive flood somewhere in America in which more than a thousand people die" to be less likely than "an earthquake in California, causing massive flooding, in which more than a thousand people die." The second is actually less probable, but it offers an easily imagined and meaningful cause.[63] Anecdotes are more readily available to our mind-brains than statistics, easier to understand, and consequently more persuasive. Related examples we discussed earlier include the Linda problem and the pickpocket story. Some people engage in complicated mathematics to find numbers in the book of Revelation that are relevant for today. We look for meaning where there is none.

Many of us have unexpectedly run into someone we know when shopping downtown. We tend to interpret it personally and meaningfully, perhaps wondering why God put this person in our path. It's always possible that God orchestrated the meeting but remember that coincidences occur more often than we think. It is actually quite common to encounter someone we know, among our many acquaintances, anytime we are in populated areas. We focus on one specific interpretation of our experience, rather than the larger category of possibilities—maybe you shop frequently, maybe you have a large number of friends who also like being downtown.[64] Because we prefer meaning, we assume causal effects when there is merely a correlation between events. For the same reason, we prefer to attribute cause to an external agent rather than to random or unknown factors. Hence, "God caused the pandemic to teach people a lesson" is much more satisfying than "there is no particular cause" or "there are many different causes" for the pandemic.

Philosopher-statistician Nassim Taleb uses the term *narrative fallacy* to describe our preference for simplified stories over raw truths.[65] Indeed, we often invent explanations, weave causal stories, or connect unconnected things. Taleb references an example given by novelist E. M. Forster: Compare "the king died and the queen died" with "the king died and then the queen died of grief." Even though the second statement is longer, it is preferred and more easily remembered because it has a single narrative and a causal explanation. A well-known study had participants select the best among identical pairs of socks. When asked to explain their selection, which must have been random since the socks were the same, they justified their choice in terms of color and texture.[66] We prefer specific, concrete stories to mundane facts. Taleb points out potential costs to this fallacy, such as our outrage at an extreme act of terrorism while we ignore the subtle but overall more harmful effects of environmental neglect.

Psychologist Frank Keil has specifically researched causal conceptions in adults and children.[67] In one study, people were asked to rate their understanding of how a device or natural phenomenon works (note the causal implications of the word *how*): they typically gave themselves a high rating. However, their self-rating decreased after they were asked to explain exactly how the device works. We tend to have shallow and inadequate understandings, but think they are accurate and adequate. Keil labels this the *illusion of explanatory depth*. He argues that we need to find simple causal interpretations in order to navigate a world of causal complexity. Recall that Christians often assume that the health benefits of religion are divinely caused—this is much easier to do than considering multiple different possible interpretations.

Our need for meaning, simplicity, and certainty also explains why people are superstitious and believe conspiracy theories, such as the ones about Covid-19 being instigated by evil politicians. Superstitions result from a combination of the limitations of our cognitive processes, our sensitivity to coincidence, our need for meaning, and our need for control.[68] They create a magical cause-and-effect connection. Wagner and Morris studied children between the ages of three and six who sat next to a doll that randomly dispensed rewards. No work was required from the children, but 75 percent of them engaged in ritualistic behavior, such as a smile or dance.[69] It is possible they were just passing the time with activity, but also likely that they were uncomfortable with an effect that was not associated with a cause, and therefore invented one. Getting something for nothing is rare in life. Assuming a cause-and-effect connection between an action and a consequence helps us to find meaning and gives us a sense of being in control. Individual superstitions become concerning when they develop into conspiracy theories. These can be fueled by the internet and social media. Our beliefs can affect the beliefs of others, which is why we need to understand and take responsibility for them.

WHAT ARE OUR EMOTIONAL AND MORAL LIMITATIONS?

Consider Adam and Eve: They were tempted by the promise of knowledge and certainty, they were easily persuaded to disobey, they were afraid and hid from God, they had difficulty admitting wrongdoing, and blamed each other. Well, not much has changed. We don't know exactly what the first humans were thinking, but they had the same mind-brains as us. These mind-brains make mistakes at emotional and ethical levels as well as mental ones, although, of course the systems are intertwined.

Most of our cognitive limitations can be considered side effects of an otherwise efficient and beneficial system that makes quick judgments for optimal daily functioning. As we have seen, these can go spectacularly wrong at times. Cognitive processing errors are common and not due to lack of intelligence or education. They are not usually intentional; at most we can be blamed for being careless. Sometimes though, judgment errors cannot be explained by brain miswiring. Some errors can be attributed to, or compounded by, selfishness, pride, and fear. They perhaps relate more to ease of conscience than cognitive ease. Of course, it is near impossible to sort out when mistakes are because of pride, when they are because of our cognitive processing systems, or when they result from some combination of the two.

Self-Serving Biases

Paul advises us not to "think of yourself more highly than you ought to think" (Rom 12:3). Yet many of us do this without realizing it. Our cognitive laziness can lead us to egocentric decisions. Because we can only attend to some of the information our mind-brains receive, our selection is often self-serving. When it comes to explaining how and why things happen, we are frequently overconfident, assuming we are right and others are wrong.

Recall our tendency to ignore probabilities and randomness in making judgments about causation. Even experts are not immune.[70] Philip Tetlock has done extensive research on political judgment and forecasting. He has found that experts in their field are often worse predictors of trends than nonexperts, and suggests that this is because they are overconfident and resist admitting error.[71] After all, they need to maintain their image as an "expert." This relates to the illusion of explanatory depth: we think we know more than we actually do. Interestingly, our overconfidence is stronger for causal knowledge than for simple knowledge of facts. This perhaps partly explains why many people are confident in their claims that God caused some event in their lives.

Have you ever noticed that anybody driving slower than you is an idiot, and anyone going faster than you is a maniac? Jokes like this demonstrate that we have some awareness of our tendency toward self-serving judgments. However, most of us still think we're better than others with respect to personal characteristics, knowledge, and abilities. One study showed that people applying for marriage licenses correctly stated the divorce rate to be 50 percent but predicted the success of their own marriages to be close to 100 percent.[72] A national survey on obedience to the Ten Commandments found that respondents typically considered themselves to be twice as obedient than everyone else.[73] People are not necessarily being mean, they merely have incorrect assumptions. It is easier to see "the speck in your neighbor's eye . . . " (Matt 7:3). We also sometimes get the arrow of causality backwards by assuming that our good qualities cause our successes, rather than that success shapes character and causes good qualities. Our inflated self-image affects our views on causation and helps explain why we are quick to blame others for causing problems in the world.

We've likely all experienced heated discussions on religion and politics. In our desire to validate ourselves, we typically only look for information that supports our views, or talk to people who agree with us. In psychology, this human tendency is known as the *confirmation bias*. Recall how we ignore silent evidence, and only include information that affirms our beliefs. Those who are opposed to vaccines don't look at websites that demonstrate the safety and effectiveness of immunization. (And this is compounded by internet algorithms that base results on our previous searches, but that's another story.) With respect to the Roman Catholic process of canonization of saints, it was observed that, when the devil's advocate position was removed, there was a dramatic increase in the number of persons who were declared saints. This can be explained through the confirmation bias, only looking for supportive evidence.[74] Self-serving biases may contribute to the tendency of Christians to only report positive answers to prayer. This is also an example of a *reporting bias*—we only mention positive outcomes for events and/or information that boosts our egos.

Most games involve a combination of skill and randomness, such as dice tossing. Yet I've noted that when my friends win, they are somewhat smug; when I win, they tell me I was just lucky. Studies have demonstrated that we usually attribute accomplishments to skill rather than chance, even when the latter is more correct.[75] Remembering our predilection for meaningful explanations, successes are accompanied by a much better anecdote and causal story than are random processes. People typically accept more responsibility for good deeds than bad ones.[76] When we succeed, we take credit, but when we fail, we blame others or circumstances. Yet remember that most events have multiple contributing causal factors. I wonder if Christians who praise God for good outcomes and blame the devil for bad ones are indirectly being self-serving because they align themselves with God and thus feel affirmed in their faith.

Recall our previous discussions on randomness, attribution, and the locus of control. Because we don't like ambiguity and randomness in life, we often overestimate the degree of personal control we have over events. One study found that people who had chosen their own lottery ticket (i.e., they had some control) were more reluctant to trade it for a better option than those who had been given the ticket randomly. This makes no sense given that all the tickets were random. But we have an *illusion of control*.[77] We make causal associations between unrelated things and choose what we want to believe. *Magical thinking*, the belief that what we wish and hope can affect outcomes, is a type of this illusion.[78] It is normal in young children but also common in adults: many people avoid the thirteenth floor of a building or treasure "lucky" objects. Seeing meaning in coincidences is also a type of magical thinking. Even churchgoers participate in luck-related behavior such as knocking on wood, although may not admit to it.[79] Magical thinking is the basis of superstitions. There is much that we cannot control in the world, and when we act and believe as if we have control, we are being dishonest.

In fact, self-deception is universal.[80] This almost automatic behavior even occurs in children and animals. It functions to decrease anxiety and increase self-esteem. It is common in addiction: "I have my drinking under control." But we all do it at times, such as assuming we are more obedient to the Ten Commandments than other people. With respect to cause-and-effect relations, we tend to view ourselves as victims and others as perpetrators. Sometimes deceiving ourselves involves deceiving others—there is no need to change our beliefs if we can get others to agree. We look for supporting evidence for our dishonest views, and prey on others who are susceptible to persuasion. Although some self-deception is trivial, it is a misrepresentation of reality, which is not how responsible Christians should view the world. Self-deception can also be harmful to others. If we are uncomfortable with randomness in life, such as our own risk of getting COVID-19, we may convince ourselves that our friend only got sick because she went to the grocery store. Sharing our opinion with that friend is unkind to say the least.

Our self-serving tendency is universal, whether we want to admit it or not. It has serious implications for our ability to judge causation accurately. But its cause is more than simple selfishness and pride. It is rooted in our emotional insecurities and fears of uncertainty.

Fear and Pride

The COVID-19 pandemic understandably evoked fear. Many of us were also too proud to admit our fear. We like the world to be neat and orderly, we like to be in control, and we like to be right. When we see chaos and ambiguity, our mind-brains often automatically change our thinking to restore some order to our lives. So people may say, "The coronavirus is no different than the 'flu'" or "I'm healthy, I won't get it." Consequently, we create many cognitive illusions to fulfill our desires, and to decrease our fears and anxieties.

Humans typically think that their beliefs, judgments, and conclusions are correct. In one classic experiment, subjects had to find the rule in the number sequence 2, 4, 6. They could suggest other three-number sequences and were told if these were correct or not. The rule was numbers in ascending order, and a helpful test would have been suggesting numbers in descending order. Most people failed because they only asked questions that confirmed their assumptions. Furthermore, they attempted to justify their incorrect choice.[81] This illustrates the confirmation bias, our tendency to assume we're right, and our reluctance to admit mistakes.

We've all heard variations of people gloating over their "rightness": I knew it was going to rain today (even though the weather is unpredictable); I knew you were going to get that job (even though there were a hundred applicants); I knew God would heal you; God told me you were going to have a boy. The I-knew-it-all-along phenomenon, or the *hindsight bias*, relates to our overconfidence and illusions of understanding.[82] In our attempts to control an uncontrollable world, we create meaning by assuming we understand the past, and therefore can also understand the future. We presume that things will happen the same way. But, as we have seen, our reconstructions of past events are less than perfect.

In her review of the history and psychology of being wrong, journalist Kathryn Schulz notes that the delight of being right is universal.[83] Even the terms we use when we are wrong (losing face, eating crow) demonstrate our repulsion to it. We forget about other correct accounts and are blind to our own mistakes and illusions. However, we enjoy pointing out when others are wrong. Logically, if we are right, then those who disagree with us must be wrong, and we are entitled to correct them. Schulz suggests some common ways we explain why others are wrong:

- The Ignorance Assumption: "Those who disagree with me just don't know the facts."
- The Idiot Assumption: "They know the facts but don't have the brains to interpret them correctly."
- The Evil Assumption: "They know the facts and how to interpret them but are just plain wicked."

We have likely heard all of these from politicians and fearmongers. Conspiracy theorists and cult leaders make strong truth claims that include assertions that others are wrong. These function to allay fear, reduce uncertainty, and increase self-esteem.[84] It is easier to blame or trust someone else than to accept the complex nature of causation, including ourselves as contributory factors. *Groupthink* is the term used for decisions and judgments that are strongly influenced by the beliefs of our own group, such as a particular church denomination.

In the history of Christianity, the Millerite story is well known. Miller and his followers predicted that the world would end October 22, 1844 CE. When it did not, they creatively explained away their predictions by adjusting the date or suggesting it's always best to be prepared. When we are proven wrong, our pride works hard to recover. We deny and/or distort facts and deceive ourselves. Schulz describes classic patterns of how we rationalize our errors:

- The Time-Frame Defense: "I was wrong but wait until . . . "
- The Near-Miss Defense: "I was wrong but only by a little."
- The Out-of-Left-Field Defense: "I was right until (an extremely unexpected/unusual event) happened."
- The Better-Safe-Than-Sorry Defense: "I was wrong, but it was still better to believe . . . than not."[85]

Recall the woman who justified her divorce by saying that God only wanted her to be married for two years. She likely felt discomfort with believing that divorce is contrary to biblical teaching, and being divorced; therefore, adopted a new belief that God wanted this to happen. The theory of *cognitive dissonance* is helpful in explaining how people generally like their beliefs and behaviors to match.[86] Inconsistency, sometimes caused by new information, leads to emotional and psychological distress. People then seek to reduce this discomfort by resolving contradictions, either through changing a behavior or a belief. Those who smoke know that it causes cancer, but they also enjoy it and can be very creative in finding ways to reduce their psychological distress at the inconsistency: Life is short, why not enjoy it; I only smoke a few; There are other causes of cancer. The ancient fable about the fox that declared the grapes to be sour when he could not reach them is an example of cognitive dissonance reduction. We change our stories, justify our behaviors, and/or deny facts in order to affirm our beliefs in the face of evidence that challenges them. We are too proud to admit our errors.

The ways we understand how and why things happen is strongly and subconsciously influenced by our fears of uncertainty and our pride. We seek to confirm and justify our beliefs to prove ourselves right. We are quick to blame others. We make causal attributions and find meaning inappropriately to reduce feelings of fear and discomfort, and to allay our anxieties.

Uncertainty and Anxiety

I have had the privilege of counseling many clients with tragic beginnings to their lives. Abuse and neglect take their toll. When children grow up in an environment that is not safe and/or unstable, one of the ways they cope as adults is to create their own stability: they may restrict what they eat because it is one area they can control; they may check the lock on the door ten times, because it helps them feel safe; they may avoid crowds or close relationships, or think in black-and-white terms. Even people who grew up relatively secure are uncomfortable when life is unpredictable and/or unknown, such as during the 2020 pandemic. Uncertainty is frustrating, even terrifying. If we don't know what's around the corner, we may not be able to protect ourselves. Humans, to varying degrees, have a low tolerance for unpredictability, lack of control, and ambiguity. We do whatever we can to reduce it.

Studies have shown that women whose husbands are missing in action have problematic grief experiences. Even animal experiments have demonstrated that rodents prefer stronger *signaled* shocks to lower *unpredictable* ones.[87] We feel less stressed when our environment has more predictability. Superstition and magical thinking are also responses to unpredictability. We feel much more in control when we can find a cause for a problem, even if it requires imaginative reasoning. It is more satisfying to think that COVID-19 was manufactured and patented by pharmaceutical companies than to explain it as caused by many random factors. This belief also provides an easy target for our anxiety, expressed as anger. Uncertainty and anxiety are intertwined.

When our friends go through unexpected relationship breakups, we hear similar stories: He was a loser; I'm already moving on. In our aversion to ambiguity, we seek quick, easy answers, and cognitive closure. We respond to problems with urgency and permanence—resolving uncertainty as quickly as possible, and for as long as possible. These responses can result in us making quick, often-incorrect judgments.[88] When we accept the first answer we find, we may miss other explanations, and see meaning in the wrong places. When the pandemic started, the first thought that came to the minds of some Christians was that God caused it and is in complete control of it. This belief brings closure to the issue and alleviates our anxiety. But if we don't consider other factors, such as our own responsibility, we may not react appropriately by practicing physical distancing or wearing a mask.

This widespread dislike of uncertainty has been addressed in existential philosophy.[89] The German term *angst* describes feelings of discomfort, tension, emptiness, and fear, which are usually unfocused. These are a universal consequence of living in an unpredictable and mostly unknowable universe. We are torn between wanting to explore, or exercise our freedom, and being afraid of hurt. Angst is a result of the tension between our creaturely limitations and our spiritual ability to transcend and reflect on them. Simply put, there is a God; it is not me. Existential anxiety is inevitable in humans who are free but finite, frail beings born into a world that incites discomfort. It is natural, but we can choose how to respond to it. Recall that Adam and Eve did not respond well.

HOW ARE CHRISTIAN AND PSYCHOLOGICAL UNDERSTANDINGS RELATED?

As Paul states, "All have sinned and fall short of the glory of God" (Rom 3:23). The term *sin* is not typically found in psychology and is not really popular in Christianity either. However, I believe that the concept of sin has explanatory power in understanding some of our cognitive limitations and self-serving biases. In my counseling practice, I have frequently heard people claim that they heard God tell them to follow a certain course; when it fails, they either say that God had a better plan for them, or they deny having claimed what they heard in the first place. In our pride, we don't like to admit being wrong; therefore, we invent new narratives to justify our previous explanations. We all sin, but it is a complex issue.

We discussed earlier that the Bible sometimes associates illness and sin, and also that we are quick to judge others as sinful. However, sin is often subtle. It can be considered turning away from or rejecting God. It can involve pride, thinking we are above God and others, or sloth, failing to fulfill our God-given commands.[90] If we lack knowledge about how the world works, this is not sinful. But if we fail to attempt to understand the world, including ourselves, as best we can, this could be considered sinful. Or if we confidently claim that we *do know* how and why things happen, this may be pride. Interestingly, without referencing sin, Kahneman thinks we have an "almost unlimited ability to ignore our ignorance" and Taleb suggests that we all have hubris with respect to the limits of our knowledge.[91]

Myers, a Christian psychologist, suggests that sin is our "disinclination to recognize [our] creaturely limitations and dependence on God."[92] I would add that we are also disinclined to recognize the complexity of the world. Being anxious about ambiguity is not sinful. But seeking to resolve our uncertainty through means other than God, such as false beliefs, could be. Paradoxically, both our need to take control and our lack of self-control, such as when we make a conclusion about causation too quickly, can be considered sinful. Our fear of change and inconsistency represents mistrust in God. This may lead us to adopt beliefs that provide (false) security and increase our sense of confidence and control. We may delude even ourselves by proclaiming, "God told me . . . " Paradoxically, people's strong proclamations (with implied causal attributions) about divine control over everything in life may not necessarily reflect a strong faith, but point instead to their own insecurities and desire for control.

The relations between sin, cognitive limitations, and understanding causation are complex. Not all our inaccurate judgments are sinful. Sin usually implies intent, but many mental short-cuts are innate and unintentional. Remember that most aspects of creation contain limitations: gravity keeps us on earth but can also cause injury. Similarly, fast, automatic thinking helps us function efficiently in the world, but can mislead us at times. However, when we use it inappropriately, this may be considered sinful. When we know that we should engage our rational brains, but choose easier methods, surely we sin. When we focus our attention too narrowly, we miss "seeing the gorilla," or miss hearing God.

CONCLUSION

I recently heard the following about the COVID-19 pandemic: There's much we don't know; Sometimes stuff just happens; We should worry less about figuring out the cause and more about finding a cure and comforting the afflicted. Clearly, not everyone misjudges cause and effect in the world. This chapter has been necessarily long and sobering, but hopefully also enlightening. So far, we have seen that creation, especially causation within it, is incredibly complex, usually involving the interaction of multiple variables. It is best understood through probabilities and network models. A Christian conception of causation is compatible with a scientific one, with the addition of an awesome God who lovingly engages with his world. This God also gives us responsibility to understand how and why things happen. He has given us amazing mind-brains.

In sum, we function effectively in the world using perception, reason, intuition, and emotion. We quickly recognize patterns and assign meaning to events, which helps us make decisions. These mental processes are intertwined, and we are usually unaware of them. However, there is a downside to our cognitive processing. The automatic processes that allow us to quickly see patterns can also make us biased. We jump to conclusions. We take the easy and self-serving route. We abhor uncertainty. Our predilection for meaning leads to inaccurate judgments of causation. Indeed, "why intelligent people [do] foolish things is no surprise."[93]

We have some awareness of our cognitive limitations; evident in jokes such as the "retrospectoscope," a medical instrument that benefits from hindsight, and "Murphy's law," or, whatever *can* go wrong *will*. But I think we need more awareness. Understanding the strengths and weaknesses of our cognitive processes is important for Christians who want to follow a godly path and exercise wise spiritual discernment. Our natural inclinations toward rapid appraisals and causal attributions can lead to costly misconceptions of reality. Continual reliance on God can protect against overconfidence and hubris in our judgments regarding causation in creation. Having read this far (thank you) you are already more aware than the average person. This awareness can be supplemented with specific strategies for improving our understanding of how and why things happen.

Who has put wisdom in the inward parts, or given understanding to the mind?

JOB 38:36

ENDNOTES

1. Farrer, *Faith and Speculation*, 68.

2. E.g., Kalat, *Biological Psychology*; Boleyn-Fitzgerald, *Pictures of the Mind*; Jeeves and Brown, *Neuroscience, Psychology*; McGilchrist, *Master and Emissary*; Ellis and Newton, *How the Mind*; Newberg, *Why We Believe*, 49.

3. Other labels are fast-slow, intuition-reason, emotional-rational, and low road-high road. Amos Tversky and Daniel Kahneman pioneered this concept. Kahneman, *Thinking, Fast and Slow*. See also Goleman, *Social Intelligence*; Haidt, *Righteous Mind*. These processes roughly correspond with right and left hemispheric functions, although there is much overlap. Iain McGilchrist, in his provocative book *The Master and his Emissary*, suggests that right hemispheric processes of emotion and intuition are primary but have been neglected in the Western world. Our fragmented, mechanistic, indeed empty world has arisen from the unchecked action of a dysfunctional left hemisphere. The prioritizing of focused attention has led to an impoverished view of the world. McGilchrist believes language and linearity need to be transcended; we need imagination in order to truly understand the world.

4. E.g., Baillargeon, "Infant's Understanding"; Leslie and Keeble, "Do Infants Perceive Causality?"; Spelke and Kinzler, "Core Knowledge."

5. Van Berkum, "Sentences in Context."

6. Ambady and Rosenthal, "Half a Minute."

7. Bechara et al., "Insensitivity." The task was developed to assess effects of brain damage on decision making.

8. The concept of intuition in medicine is fairly new. It is perhaps especially helpful for radiologists who need to detect subtle changes and consider their relevance within a clinical context, but practitioners such as anesthesiologists may have better intuition because they receive more frequent and immediate feedback. Kahneman, *Thinking, Fast and Slow*, 239–42; Groopman, *Second Opinions*.

9. Kahneman, *Thinking, Fast and Slow*, 240.

10. "Nature appears to have built the apparatus of rationality not just on top of the apparatus of biological regulation, but also *from* it and *within* it." Damasio, *Descartes' Error*, 128.

11. E.g., Rolls, *Emotion and Decision-Making*; Frijda et al., *Emotions and Beliefs*; Newberg, *Why We Believe*; Gorman and Gorman *Denying to the Grave*; Goleman, *Emotional Intelligence*.

12. Lerner et al., "Heart Strings."

13. Risen and Critcher, "Visceral Fit."

14. E.g., Eysenck and Keane, *Cognitive Psychology*.

15. Michotte, *Perception of Causality*.

16. Heider and Simmel, "Study of Apparent Behavior."

17. By Grade 4, most children develop natural explanations. Kelemen, "Why Are Rocks Pointy?"

18. This is slightly stronger among those with religious affiliation, and a high degree of paranoia or empathy. Banerjee and Bloom, "Why Did This Happen?"; see also Banerjee and Bloom, "Does Everything Happen?" This relates to the *just-world fallacy* that good actions are rewarded, and bad ones punished. Lerner, *Just World*.

19. Barrett, *Born Believers*, esp. 15–42; Keil and Newman, "Order, Order Everywhere."

20. Molina et al., "Animate-Inanimate Distinction."

21. Barrett, *Born Believers*.

22. Gilbert et al., "Illusion of External Agency."

23. E.g., Berthoz, *Emotion and Reason*; Ariely, *Predictably Irrational*; Lehrer, *How We*

Decide; Rolls, *Emotion and Decision-Making*; Keil, "Explanation and Understanding."

24. Haidt, *Righteous Mind*, 45.

25. The theory is more complex than my brief summary implies; there are primary and secondary appraisal processes. Lazarus, *Psychological Stress*; Lazarus and Folkman, *Stress, Appraisal*; Scherer et al., *Appraisal Processes*.

26. This theory was originally suggested by Fritz Heider, *Interpersonal Relations*; see also Fiske and Taylor, *Social Cognition;* Weiner, *Attributional Theory;* Jones et al., *Attribution.*

27. This theory was first developed by Julian Rotter, "Internal versus External Control."

28. Clore, "Rationality of Emotion," 213.

29. Myers, *Intuition*, 51.

30. Haidt, who likens the "emotional" brain to an elephant being ridden by "conscious reasoning," claims the elephant rules (*Righteous Mind*, 61–83). Berthoz similarly suggests, "passion trumps reason, because reason has forgotten to make room for passion" (*Emotion and Reason*, 283).

31. See summaries in Kahneman, *Thinking, Fast and Slow*; Myers, *Intuition*; Haidt, *Righteous Mind*; Lehrer, *How We Decide*; Taleb, *Black Swan*. Research on cognitive processing has impacted many fields (business, economics, law, healthcare) but is not without its critics. E.g., Stein, "Are People Probabilistically Challenged?"

32. E.g., Goldstein, *Sensation and Perception*.

33. "Optical Illusions." There are many other examples available on the internet and social media.

34. Simons and Rensink, "Change Blindness."

35. Simons and Chabris, "Gorillas in Our Midst." Google the latest version for fun: "The Monkey Business Illusion."

36. Wilson and Schooler, "Thinking Too Much."

37. Schwartz et al., "Ease of Retrieval."

38. Engel and Singer, *Better than Conscious?*

39. Kahneman, *Thinking, Fast and Slow*, 115.

40. Tversky and Kahneman, "Law of Small Numbers."

41. Yamagishi, "12.86% Mortality."

42. Gilovich et al., "Hot Hand in Basketball."

43. Kahneman, *Thinking, Fast and Slow*, 183.

44. Tversky and Kahneman, "Extensional Versus Intuitive"; Kahneman, *Thinking, Fast and Slow*, 146–65.

45. E.g., Kahenman, *Thinking, Fast and Slow*, 114–18, 422–23; Taleb, *Fooled by Randomness*.

46. This is known as the *availability heuristic*. Kahneman, *Thinking, Fast and Slow*, 7–9, 129–35.

47. Alter et al., "Overcoming Intuition"; Kahneman, *Thinking, Fast and Slow* 62–67.

48. Lichtenstein et al., "Lethal Events."

49. Zajonc, "Effects of Mere Exposure"; Jaccoby et al., "Becoming Famous Overnight."

50. Kahneman, *Thinking, Fast and Slow*, 73; this "Moses illusion" sets up a misleading biblical context.

51. Kahneman *Thinking, Fast and Slow*, 322–33.

52. Schwartz et al., "Ease of Retrieval."

53. Tulving et al., "Priming Effects." There is semantic activation without conscious identification. See also Kahneman, *Thinking, Fast and Slow*, 52–58.

54. Kahneman, *Thinking, Fast and Slow*, 363–74; McNeil et al, "Elicitation of Preferences."

55. Hassin et al., "Spontaneous Causal Inferences."

56. Kahneman, *Thinking, Fast and Slow*, 114; Stuart Vyse refers to the *principle of contagion*, in which things once associated, remain so (*Believing in Magic*, 5–12).

57. Multiple studies have demonstrated the falsity of this belief. E.g., Gorman and Gorman, *Denying to the Grave*.

58. Taleb, *Black Swan*, 100–101.

59. Stanovich's term; *Intelligence Tests*, 70–85.

60. Related by Hastie and Dawes, *Rational Choice*, 123.

61. Kahneman, *Thinking, Fast and Slow*, 98–99.

62. Friesen, *Decision Making*, 127–47, 243–55, 267–69.

63. Tversky and Kahneman, "Extensional Versus Intuitive."

64. Falk and Macgregor, "Surprisingness of Coincidences." See also Vyse, *Believing in Magic*; Mazur, *Fluke*; Sloman, *Causal Models*, 60–67.

65. Taleb, *Black Swan*, 62–84.

66. Nisbett and Wilson, "More Than We Can Know."

67. E.g., Keil and Wilson, *Explanation and Cognition*; Johnson et al., "Simplicity and Complexity"; Keil, "Running on Empty?"; Keil, "Explanation and Understanding"; Rozenblit and Keil, "Folk Science."

68. Superstitions are unrelated to culture, intelligence, or psychopathology. Demographical studies suggest that women, younger people, those with an external locus of control, low self-efficacy, and conservatism have a higher incidence of superstitious beliefs. Vyse *Believing in Magic*, 237–60.

69. Wagner and Morris, "'Superstitious' Behavior." Behaviorist B. F. Skinner famously demonstrated that pigeons, when given food at regular intervals, developed ritualistic behavior ("'Superstition' in the Pigeon").

70. This has been called the "curse of expertise." Fisher and Keil, "Curse of Expertise." See also Kahneman, *Thinking, Fast and Slow*, 222–33.

71. Tetlock, *Expert Political Judgment*; Tetlock and Gardner, *Superforecasting*. Sociobiologist Robert Trivers points out that overconfidence is older than language and very dangerous (*Folly of Fools*, 13–14). Interestingly, it is more common in males than females.

72. Baker and Emery, "Every Relationship."

73. Rosenblatt, "11th Commandment."

74. E.g., Zaleski, "Saints of John Paul II."

75. Kahneman, *Thinking, Fast and Slow*, 209–21.

76. Ross and Sicoly, "Egocentric Biases."

77. Developed by Ellen Langer, "The Illusion of Control." Theologian Kate Bowler thinks "control is a drug" and "we want to tell ourselves a story—any story—so we can get back to certainty" (*Everything Happens*, 84, 160).

78. E.g., Serban, *Magical Thinking*. Note that religion is not magical thinking because it has social and historical roots, and incorporates critical thinking. Vyse, *Believing in Magic*, 3–15.

79. Francis et al., "Unconventional Beliefs." This is interesting in relation to the study mentioned earlier that showed Christians reacting unfavorably to the concept of luck (Stevens, "Grounded Theology").

80. E.g., Barnes, *Self-deception*; Trivers, *Folly of Fools*, 15–18, 139–56.

81. Wason, "Failure to Eliminate Hypotheses."

82. Kahneman, *Thinking, Fast and Slow*, 199–207; Taleb, *Fooled by Randomness*, vii –xvii.

83. Schulz, *Being Wrong*, 3–43.

84. Gorman and Gorman suggest common factors in successful conspiracy theories: a charismatic leader, the nature of risk prediction, a fear of complexity, confirmation

biases, filling knowledge gaps, and the internet (*Denying to the Grave*, 7, 35–64).

85. Schulz, *Being Wrong*, 201–19. More recently, Festinger and colleagues studied a religious group that predicted the end of the world, and the cognitive dissonance reducing strategies they used when this did not occur. They noted that even clear disconfirming evidence can increase conviction and proselytizing (*When Prophecy Fails*).

86. Festinger, *Cognitive Dissonance*.

87. Lazarus and Folkman, *Stress, Appraisal*, 82–116; De Berker et al., "Computations of Uncertainty."

88. Kruglanski and Webster, "Closing of the Mind"; Holmes, *Nonsense*.

89. This idea is associated with the German philosopher Heidegger, and was developed by Kierkegaard (*Concept of Anxiety*) and Niebuhr (*Nature and Destiny of Man*, 178–240). See also Gordon, "Impermanence of Being"; Cooper, *Sin, Pride*, 40–45, 158–62; White, "Personality of Sin."

90. E.g., Biddle, *Missing the Mark*, 32–76, 136.

91. Kahneman, *Thinking, Fast and Slow*, 201; Taleb, *Black Swan*, 138.

92. Myers, *Inflated Self*, 93. He further states, "One of the brute facts of human nature is our capacity for illusion and self-deception" (xiv).

93. The title of a chapter in Stanovich, *Intelligence Tests*, 59–69. He uses the term *dysrationalia* to describe "the inability to think and behave rationality, despite adequate intelligence" (2).

7

What Are Some Wise Ways to Evaluate Causation?

A SURVEY DONE TWO months into the 2020 pandemic found that people who had relationships in their lives based on covenantal values, like sacrifice and support, struggled less than those whose approach to relationships was self-valuing. In addition, those who attended church regularly were also more resilient during lockdown. The author wisely advises, "Be authentic. Be supportive. Be resilient."[1] This study did not consider people's views on what caused the pandemic, but I think it is interesting to ponder if faith enables better judgment.

To reiterate, an accurate perception of how and why things happen is crucial. Beliefs lead to behavior, and inaccurate ones may lead to actions that harm us, such as failing to protect ourselves against COVID-19 because we think it's a hoax. Inaccurate perceptions may also harm others, such as assuming someone's sickness is caused by sin. As Christians, we have God-given responsibility to accurately understand cause and effect in the world. Indeed, I believe we are called to integrate our faith with our knowledge of the world. We need to focus on truth as best we can, even if it causes uncomfortable emotions. Our beliefs should reflect reality, regardless of how we feel about that reality. And, knowing when God has acted and when we have worked with him can be spiritually edifying and give meaning to our lives.

Recall laws and limits, dispositions and diversity, patterns and probabilities, chaos and cooperation. As we have seen through our examination of causation in the Bible, theology, and the natural world, there are seldom simple cause-and-effect associations between God, humans, evil spirits, and inanimate factors. There are layers and levels, and different ways to frame causation. Consequently, figuring out how and why things happen in the world can be challenging. From a Christian perspective, this includes not only cause and effect in the created world, but also God's action in this world—identifying this last is commonly known as discernment. Evaluating causation is challenging enough; it is compounded by our sinful natures and mind-brains that are prone to judgment errors.

However, there is good news. We can receive wisdom and guidance from both psychological research and theological reflections. Christian spirituality and its approach to discernment is especially helpful. All that we have learned so far in this book can be applied to our daily evaluations of how and why things happen in the world.

WHAT PSYCHOLOGICAL STRATEGIES CAN IMPROVE OUR JUDGMENTS OF CAUSATION?

A friend recently asked, "Do mosquitos cause COVID-19?" Given what we've learned in the last chapter, we could speculate that she had some bites from a recent camping trip that were itching, making her think about mosquitos (recall the phenomena of association, availability, and priming). Perhaps, given the pandemic, she was also anxious and looking for an easy resolution to the uncertainty. Increased knowledge increases our sense of control. To address her question, it would help to understand *why* she is asking it before advising some fact checking. Remember, emotions are more persuasive than logic.

In general, we think that we usually make logical judgments, but often our rational mind-brain is only endorsing intuitions that come from our automatic mind-brain. We tend to overestimate causality and view the world as more explainable than it actually is. As Taleb notes, we frequently confuse luck with skills, probability with certainty, randomness with determinism, conjecture with certitude, coincidence with causation, and theory with reality.[2] Most of these biases can be explained by our overreliance on our intuitions and emotions. However, many are also a result of our pride, fears of uncertainty, and tendencies to be self-serving. Knowledge of cognitive processes can improve our judgment skills.

A first strategy is to gain awareness of the nature of human decision making and mental limitations, as revealed by psychology research.[3] We can remind ourselves of some of the common factors that influence our judgment: experience, expectations, emotions, ego, and ease. A second, and related, strategy is to know which processes are best applied to which situations, or what tools to use and when to use them. When we have to judge quickly, like changing lanes to avoid ice, we should rely on our automatic systems. Similarly, when we want to recall knowledge, such as in multiple-choice exams or finding lost keys, we can benefit from "thinking" less. However, we need to recognize when we are in a cognitive minefield, such as highly ambiguous or emotional situations, because these have a high risk of error. Religion and politics are good examples of such situations. Similarly, circumstances that involve randomness and probability require careful judgment. When we encounter a new problem, we cannot rely on our automatic judgments because we lack previous experience; consequently, we need to use our rational mind-brains. When a decision is not that important, such as where we travel on vacation (post-pandemic), we should learn to trust our intuition and emotions because they often reflect subconscious desires and knowledge. However, most of the time, when judging cause and effect, especially if considering God's role in an event, we need to slow down and consider a few different possible explanations before choosing one. We can remind ourselves of what we do not know and what may be unknowable. We can review similar cases and avoid generalizing from our past experience to our current situation. We should engage in exploratory rather than confirmatory thought. It is usually wise to solicit contrary evidence and second opinions.

A third strategy is to practice our cognitive skills and seek feedback. Encouragingly, we can learn from repeat observations and experience. Train your brain. Develop checklists. Look for perceptual illusions. Embrace change and creativity. Consider the big picture. Frame your question in three different ways. Try arguing in support of a political position that's opposite to what you believe. Remember that making mistakes is very common. These can be mitigated, not only by learning about cognitive processes, but by adopting a posture of curiosity and humility. This involves listening more often than speaking; learning from our mistakes; consulting others, especially experts; and choosing our words wisely, using terms like *perhaps* and *probably* when we make causal assertions.[4] Such strategies may help us become wise evaluators in our wise and wonderful world.

A fourth strategy is to learn to *embrace* uncertainty rather than avoid it. Remember, uncertainty in life is certain, and not necessarily detrimental. It can inspire us to explore the creativity inherent in the world as well as developing our own creativity. Accepting ambiguity can increase motivation, encourage empathy, and improve our problem solving and decision making abilities.[5] Paradoxically, it can also decrease our anxiety. Similarly, some degree of discomfort is beneficial. It can increase success and resilience. Research shows that humans function optimally at a midpoint between boredom and anxiety.[6] If life is too predictable, we stagnate—recall the donkey who died because it avoided risk.

In psychotherapy, we help clients recognize how their (often inaccurate) attributions of causation affect their feelings. Some parents feel completely responsible for the failures of their children and forget about all the other influences that affect children. Some Christians "blame" God for everything, without admitting their own responsibility for their choices. Therapists help people understand that there are usually many causes and possible interpretations in challenging life situations. We teach self-awareness and the connections between belief, emotion, and appraisal.[7] We educate clients about common so-called cognitive distortions, such as black-and-white thinking, fortune-telling, overgeneralizing, or jumping to conclusions. We help people realize when their thinking is self-serving, and when they need to accept uncertainty.

Psychology, like most fields, has some paradoxes. Recall that embracing ultimate meaning in life is wise, but seeing "meaning" everywhere is not. Sometimes we help people gain more control in their lives; other times we encourage them to loosen their control and understand the anxieties that underlie it. In some situations, people's feelings of helplessness, or lack of control over a situation, lead to depression.[8] It is clearly healthy to have some degree of control in some aspects of our lives, but not to an extreme. We need to realize that we cannot "cause" everything to happen and that sometimes stuff just happens. Interestingly, this relates to our earlier theological discussion on how God in his sovereignty and wisdom does not need to control everything. Faith can help people find appropriate meaning and control in their lives.

WHAT SPIRITUAL STRATEGIES CAN IMPROVE OUR JUDGMENTS OF CAUSATION?

The author of Hebrews claims, "Solid food is for the mature, for those whose faculties have been trained by practice to distinguish good from evil" (Heb 5:14). Unfortunately, he does not explain exactly how to train our faculties. This verse, the end of a warning to abide by the truth of Christ, contains three concepts: practice, spiritual maturity, and telling good from evil. The last, and perhaps the first, is usually discussed within Christian spirituality under the topic of discernment. This subject could also incorporate our evaluation of how and why things happen in the world, including when and how God acts. However, discernment is both challenging and frequently misunderstood—hence the need for practice and maturity.

Spiritual Discernment

What caused the Covid-19 pandemic? Does God want me to work from home? Why did my friend get sick? How can the church combat evil? The diversity of these questions illustrates the diverse nature of spiritual discernment. Recall that one of my motivations for writing this book was my observation that many people talk about discernment without really knowing what they are asking. Having a better idea of what exactly discernment is will help us in understanding causes and effects in the world.

"My eye has seen . . . my ear has heard . . ." (Job 13:1). The Old Testament uses various terms that mean discernment; they are usually associated with sensory perception.[9] The Greek word translated as discernment is *diakrisis*, meaning to separate, sort out, or distinguish (1 Cor 12:10; Heb 5:14).[10] Biblical teaching about discernment also involves the ideas of testing false prophecy and distinguishing between good and evil (1 John 4:1). Remember, Scripture does not focus on cause and effect but on a relationship with God, through Christ and the Spirit. Typically, when people encounter God, they don't receive detailed life instructions, but instead become aware of the divine presence, and experience refreshment, peace, love, and joy. Remembering the overall focus of the Bible and its emphasis on communities rather than individuals, these are things that impact the kingdom of God. This should guide our discernment practices. Spiritual discernment, something required of all Christians, can be considered both a gift and a virtue that can be developed through practice and grace.

Ignatius of Loyola described dense complexes of motives in decision making. Francis of Assisi received divine visions and also asked others to pray for him regarding decisions. The concept of discernment has a long history. It uses the language of guidance, direction, and seeking, and refers to the will of God, the voice of Jesus, and the presence of the Holy Spirit.[11] Although there are several definitions of discernment, they have in common the idea of identifying situations that are significantly related to God or not.[12] Theoretically, those who believe that God is omni-causal would not need to practice discernment, because the only thing to "discern" is God. There are many aspects or types of discernment: identifying a demonic spirit, engaging in personal or corporate decision-making, identifying false prophets, finding God's will, and hearing God's voice—these are often interrelated.[13] I would add identifying God's action in current and historical events to the list.

It is interesting that those writing on spiritual discernment seldom discuss ways to recognize divine action; they perhaps prioritize guidance for human action. Some scholars who write about God's action in the world doubt that we can discern it, or at least only in hindsight.[14] I think that we should be cautious and humble in our attempts to discern divine action, but are nevertheless responsible to do so. God wants to be known and want us to work with him in the world. Therefore, it helps to have some idea of how to tell when and where he acts.

Discernment is typically framed in binary terms: God/not God. Yet, as we have seen, there are many causative factors in the world. "Not God" could include human selfish and/or evil desires as well as evil spirits. There are also some neutral categories. Sometimes things happen because of the nature of the created world—recall dispositional causation and undesired events that are simply side-effects of normal processes. Some human decisions and actions, such as what we eat, are not significantly related to God but are not opposed to God either. One of the most common insights I receive when praying for guidance is to trust my own judgment. Remember, God is flexible and will walk with us on many possible pathways.

I am viewing discernment broadly, but I think it is essential that we understand all the different aspects. We could categorize our questions as important or unimportant, pertaining to individuals or groups, relating to the past or the future, and seeking guidance or discerning divine action. Our answers could include God (good), Satan (evil), human (good, evil, or neutral), and natural (mostly neutral but influenced by good and evil agents), bearing in mind that sometimes more than one may apply. I suggest it is helpful to focus on the specific aspect of discernment we are interested in, such as guidance for a decision, whether God caused the pandemic, or whether evil spirits are influencing someone. As well as knowing *what* discernment is, we can benefit from knowing *how* we practice it.

Processes in Discernment

I had an experience once, when meeting a candidate for a pastoral position, of instinctively feeling that there was something untrustworthy about him. I couldn't explain my thoughts and didn't share too much, but voted against continuing the process. The church's search committee later discovered that this candidate had exhibited some behaviors in the past that shed doubt on his character, and he was eliminated. My discernment, based on intuition, was confirmed through logical processes. I wish I could say this happened frequently.

Remember that, although God wants to talk to us, we are limited in our ability to listen, interpret, and judge. Consequently, errors are common and many Christian discernment strategies are misguided. As biblical scholar Bruce Waltke points out, following God's will is based on an ongoing relationship with him, not specific arbitrary signs. Therefore, common practices such as "Bible roulette," following hunches, or seeing God's will in coincidences are not biblical. And, basing our decisions on a feeling of peace is unreliable.[15] Although not always easy, discernment is not miraculous and mysterious, but something that can be understood.

Discernment may seem difficult when we are unclear about the question we are asking or the judgment processes we are using. Since spiritual communication is mediated through our mind-brains, and since discernment, like most human experience, involves elements of knowledge, judgment, and decision, cognitive psychology research can be helpful. We saw that spiritual knowledge can be acquired through both rational and nonrational means, and that biblical terms for discernment allude to both sensory and analytical processes. Recall that Augustine referred to both analysis and wisdom in learning.[16] There are interesting similarities between discernment strategies and the two types of cognitive processing. We make judgments using both System 1 (emotions/intuition) and System 2 (reason/logic) processes. Interestingly, many writers on discernment implicitly refer to these.

John Wesley, in his classic advice on theological reflection, points to the importance of Scripture, Christian tradition, experience, and reason.[17] He seems to emphasize reason (all except "experience" involve rational processes), but others suggest that intuition is the primary way we hear God's voice.[18] Recalling that cognitive processes are intertwined, it makes more sense that both automatic and intentional strategies are necessary. One process may be more prominent depending on the type of discernment question we are asking. If I seek awareness of God's presence, intuition and imagination are helpful. If I seek guidance about a job decision, rational reflection and Bible study may be appropriate. If I seek the cause of something, at times I may use my automatic processes, relying on meaningful associations between events, but other times I may need knowledge of how and why things happen in order to make a rational judgment.

Evangelical Gordon Smith refers to the "inner witness of the Spirit" and a "direct impression on our inner consciousness"—both intuitive experiences. But he also claims that discernment is deliberate. He describes it as "a way of knowing and seeing that is experienced as a profound interplay of intellect and emotion."[19] Dallas Willard similarly notes that impressions sometimes just feel right; he relates sensing God's presence to our intuitive ability to know when someone is staring at us. But he insists that we should be guided by "reasonable, intelligible communication, not by blind impulse, force or sensation alone."[20] Willard refers to three interdependent "lights" in discernment: circumstances, impressions of the Spirit, and biblical passages. If these point in the same direction, we are likely correctly discerning God's guidance. He believes that one alone, such as a closed door of circumstance, is unreliable. Willard also emphasizes our responsibility in making judgments: sometimes the Spirit counsels us to decide for ourselves.

Being informed about the psychological and spiritual processes we use can help us improve our discernment abilities, including who/what causes things to happen in the world. We can "train our faculties." This may involve self-awareness: examining our motivations (e.g., subconscious desires for pleasure, honor, or power) and emotions (fear, anger, or sadness) before making judgments. We can also employ rational methods, such as considering the context of a situation, understanding all the issues, framing decisions in terms of manageable choices, and listing pros and cons of each option.[21] Perhaps most importantly, we can cultivate humility and open mindedness.

Recall my patient who thought God wanted her to experience depression. Her beliefs potentially hindered her ability to recover. An important aspect of self-awareness is recognizing our underlying assumptions about how and why things happen. If we presume all sickness is caused by sin, we will have difficulty hearing other possible interpretations.[22] Because we like early cognitive closure, we may stop listening when we find an answer we like. Our assumptions about how God acts in the world also impact our discernment. God indwells and works from within creation, rather than intervening, apparently arbitrarily, from outside. He reveals the light and life within, that are often covered by dirt and darkness. Given that the Lord shines strongest in the body of believers, it makes sense to look for his presence and action within the church and its mission. Remember, miracles always have a theological purpose, such as revelation. How we evaluate these depends on our purpose and assumptions. A physicist might assess a miracle based on the probability of the event and the reliability of the person who witnessed it. But a theist would judge it according to its function as a sign of God's activity and its compatibility with what is known about divine purposes.[23] I suggest that we integrate our faith with scientific knowledge: a low probability event with spiritual significance, associated with much communal prayer, perhaps has a high probability that God acted directly in the situation.

A helpful theological assumption is that God wants to work coopera-
tively with his creatures. Therefore, it can be difficult to distinguish whether
God caused something directly, a person caused it, or God and human
acted together. Recall that biblical texts often suggest much overlap between
divine and human causation. I'm not sure it is necessary to make sharp dichotomies between divine and human action when the activities function
to further the kingdom of God. It is reasonable to conclude that God is
involved when we see spiritual fruits. And, instead of expressing humility
(often false) in claiming "It wasn't me, it was only God," we can accept some
credit for our obedience in cooperating with God.

On one occasion I suggested that a counseling client, who compen-
sated for low self-esteem by hard work, pray for insight. She reported that
God told her to "knuckle down." I pointed out that, although *she* tended to
beat herself up, the voice of Jesus is usually gentle and encouraging, and perhaps it was her own voice she heard. An important process in discernment,
especially applicable for important communal decisions, is evaluating what
we think we have heard. This could be seen as a second step—a rational
process following an intuitive one. It is similar to criteria commonly used to
appraise any spiritual experience. First, we can examine the *content* of our
spiritual impression: Is it in line with Scripture and tradition? Is it oriented
towards God and not self? Is it confirmed by others? Does it glorify Christ?
Second, we can consider its *tone*: Is it loving and gentle? Finally, we should
examine the *fruit* of our discernment: Does it lead to growth in purity and
devotion? Spiritual transformation?[24] So if someone reports that God told
them to act in an R-rated movie, we might question their discernment. If
someone says that God caused their cancer, we might question whether this
glorifies Christ. We could also clarify that God may use their suffering to
produce spiritual fruits, but that this is different from God causing it. Remember the importance of asking the right question.

Both rationality and intuition, experience and evaluation are important in Christian discernment. A key component is identifying which process we are using and knowing which is appropriate to the situation. We
can learn from our experience, research on thought processes, and teaching
and feedback from Christian communities. With practice, our minds are
illuminated and our judgments clearer. We can come to know ourselves, the
world, and God better.

Spiritual Maturity

Here's one of my favorite guiding verses for prayer: "If any of you is lacking in wisdom, ask God . . . and it will be given you" (Jas 1:5). James also points out that "wisdom from above is first pure, then peaceable, gentle . . . without a trace of partiality or hypocrisy" (Jas 3:17). Because evaluating how and why things happen, recognizing God's work in the world, and discerning his direction for us can be challenging, wisdom is essential. Christians can rely on the indwelling Holy Spirit who "guides us into all the truth" (John 16:13). Like any close friendship, a close relationship with the Lord enables us to hear and understand him more effectively. Living in the light helps us to see the truth. Knowing the effects of the wind in the world helps us to see divine action. When we are obedient, focusing on the Spirit within, we can better discern the degree of God's involvement in a specific situation.

Practices that foster spiritual maturity may aid our discernment abilities. Unsurprisingly, much of the discernment literature emphasizes the importance of a relationship with God, which prepares us for discernment.[25] To improve our wisdom and ability to evaluate causation in creation, we can cultivate a godly character through Bible study and prayer. We can engage in spiritual disciplines, such as solitude, silence, and meditation, in order to open ourselves to the presence of God and be in tune with his Spirit. Such practices may also decrease anxieties that may cloud our judgment and allow us to focus our eyes on our Lord rather than ourselves. Prayer, especially when we listen more than speak, not only helps us grow spiritually, but aids our ability to hear God and make correct judgments. It calms our fears, but, of course, is not just a therapeutic technique. We can also actively participate in a Christian community and consult others, especially those who know us well, on matters requiring wise discernment. With respect to cognitive limitations, this practice may also counteract self-serving biases.

Growing in faith may help us cope with the uncertainties that are inevitable in life. A strong faith is an antidote to the fears and anxieties associated with events like the COVID-19 pandemic. Instead of looking for easy answers or adopting false beliefs that decrease our anxiety, we can rely on "our ever-present help in times of trouble" (Ps 46.1). We can trust a certain God in an uncertain world. Writers on Christian spirituality suggest that discomfort leads to spiritual growth; commonly referred to as a "wilderness experience" or a "dark night of the soul." David, Job, and Habakkuk all experienced angst that aided their faith in God. Indeed, it may be that God is *most* present during anxious and uncertain moments of human history.[26] Remember that not all discomfort should be embraced (if we have a fever, we should see a doctor) and that just because God can use our discomfort for good does not necessarily mean he causes it.

Focusing on becoming Christ-like, turning toward the light of God, and listening to the guidance of the indwelling Spirit are our priorities. As we grow in faith and wisdom, we will develop wise discernment skills.

WHAT ARE SOME WISE, PRACTICAL WAYS TO DISCERN CAUSATION?

Paul Young, in his otherwise excellent book *Lies We Believe About God,* agrees with the popular notion that there is no such thing as a coincidence. He gives an example of praying for guidance before giving a presentation. The passage he chose was life changing for one person.[27] However, I think his interpretation is based on a misunderstanding of both causation in the world and spiritual discernment. Guidance from the Holy Spirit and consequent results (that we may not always see) is not coincidental. But this is very different from finding a convenient parking space or unexpectedly meeting someone we know. We have discussed many other examples of confusion about causation and discernment. The good news is that we can use many practical strategies to enhance our discernment accuracy and, in so doing, become wiser.

Considering everything we have discussed in this book, I suggest that we all can benefit from better awareness of the nature of:

- God's interaction with the world, which is loving and flexible, but not omni-causal.

- human responsibility in understanding how and why things happen, and working with God in making things happen.

- our cognitive processing abilities in making judgments about causation.

- the created world, in which causation is usually multifactorial and best understood in a probabilistic manner.

- spiritual discernment.

Different disciplines examine different aspects of causation and there is interesting overlap. Both Christian theology and cognitive psychology point to the importance of wisdom and humility in making good judgments. The author of Hebrews advises us to "train our faculties." Spiritual and mental interrelate. Humility can include recognizing our tendencies for egocentric biases, our preference for cognitively-easy judgments, and our preference for meaningful stories. Self-knowledge involves awareness of our thinking processes and biases, our emotions, and motivations. Recognizing the context of discernment may include noting mental availability and association. Furthermore, acknowledging our need for certainty and control, our preference for meaning and anecdote, and our self-serving biases may enhance our relationships with God and others. Both cognitive psychology and Christian spirituality note the importance of attending to intuition, albeit with caution. We do not want to miss the still, small nudges of the Spirit, but we also do not want to rely excessively on our emotions. Perhaps hearing the voice of Jesus improves with experience, like musicians who can recognize certain tones only with practice.

Philosophy, mathematics, science, and theology all describe causation as involving numerous different factors, both naturalistic and personalistic, interacting in ways that are difficult to identify. God has created a wonderful world in which causation is intrinsic and sometimes overdetermined. Numerous pathways intertwine to produce order, although sometimes unwelcome side effects of these processes occur. In the intricate web of causation, precision is impossible but is improved by using statistical concepts. God walks with us through the twists and turns of the webs of life, and calls us to follow him, making wise decisions, and working with him to build his kingdom. We are to restore the brightness to our beautiful world, counteracting sin and evil. However, for now we see through dirty glasses; therefore, discernment is difficult but critical.

I suggest five ways that we can better perceive and practice spiritual discernment, especially with respect to understanding how and why things happen. These are guidelines for our discernment questions; not all are applicable in all situations. There are many possible approaches, but what we have learned about causation can inform our discernment practices.

First, we need to be *God-aware*. Consider the theologically and spiritual significance of an event, the ways in which God works, and the possibility of human cooperation. Although we can praise God in all circumstances, it does not mean he *directly acts* in every circumstance. We can ask:

- Is this event compatible with biblical accounts of divine action?

- Is it in line with the loving character of God?

- Does it glorify God? Further his kingdom?

- Is/was it associated with intentional prayer?

- Do we see fruits of the Spirit? Does the event lead to increased love for God and neighbor? Spiritual transformation?

Second, we need to be *situation-aware*. Consider philosophical, statistical, and scientific aspects of causation: types (Aristotle's material, formal, efficient, and final levels; not all present in every situation), necessary and sufficient conditions, temporal and spatial relations between cause and effect, base rates (prior probabilities of an event occurring), counterfactuals (alternate interpretations), intrinsic or dispositional causation, and web-like processes in many aspects of nature. Not all factors are relevant to every circumstance, but it is better to consider multiple possibilities. At times we may need to conclude that discernment is either unnecessary or impossible. We can ask:

- Is this event common or rare?

- Is it important? i.e., is discernment necessary?

- Is it part of the typical, naturalistic causal structure of creation?

- Could it be explained through randomness?

- Is it a result of a complex, dynamic system?

- What are all the possible explanations for this event?

- What would have happened if the event did not occur?

- Does this event require an agent or an ultimate cause?

Third, we need to be *self-aware*. The God who created our cognitive processes wants us to use them appropriately and responsibly. Consider our mental and moral limitations, and the spiritual fruit of humility. Consider the value of consulting others and practicing discernment in community. Consider which theological questions are best addressed by which cognitive process. We can ask:[28]

- Why are we asking the question of causation?

- Is there a different/better question we could ask?

- What are our motivations? What are our assumptions, desires, and/or hopes?

- Are we willing to accept the unknown and uncertain?

- Are we cooperating with God? Aligning ourselves with his overarching purposes?

Fourth, we need to be *precise*. Talking about God and his action is too important a topic for glib statements like "God's in control." We should choose our words carefully and be clear about our meaning. We need to be responsible and precise with speech and behavior, and consistent in what we believe and how we act. Before we even practice discernment, we can pray for insight about how to pray. Considering categories of discernment, we can ask:

- Are we requesting spiritual guidance, or attempting to discern the cause of something?

- What level of reality are we considering? Are we asking a scientific or a spiritual question?

- Are we asking questions about observation (what is), intervention (what if), or imagination (why)?

- Are we asking a specific, personal question or a general, broadly-applicable one?

- Are we asking about ultimate meaning, explanation, reassurance, or guidance for future actions?

Finally, we need to be *wise*. There's a saying that knowledge means realizing a tomato is a fruit, but wisdom is not using it in a fruit salad. Wisdom involves knowing when and how to apply the suggestions in my previous four points, knowing which questions to ask in which situations. I have suggested some guidelines for discernment but not step-by-step instructions. Wisdom relates to humility, knowledge, practice, and experience. It is wise to work out our salvation daily, and immerse ourselves in spiritual practices and community. It is also wise to follow, though not blindly, the wisdom of great Christian teachers, and the knowledge acquired by science regarding the nature of nature and the nature of ourselves. This can help us have realistic expectations regarding causation and its detection. Discernment is multifaceted, involving both intuition and reason, both spiritual experience and evaluation of that experience, both pre-reflective and reflective processes.

Let's revisit what caused the COVID-19 pandemic. This event is rare and has affected multiple levels of reality; therefore, the question is important. With respect to self-awareness, some may ask out of curiosity, but others may ask because they need reassurance, or someone to blame. The question could be phrased more precisely in terms of whether we're asking a spiritual *why* question or a scientific *what is* question. Possible causative factors include nature, God, humans, and evil spirits, remembering that these may overlap. The scientific question (Aristotle's material, formal, and efficient levels) requires situation awareness. One level is the coronavirus itself, likely a genetic mutation. Another level is the transmission of the infection. Illnesses are complex dynamic systems usually caused by natural processes. There are likely many interacting causative components. In other words, Covid-19 can be explained without needing an agent or an ultimate cause. However, with respect to the spread of the illness, irresponsible human behavior, possibly influenced by evil spirits, is likely a factor. Finally, with respect to the spiritual questions and God-awareness, the pandemic does not glorify God, further his kingdom, or cause spiritual transformation (although our responses to it may). Therefore, it is unlikely that God directly caused the pandemic. This is not the only possible way to address the question, but gives us a sample scenario of how to apply the guidelines I've suggested.

Of course, not every strategy works for every situation, or every decision about causation. One could use scientific, logical means to explain to a five-year old that the noise in the room is caused by the wind, not a monster. However, it is more loving and effective to give the child a hug of reassurance and open the window for her to experience the wind. Guidance can help but wisdom is essential.

It takes wisdom to discern accurately and also to decide whether and how to share our knowledge. When I think that I hear God's voice, I may tell a few trusted friends if any. If God is truly speaking, others who are in tune with the Spirit will also hear his voice. If we do share our experience, we need to consider our motivations in doing so; whether we seek to edify ourselves or others. We also need to choose our words wisely. We can use the languages of probability and doubt to express our thoughts on divine action: "I think it is very likely that God orchestrated that event." At times metaphorical language may be more apt: "At one point, I sensed a lightness and brightness flowing through that dark situation." Regardless, we can trust that God wants to be known, and wants us to draw closer to him. I believe he honors our efforts to do so.

CONCLUSION

I once supported a friend who was recently separated. She stated, "God has a plan for this." When I questioned her assumption, she was quite defensive and upset. I realized that perhaps my timing was not the best. A few months later, having gained a little wisdom, I kept quiet when she concluded that her ex-husband, not God, was responsible for the marriage breakdown. Wisdom involves not just knowing why things happen and why people need easy explanations, but also knowing when and how to question their beliefs about causation.

In this chapter I have sought to integrate what we have learned in previous chapters and apply it to our evaluations of how and why things happen.

We can adopt strategies derived from both cognitive psychology and Christian spirituality, which, as we have seen, have interesting areas of overlap. Knowing some scientific perceptions of causation and some theological views on God's interaction with the world can help clarify our discernment questions. In particular, I suggest that guidance from Christian spirituality as well as personal maturity can help us make wiser judgments and mitigate some of the errors we are prone to. My many suggestions may seem overwhelming, but remember that these are guidelines; not all are needed all of the time. Even using a few can benefit us. I suspect many people may already be applying some of these strategies, but don't stop reading yet . . .

. . . let the wise also hear and gain in learning, and the discerning acquire skill.

PROV 1:5

ENDNOTES

1. Strom, "Weathering the Storm."

2. "We favor the visible, the embedded, the personal, the narrated, and the tangible; we scorn the abstract." Taleb, *Fooled by Randomness*, 262.

3. E.g., Kahneman, *Thinking, Fast and Slow*, 239–41, 417–18; Lehrer, *How We Decide*, 243–50; Perkins, *Outsmarting IQ*. Psychologists Gilovich and Ross suggest that awareness and adoption of appropriate cognitive strategies is a hallmark of wisdom (*Wisest One*, esp. 267–70). A new area of study, intellectual humility, comes to similar conclusions. E.g., Leary et al, "Intellectual Humility."

4. Tetlock and Gardner have delineated the qualities of those who are highly accurate: cautious, humble, open-minded, curious, and reflective, with probabilistic and nondeterministic views, and a pragmatic and analytical forecasting style (*Superforecasters*, 191). See also Schulz, *Being Wrong*, 273–95.

5. Holmes, *Nonsense*.

6. The 1908 Yerkes-Dodson law shows that selective attention increases with increasing stress but, at a certain point, anxiety can erode performance. Yerkes and Dodson, "Strength of Stimulus." Amanda Lang suggests that the ability to live with discomfort is a hallmark of successful people; *Beauty of Discomfort*. See also Goleman, *Social Intelligence*.

7. This is known as cognitive behavioral therapy; its development is associated with Aaron Beck (*Depression*) and Albert Ellis (*Reason and Emotion*).

8. Seligman, *Learned Helplessness*.

9. E.g., Avrahami, *Senses of Scripture*.

10. E.g., Johnson, *Scripture and Decision Making*.

11. Discernment has been discussed primarily in Roman Catholic spirituality, associated with the work of Ignatius of Loyola. This classic approach advises paying attention to signs of the peace of Christ, and recognizing the work of the Spirit during times of consolation and desolation. E.g., Gallagher, *Discernment of Spirits*.

12. E.g., Howard, *Touch of God*, 11. He draws on work by Ignatius, Edwards, and Gelpi. He suggests that Protestants emphasize discernment as finding God's will, whereas Charismatics stress hearing God's voice.

13. E.g., Howard, *Touch of God*, 4–12. See also McIntosh, *Discernment and Truth*, 5–10.

14. Polkinghorne argues that it is hidden "within the unpredictable flexibility of cosmic process" (*Science and Providence*, 52). See also Brümmer, "Farrer, Wiles," 8–10; Gruning, *How in the World*, 23–26.

15. Waltke, *Will of God*, esp. 3–21. See also Friesen, *Decision Making*, 127–47, 243–55, 267–69; Howard, *Touch of God*, 291–331.

16. He also used the language of the spiritual senses. E.g., Tornau, "Saint Augustine"; McIntosh, *Discernment and Truth*, 215–55; Westerholm, "On Christian Discernment."

17. E.g., Outler, *John Wesley*.

18. Psychologist William James claims that in religious experience, instinct leads and intelligence follows (*Varieties*, 242–6, 431). Evan Howard somewhat similarly suggests that experience leads to understanding which then leads to judgment and action (*Christian Spirituality*, 371–401).

19. Smith, *Voice of Jesus*, 53. Further, it is "never so mysterious that we cannot speak with clarity of how we make decisions" (133). See also Howard, *Touch of God*, 40–50; Parker, *Led by Spirit*, 175–205.

20. Willard, *Hearing God*, 69; also 217–25, 266. This idea of discernment involving both intuitive and intellectual processes is common in the Roman Catholic tradition (McIntosh refers to affective, noetic and relational aspects; *Discernment and Truth*, 82–124; Dougherty mentions "awareness of inner stirrings without analysis"; *Discernment*, 5–10) and in Christian piety (e.g., Jersak, *Can You Hear Me?*, 41–70).

21. E.g., Waltke, *Will of God*, 86–103; Smith, *Voice of Jesus*, 134–38, 146–53; Dougherty; *Discernment*, 48–62.

22. E.g., Howard, *Touch of God*, 291–331.

23. Knight, *God of Nature*, 36–40.

24. E.g., Howard, *Christian Spirituality*, 371–401; Willard, *Hearing God*, 231–32; Smith, *Voice of Jesus*, 89–127; Clouser, *Knowing with the Heart*, 43–66.

25. E.g., Barton, *Pursuing God's Will*; Boyd, *Present Perfect*; Howard, *Christian Spirituality*, 371–401; Howard, *Touch of God*, 291–331; Smith, *Voice of Jesus*, 27–30, 208–10; Waltke, *Will of God*, 104–20.

26. E.g., Turner, *Darkness of God*; Bingaman, "Pastoral Theological Approach."

27. Young, *Lies We Believe*, 155–64.

28. Yancey suggests similar questions when prayer for healing: "Am I expecting a miracle as an entitlement?"; "Am I using the benefits of common grace?" (medicine, the healing capacity of our bodies); "Do I wrongly blame God?"; "Am I prepared that healing may not occur?" (*Prayer*, 259–66).

8

Conclusion

I REMEMBER A PASTOR saying that when things go wrong, such as an illness, we tend to doubt God. But doubt originates with Satan; instead we must trust that God is in complete control. Note the inconsistency: if God is in control, then how can the devil cause doubt. I agree about trusting the Lord. However, Christian faith does not mean that God causes all things. We can trust God, but bad stuff still happens in life. We also need to own our doubts and take appropriate responsibility for our problems, rather than blaming the devil.

If we view God as omni-causal, we misconstrue biblical teaching on the nature of divine sovereignty. I believe that by better understanding the nature of causation and the nature of God's interaction with our wise and wonderful world, we can better evaluate how and why things happen, without glibly assuming God causes everything. We can also be better informed about responsible behavior, and we can be transformed at a spiritual level. Fringer and Lane summarize how important it is for Christians to have accurate views: "If we are truly responsible for what we know and what we do, then our challenge is to make sure our seeing is not clouded by wrong believing and that our believing is not distracted by a limited view of God, Scripture, or our world."[1]

What caused the 2020 pandemic? This book centered around this global disaster and people's various views on its cause. COVID-19 illustrates the complex nature of causation, common misunderstandings of it, and the fact that there's not always a deep reason for every event that happens in life. I believe that Christians are tasked with comprehending both Creator and creation. Our knowledge of causation, albeit imperfect, can guide our actions in the world as well as our relationship with our Lord.

My aim in this book has been to review causation in the created world through the lens of Christianity in order to increase our understanding of cause, effect, explanation, and divine action—the way the world works and the way God works. To assist with this project, I gleaned knowledge from various disciplines, including philosophy, statistics, natural sciences, psychology, biblical studies, and Christian theology. Multidisciplinary works cannot cover every detail and nuance of every topic. I wonder if my book's argument may reflect its content and process. Like the world we live in, my writing is a dappled collection of information, chosen according to my priorities, with some content rejected in the final compilation. There is an overarching structure, with connection and disconnection between elements. I prayed for wisdom in writing and like to think the Spirit is interwoven with the words, perhaps more prominent in certain places for certain readers. However, I am (mostly) aware of my human limitations. There may be areas of disagreement, but I hope to at least have raised some awareness and stimulated thought about the important question of how and why things happen.

Recall the children who ask why apples are red, or learn that a fire is hot, or invent purposeful explanations for things. Assumptions about causation are a fundamental part of daily life, intuitive and instinctive. They guide our decisions, both trivial (flipping a switch to turn on a light) and critical (using the right treatment based on an understanding of the cause of an illness). At times we don't think about causes; other times we insist on explanations. We fear uncertainty and ignorance and want to know *why*. Christians also want to know God's role in causation.

In considering some philosophical, psychological, and scientific conceptions about causation, we saw that reality and truth are complex. There is much that is unknown, much beyond our five senses, and many paradoxes. Viruses are used to manufacture vaccines against those same viruses. Similarly, we use our minds to study our brains, but our minds are "caused" by our brains. And our mind-brains produce "realities," like dreams and optical illusions, that are not real. Our beliefs and our interaction with the world affect what we learn. There are also inherent limitations related to knowledge, scientific methods, and mental processes. We learn in various ways: rational, intuitive, experiential, authoritative, tacit. But our cognitive interpretations and judgments about the information we acquire are often deeply flawed. Christianity reminds us of the importance of humility when we consider how and why things happen.

Think about the network of events and decisions in your day so far: one thing led to another and you likely missed half of what happened, let alone trying to figure out what caused what. Philosophy offers ways to conceptualize causation. We can recognize cause-and-effect connections when they are associated in space and time, when we have previous experience and knowledge of such relations, and when we know someone's intent in making something happen. We can consider causality at different levels, both scientific and spiritual, recognizing that not everything has an ultimate cause. We ask, *what is, what if,* and *why.* The best models for appreciating causation are nonlinear, web-like, and probability based.

Numbers, patterns, and graphs can be fun but frightening. The fields of mathematics and statistics help us understand connections between small and large numbers, specifics and generalities. Knowing the prior probabilities of events is important for evaluating causation: we should not assume an event is a "Godincidence," unless we know how often it usually happens. Statistics can tame unpredictability, allowing us to make predictions with large samples and over time. Some cause-and-effect relations cannot be known—they are random. This is especially true at the quantum level and at the level of large dynamic systems. The novel coronavirus developed from a random mutation and spreads in so many ways that precise prediction is impossible. Randomness can scare people, but it is not the same as purposelessness. It is part of God's good creation. We see it in farmers who sow seeds and use it when we play games.

Cards and coins, sunflowers and pineapples, bunnies and weeds, snakes and bicycles, dust particles and moon craters: The Lord God made them all. He created a world in which order and disorder dance together. A world of freedom and possibility. In the intricate multidirectional flow of causation, there are regularities, redundancies, and randomness. Order can emerge from chaos and chaos can develop into order. Various aspects of creation are self-organizing, self-causing, and/or self-perpetuating. Mind has some power over matter. Exact causes are difficult to determine, and sometimes stuff just happens. In our daily lives, causative factors intertwine, coincidences occur more commonly than we think, and randomness can be purposeful.

A man is born crippled for no reason. Paul is given a thorn in his side by both God and Satan. There are many causes for illness described in the Bible, although not in a systematic way. What we can infer about how and why things happen, unsurprisingly, fits well with scientific observations of causation in the world. The Creator cares deeply about his creation but does not micromanage it. Neither can he be manipulated to help us feel better. There is natural order in the infrastructure of creation. The Spirit guides human affairs, focusing on those who are obedient and allow him to work through them. But he gives us freedom and responsibility to care for each other and the world. God has an overall purpose for the salvation and redemption of the world, but this does not translate into a specific individual plan for each person's life. Not everything that happens is meaningful, although I suspect the Lord is involved in more than we realize. The Spirit blows through our wise and wonderful world in various ways, restoring the brightness of creation. Divine action is best understood through multiple analogies or models: a loving parent, a creative artist, wind, waves, or light.

However, most people prefer black and white explanations. Despite the complex nature of creation and God's interaction with it, humans tend to conceptualize causation in a simplistic manner. We make judgments quickly, based on intuitions, emotions, and prior beliefs. In particular, we are primed to misinterpret causation, favoring stories with personal meaning. This process is not always appropriate to the situation and affects our ability to properly evaluate causation. Our mind-brains and our sinful natures like meaning, certainty, and control; we misunderstand statistics and randomness, often deceive ourselves, and dislike being wrong. There is a mismatch between reality and our interpretation of it. Fortunately, this can be mitigated through education and self-awareness. Furthermore, improving our knowledge of how and why things happen can inform our Christian ministries. This is the reason I wrote this book.

WHAT'S WRONG WITH COMMON CHRISTIAN CONCEPTIONS OF CAUSATION?

During the COVID-19 pandemic some Christians claimed, "It's in God's hands," but they still washed their own hands. As I have mentioned, many people have unhelpful and inconsistent beliefs about causation, especially with respect to God's action in the world. These are often expressed in clichés or misinterpretations of biblical verses: God has a plan. God is in control. Everything is sifted through the fingers of God. It's God's will. Everything happens for a reason. All things work out for good. When God closes a door, he opens a window.

Christians commonly offer these clichés in various forms as advice to those who are suffering. They mean well but, likely because this understanding is biblically inaccurate and often associated with the comforter's own insecurities, cognitive conflicts arise. This requires people to explain their misguided advice: God is punishing you for your sin. God has caused this problem because he loves you. God will change things, just be patient.[2] It is also common for people to confuse or conflate "God has a plan for your life" with "God is with you." But control and comfort are different things. Similarly, just because God *can* bring good out of a bad situation, does not mean that he *causes* it in the first place.[3]

As we have seen, such statements reflect an inaccurate and inconsistent view of God and his relationship to creation. We are not simply the passive underside of a tapestry he is weaving but are given responsibility to work with God in the world, as co-weavers. The sovereign Lord is not Santa Claus, but a God of infinite patience and love who values relationship over control. He is always with us through his Spirit to comfort, guide, and teach us through various circumstances of life, but these circumstances are usually caused by numerous interacting factors. Doors and windows are made to be opened and shut. Sometimes another person slams the door in our face, sometimes the wind blows it shut, sometimes we don't push the handle to open the door.

Assuming that God causes every event in life is potentially harmful. First, such a view can be egocentric and self-serving. Recall our inclination towards cognitive ease, certainty, and a simple narrative of cause and effect. When we are unable to control a situation, it comforts us and reduces cognitive dissonance to believe that God is in complete control and has a divine plan. We can thus avoid any challenges to our own psychological and spiritual growth. Worse, we can use a view of an omni-controlling God to excuse our own behavior. Fringer and Lane summarize:

> Those holding to a hermeneutic of authority often justify their actions and manipulations as the acts or will of God. Throughout history, many persons who claim to live under the dominion of the God of control have acted in this God's name and claimed his authority but have lacked any of his character.[4]

Second, such a view may lead us to abdicate our God-given roles and responsibilities in caring for self, other, and creation. If we attribute causation to God's hands or God's will, we may fail to exercise our own hands and will. With respect to self, people sometimes "blame" God for their own bad decisions. Young Christians may ask God to take away a potential partner if they are not *the one*. Consequently, they fail to learn self-awareness, character judgment, and wise decision-making skills. This relates to a common misconception about finding God's will. As we have seen, God's general will for humanity is clear in the Bible but there is no evidence of any specific, individual life plan. Indeed, it can be scary to think what may happen if we miss God's "one will" for our lives.[5] The so-called prosperity Gospel advocates health and wealth as our right. This can lead to people failing to take responsibility for their own health choices. Conversely, if we believe that suffering has a divine purpose, we may avoid helpful medical care. When we "trust" that God is in control, we may fail to care for others and the environment.

Third, if we claim that God orchestrates everything for some mysterious divine purpose, we can end up hurting others, either by claiming that God has a reason for their suffering or by blaming the sufferer. People may be well intentioned but are being dishonest. Their misguided hope may encourage denial and delay healing and/or grieving. Kate Bowler, in describing her experience with cancer, was "worn out by the tyranny of prescriptive joy." She further quips, "When someone is drowning, the only thing worse than failing to throw them a life preserver is handing them a reason."[6] Similarly, and usually subtly, Christians may accuse others of unrepentance or lack of faith. Shane Clifton, who is afflicted with quadriplegia, has written about "the dark side of prayer for healing."[7] He relates his personal experience of remaining "unhealed," and expresses his frustration with a church that fails to acknowledge the rarity of supernatural healing, the permanency of disability, and the need for communal acceptance. And of course, when we blame sufferers, we fail to recognize and deal with other causative factors. Candy Gunther Brown, in her investigation of charismatic healing, points out that "a supernaturalized model of sickness and healing encourages already-suffering individuals to internalize blame for failures that could instead be traced to systemic oppression."[8] Overall, I suggest that it is kinder to recognize the complexity of causation and the randomness of life, and to respond with integrity and compassion for those who suffer.

Many people who claim to "just follow the Bible" or "do God's will" end up distorting teachings to fit their views and give them false security. It is interesting that we disparage humans who are control freaks, yet we have no problem viewing God that way. I suggest that the word *control* is unhelpful, and that we focus on divine *sovereignty* instead. We are better served by using multiple models through which to perceive God and his relationship with creation. Understanding the complexity of causation, and the overall salvific and eschatological purposes of God, liberates the Christian from trying to understand God's reasons, and also offers hope regarding the possibility of effecting real change in the world.

WHAT ARE SOME PASTORAL IMPLICATIONS OF THIS STUDY?

Jeremiah 29:11—"'For I know the plans I have for you,' declares the Lord, 'plans to prosper you and not to harm you, plans to give you hope and a future'"—is overquoted and often misunderstood. It is addressed to the nation of Israel, not individuals, yet Christians frequently use it to reinforce their beliefs that God has a specific plan for their specific lives; that he micromanages the world. Given the complexities and uncertainties of life, I think a better pastoral response is to emphasize the two verses that *follow:* "'Then you will call on me and come and pray to me, and I will listen to you. You will seek me and find me when you seek me with all your heart'" (Jer 29:12, 13). The emphasis here is relational, not situational.

We have reviewed some suboptimal results of misconstruing causation; now we consider some better approaches by applying our knowledge of causation in creation and Christianity. Doing so can guide our practical responses and improve the consistency between our beliefs and actions. I have witnessed many examples of this: friends who simply provide comfort and care without claiming that God caused the suffering, or at least not voicing their opinion regarding reasons; pastors who acknowledge differing interpretations of biblical verses, or admit when they don't have an answer; counselors who point out the complexities and ambiguities of life and encourage us to question God; and, of course, the many theologians who have helped inform me about God's purpose and action in the world.

First, a better understanding of the nature of God and his interaction with the world can guide our ministries.[9] The triune God is sovereign and loving; he deeply cares for creation and desires relationships with his creatures. However, the type of world he has made is complex and intricate. Because creation is free, flexible, and flowing, God engages with it in the same manner. He indwells the world through his Spirit, although his light is sometimes dimmed by the sin and complexities of the world. This view of God can guide our preaching and can decrease the dissonance between what we believe and what we experience. Life is often uncertain, and suffering is inevitable, but God is with us through it. However, he does not magically remove all the difficult stuff. It is common practice in churches to relate only answered prayers, to focus on the positive. This may encourage people, but it is not necessarily accurate because it misses the silent evidence. We need to consider alternate explanations for events and be sensitive to people who have less positive experiences. Maybe we should refrain from praising God for one person's healing when the person next to them remains ill. We need to offer realistic hope, a hope through salvation in Christ, not easy answers to problems. Our relationship with God, not our assumption that he is omni-causal, provides meaning and comfort.

Second, the findings from this study emphasize human responsibility. This affirms and encourages the ministries many Christians are already involved in: caring for others through prayer, companionship, meeting physical needs, or improving social justice; preserving and caring for our natural environment; caring for and developing creation through scientific endeavors; and sharing the good news of Christ. Remember, we are called to "love your neighbor, wear a mask." Rather than being passive recipients of divine causation, we need to aim for collaboration: working with God in loving others and building his kingdom.

Third, this study has implications for pastoral counseling. If people are seeking God's will for their lives, we can explain that God will walk with us on many different paths. His light is not a pinpoint, but a ray, not a sharp laser, but a soft lamp. The Bible gives guidance about God's overall sovereign plan, and his desire for loving, virtuous, and moral behavior, but these can be accomplished in many ways.[10] We can also liberate people from fears of "missing" God's will. God is always willing to offer second chances, re-dos, and re-boots. Knowing some cognitive strategies and shortcomings can inform our pastoral care. We can ask people to clarify their questions, be aware of their motivations and assumptions, and explain their judgments. Prayer for self-awareness is always wise.

This study may offer insight for counselors regarding the perennial problem of pain. We can remind sufferers of the multiplicity of causes, and free people from misguided guilt about divine purposes. Life is complex and therefore sometimes difficult. We can assure people that God is with them, even if there is no explanation for why bad things happen. Bowler makes some suggestions of what *not* to say to a sufferer: "It's going to get better, I promise"; "Everything happens for a reason" (such as sin, unfaithfulness, or an aversion to Brussels sprouts), "God is fair," "God is unfair." Instead she suggests: "Can I bring you a meal?" "You are a beautiful person, I'm on your team," "Can I give you a hug," "Oh that sounds hard." Or else saying nothing at all.[11]

Fourth, there are implications for spiritual practices and formation. Recall the importance of accepting ambiguity in life. Henri Nouwen points out that our fears of uncertainty, which manifest as a need to be in control or a withdrawal from life, get in the way of a deeper relationship with God and fruitfulness in life.[12] Although challenging, we need to embrace discomfort, sit with our brokenness, accept the unknown, acknowledge our limits, and admit when we are wrong.

Finally, this study can impact our beliefs about prayer, especially its causative potential. There is no doubt on biblical, theological, and spiritual grounds that prayer is essential, if incompletely understood.[13] Awareness of the complexity of causation in the world, human causal effectiveness, and especially divine-human cooperation, can guide our prayer. The sovereign Lord always desires what is best for his creation and creatures, but cannot be manipulated. Prayer is based on a good relationship with God, and in turn strengthens that relationship. We can also pray for guidance in working with God to effect change in the world, knowing that we have been given freedom and responsibility. That guidance may include reminders to consider statistics and alternate pathways of causation.

Let's consider these pastoral implications for our beliefs and behaviors around COVID-19. On an individual level, knowing causative factors can guide our actions with respect to prevention and treatment of an illness: we wear masks, keep two meters apart, and get tested if we have symptoms. If we are unwell, we need to be conscientious in understanding why, caring for ourselves, and seeking assistance from experts as appropriate. As Christians, we have the indwelling Holy Spirit who can guide our response. We can pray for insight into the illness, in particular asking if there are any behaviors we need to change, any sin we need to confess, or any demonic involvement. We can then act accordingly. If our condition requires expert help, we can pray for wisdom for the health professionals who treat us. We can pray for healing, knowing that this could mean many different things. We can pray for guidance for the scientists working on a vaccine for the novel coronavirus. On the communal level, we can work with Jesus to heal and prevent illness. We can isolate if we have symptoms. We can take meals to elderly neighbors. It is important to recognize the symbiotic connection between individual sin and its structural embodiment. By keeping our environment clean, feeding the hungry, and clothing the naked, we work with God in suppressing evil. The more we spread the light of Christ, the less dark the world will be.

Although many of the pastoral practices mentioned are already present in Christian communities, this study reinforces them and offers a different framework for conceptualizing some aspects of pastoral care. Understanding the nature of causation in creation and Christianity may add consistency, focus, and motivation to our spiritual lives. However, given its complexity, correctly judging causation is not easy.

WHAT SHOULD OUR PRIORITIES BE?

The Christian's task is to "'love the Lord your God with all your heart, and with all your soul, and with all your strength, and with all your mind'; and 'love your neighbor as yourself'" (Luke 10:27); "do justice . . . love kindness . . . walk humbly with your God" (Mic 6:8); and "make disciples of all nations" (Matt 28:19). Having written an entire book on the topic, I realize that this seems hypocritical, but I think that learning about causation is *not* the most important aspect of Christianity.

Instead, a first priority is our relationship with God, made known to us through Christ and the Holy Spirit. Prayer, not just the petitionary type, is an essential aspect of this. We can develop this divine-human relationship through understanding causation in creation and Christian theology. God loves and is not far from each of us, though he may not be directly involved in every event. We need to focus on his overall purpose for the world, praising him for all aspects of nature, not just those that are personally pleasing or convenient to us. Rick Warren got it right in saying, "It's not about us."[14] Meaning is to be found not in circumstances but through our perspective and response to them. A classic example is given by Victor Frankl, a holocaust survivor. He noted that people who were able to find meaning in this hopeless situation lived better and longer.[15] Our focus should be on *big* meaning, not *little* meaning.

A second priority is Christian character. Being made in God's image means that our thoughts and actions should reflect his. Character is more important than circumstance, spirit is more important than flesh, our treasures are in heaven not earth. Christ, not causation in the world, is central; but we can never go wrong by modeling Solomon and praying for wisdom in evaluating how and why things happen. *Sapientia* is more important than *scientia*. I wrote this book to increase understanding, but I suggest that we need to increase our acceptance of non-understanding, of ambiguity and mystery.

A final priority is how we respond to God and events in the world. As we noted, biblical authors say little about causation but much about how we should speak and act. This encourages us to focus on our response to problems, rather than the causes of them.[16] As we navigate our often-messy, complicated lives, we need to prioritize being faithful stewards, recognizing that God uses broken vessels. We can alleviate suffering when possible. We can respond to illness with kind words and actions. When we realize that causation is multifactorial and that God desires human cooperation in effecting his will, we can realize that many possible responses are available to us. By participating in God's work, sharing his love, and reimagining the world and God's relationship to it, we can assist in cleansing the cosmos and restoring creation's shine and colors.

CONCLUSION

Let's summarize some concepts in this book by considering shapes. Lines: the simple arrow of causation that seldom applies in real-life situations; the experiment on conformity, in which people were easily persuaded to choose the wrong answer. Circles: the shape of the coronavirus, the apple that tempted the first humans and inspired Newton, the baby shaking a rattle. Triangles: those that bump other shapes and that people personify, Sierpinski's examples of a fractal, Kanizsa's optical illusion. Webs: the common and complex way to understand cause-and-effect relations, the websites that promote misinformation.

In *All Things Wise and Wonderful* we have sought to better understand how and why things happen in life, through the lens of Christianity. God has gifted us with a praiseworthy world, full of bright and beautiful things. It is a world that does not require constant divine intervention. He has also gifted us with freedom and responsibility in exploring creation and effecting causation. The God of love desires interaction with the world and his focus is on building his kingdom. Sometimes there is a specific reason for an event, sometimes no reason at all, sometimes 10,000 intertwined reasons. God values our cooperation in working with him to improve creation, to spread his love and mercy. Although we are tasked with understanding both God and his world, we need to recognize the intrinsic limits of knowledge in general, and our cognitive and moral limitations in particular. Humility and wise discernment are always apropos.

Despite the priorities we considered above, the concept of causation is central to life. It is human nature to ask why things happen. And it is the nature of the world, and perhaps the divine, not to provide easy answers. Yet another paradox and tension in life we need to accept. I have not intended to give definitive answers to the questions of why and how; merely to provide further questions, alternate frameworks, and possible approaches. No matter what perspective we have, our view is always incomplete. Believe it or not, I make my share of mistakes. There is definitely room for further research and clarification of some issues raised in this study. Perhaps the models and metaphors I have suggested might be developed in more detail.

I wonder if our fluid world, that appears solid, is best described through figurative language. Likewise, our solid, real Creator, who nevertheless can be elusive and enigmatic. Perhaps we can find overarching metaphors for understanding causation in creation and Christianity that fit the biblical witness and also resonate with our experience. This may not only increase our insight but may mitigate our overconfidence in our ability to comprehend causation. Perhaps we need a mixture of metaphors . . .

God made all things bright and beautiful, but they sometimes turn dim and deformed, marred by the nature of the world, the disobedience of humans, and the infiltration of evil spiritual forces. In the multiplicity, mystery, and majesty of creation, the wind whispers within and without, the light illumines, and the Spirit swirls. Complex systems and shadows make the world dappled. Webs of causation and counterfactuals threaten to overwhelm our cognitive capabilities. Yet God shines brightly, coloring the world, drawing it to him. Creation is infused with the Holy Spirit.

We have eternal hope in our Savior and Redeemer, and present-day responsibility in adding shine to the world. The seeds we sow will sprout because God made them that way, but they will do better if we water them. The world offers many trails to travel and tame. In the twists and turns of life, God never forsakes us. He is in the whirlwind, the waves, and the whimper. He cradles the world with arms and fingers open, he manages the company with input from his subordinates, he authors the book with ever-changing scenes and characters. He focuses on winning the game of chess, even though peripheral pawns may be acting up or falling down. He tenderly tends the sick as a mother hen and a healing professional.

Worship the God who is wise and wonderful and explore his wise and wonderful world. But remain open and humble about how little we understand.

For the Lord gives wisdom; from his mouth come knowledge and understanding.

PROV 2:6

ENDNOTES

1. Fringer and Lane, *Theology of Luck*, 95.

2. E.g., Bowler, *Everything Happens*, 170; Philip Yancey thinks that Christians often exacerbate the experience of suffering with explanations like "God is punishing you," "it's Satan," "it's neither—God has afflicted you out of love" (*Question that Never Goes*, 16).

3. E.g., Greear, "What if You Really Believed"; Warren, *Purpose Driven Life*, 193–6.

4. Fringer and Lane, *Theology of Luck*, 174.

5. Fringer and Lane give the example of people conflating soul mate and God's will; with such reasoning, if one makes the wrong choice, the impact could affect all subsequent choices, and in the end, no one follows "God's will" (*Theology of Luck*, 125–31). See also Basinger, "Practical Implications"; Carey, "No Secret Plan."

6. Bowler, *Everything Happens*, 118, 170. Banerjee and Bloom believe that this view "can lead us to blame those who suffer from disease and who are victims of crimes," and we may accept the status quo of poverty, inequality, and oppression if we believe it is part of a meaningful plan for life ("Does Everything Happen?").

7. Clifton, "Dark Side of Prayer."

8. Brown, "Introduction," 10.

9. E.g., Basinger, "Practical Implications."

10. Friesen points out that if Hudson Taylor had gone to Africa instead of China, he still would have been following the great commission; *Decision Making*, 81–95.

11. Bowler, *Everything Happens*, 169–75.

12. E.g., Nouwen, *Lifesigns*, 15–24, 89–91.

13. E.g., Yancey, *Prayer*.

14. Warren, *Purpose Driven Life*, 17.

15. Frankl and White, from very different perspectives, point out that meaning lies not in the events themselves but in our reaction to them. Frankl, *Man's Search for Meaning*; White, *Fall of A Sparrow*, 9–21.

16. Yancey, *Question that Never Goes*, 46–50.

Bibliography

Alter, Oppenheimer, et al. "Overcoming Intuition: Metacognitive Difficulty Activates Analytic Reasoning." *Journal of Experimental Psychology General* 136 (2007) 569–76.

Ambady, Nalini and Robert Rosenthal. "Half a Minute: Predicting Teacher Evaluations from Thin Slices of Nonverbal Behavior and Physical Attractiveness." *Journal of Personality and Social Psychology* 64 (1993) 431–41.

Anderson, P.W. "More is Different." *Science* 177 (1972) 393–96.

Ariely, Dan. *Predictably Irrational: The Hidden Forces That Shape Our Decisions.* New York: HarperCollins, 2008.

Aronowitz, Robert A. *Making Sense of Illness: Science, Society and Disease.* Cambridge: Cambridge University Press, 1998.

Asch, Solomon E. "Effects of Group Pressure Upon the Modification and Distortion of Judgment." In *Groups, Leadership and Men,* edited by H. Guetzkow, 177–90. Pittsburgh, PA: Carnegie Press, 1951.

Audi, Robert. *Epistemology.* 2nd Edition. *A Contemporary Introduction to the Theory of Knowledge.* New York: Routledge, 2003.

Aurelio, John R. *Mosquitoes in Paradise: A New look at Genesis, Jesus and the Meaning of Life.* New York: Crossroads, 1985.

Avalos, Hector. *Health Care and the Rise of Christianity.* Peabody, Mass: Hendrickson, 1999.

Avis, Paul. *God and the Creative Imagination: Metaphor, Symbol and Myth in Religion and Theology.* New York: Routledge, 1999.

Avrahami, Yael. *The Senses of Scripture: Sensory Perception in the Hebrew Bible.* London: T&T Clark, 2012.

Baillargeon, Renée. "Infant's Understanding of the Physical World." In *Advances in Psychological Science Vol 2: Biological and Cognitive Aspects,* edited by M. Sabourin et al., 503–29. Hove, England: Psychology Press, 1998.

Baker, Lynn A. and Robert E. Emery. "When Every Relationship Is Above Average: Perceptions and Expectations of Divorce at the Time of Marriage." *Law and Human Behavior* 17 (1993) 439–50.

Balaguer, Mark. *Free Will.* Cambridge, MA: MIT Press, 2014.

Ball, Philip. *Patterns in Nature: Why the Natural World Looks the Way It Does.* Chicago: Chicago University Press, 2016.

Banerjee Konika and Paul Bloom, "Does Everything Happen for a Reason?" *New York Times*, 2014, https://www.nytimes.com/2014/10/19/opinion/sunday/does-everything-happen-for-a-reason.html

———. "Why Did This Happen to Me? Religious Believers' and Non-Believers' Teleological Reasoning about Life Events." *Cognition* 133 (2014) 277–303.

Barbour, Ian G. *Religion and Science*. San Francisco: Harper, 1997.

Barnes, Annette. *Seeing through Self-Deception*. Cambridge: Cambridge University Press, 1997.

Barrett, Justin. *Born Believers: The Science of Children's Belief*. New York: Free Press, 2012.

Barrigar, Christian J. *Freedom All the Way Up: God and the Meaning of Life in a Scientific Age*. Victoria, BC: Friesen, 2017.

Barth, Karl. *Church Dogmatics*. Translated by G. W. Bromiley and R. J. Ehrlich. Edinburgh: T&T Clark, 1936–77.

Bartholomew, David J. *God of Chance*. London: SCM, 1984.

———. *God, Chance and Purpose: Can God Have It Both Ways*. Cambridge: Cambridge University Press, 2008.

———. *Uncertain Belief: Is It Rational to Be a Christian?* New York: Clarendon, 1996.

Barton, Ruth Haley. *Pursuing God's Will Together: A Discernment Practice for Leadership Groups*. Downers Grove: InterVarsity, 2012.

Baruš, Imants and Julia Mossbridge. *Transcendent Mind: Rethinking the Science of Consciousness*. Washington: American Psychological Association, 2017.

Basinger, David. "Practical Implications." In *The Openness of God: A Biblical Challenge to the Traditional Understanding of God*, edited by Clark H. Pinnock et al., 155–76. Downers Grove: InterVarsity, 1994.

Beale, G. K. *The Temple and the Church's Mission: A Biblical Theology of the Dwelling Place of God*. New Studies in Biblical Theology 17. Downers Grove: InterVarsity, 2004.

Bechara, Damásio, et al. "Insensitivity to Future Consequences Following Damage to Human Prefrontal Cortex." *Cognition* 50 (1994) 7–15.

Beck, Aaron. T. *Depression: Causes and Treatment*. Philadelphia: University of Pennsylvania Press, 1967.

Becker, Adam. *What is Real? The Unfinished Quest for the Meaning of Quantum Physics*. New York: Basic, 2018.

Benbennick, David. *Möbius Strip*. Photograph. License: Creative Commons Attribution-Share Alike 3.0 Unported. 2005. https://commons.wikimedia.org/wiki/File:M%C3%B6bius_strip.jpg

Benedetti, Fabrizio. *Placebo Effects: Understanding the Mechanisms in Health and Disease*. Oxford: Oxford University Press, 2009.

Berthoz, Alain. *Emotion and Reason: The Cognitive Science of Decision Making*. Trans. Giselle Weiss. Oxford: Oxford University Press, 2006.

Bhaskar, Roy. *A Realist Theory of Science*. 2nd ed. London: Verso, 1997.

Biddle, Mark. *Missing the Mark: Sin and its Consequences in Biblical Theology*. Nashville: Abingdon, 2005.

Bingaman, Kirk A. "A Pastoral Theological Approach to the New Anxiety." *Pastoral Psychology* 59 (2010) 659–70.

BioLogos. "Love Your Neighbor, Wear a Mask: A Christian Statement on Science for Pandemic Times." *Biologos.org* (2020). https://statement.biologos.org/

Bluman, Allan. *Elementary Statistics: A Step by Step Approach*. New York: McGraw-Hill Higher Education, 2015.

Bohm, David. *Wholeness and the Implicate Order*. London: Routledge, 1980.

Boleyn-Fitzgerald, Miriam. *Pictures of the Mind: What the New Neuroscience Tells Us about Who We Are*. Upper Saddle River, NJ: Pearson Education, FT, 2010.

Borgen, Peder. "Miracles of Healing in the New Testament." *Studia Theologica—Nordic Journal of Theology* 35 (1981) 91–106.

Bowler, Catherine. "Blessed Bodies: Healing within the African American Faith Movement." In *Global Pentecostal and Charismatic Healing*, edited by Candy Gunther Brown, 81–106. New York: Oxford University Press, 2011.

Bowler, Kate. *Everything Happens for a Reason: And Other Lies I've Loved*. New York: Random House, 2018.

Boyd, Gregory A. *God at War: The Bible and Spiritual Conflict*. Downers Grove: InterVarsity, 1997.

———. *God of the Possible*. Grand Rapids: Baker, 2000.

———. "Open Theism." In *Divine Foreknowledge: Four Views*, edited by James K. Beilby and Paul R. Eddy, 13–47. Downers Grove: InterVarsity, 2001.

———. *Present Perfect: Finding God in the Now*. Grand Rapids: Zondervan, 2010.

———. *Satan and the Problem of Evil: Constructing a Trinitarian Warfare Theodicy*. Downers Grove: InterVarsity, 2001.

Bracken, Joseph A. *Does God Roll Dice? Divine Providence for a World in the Making*. Collegeville, MN: Michael Glazier, 2012.

Bradley, James. "Randomness and God's Nature." *Perspectives on Science and Christian Faith* 64 (2012) 75–89.

Brown, Candy Gunther, ed. *Global Pentecostal and Charismatic Healing*. New York: Oxford University Press, 2011.

———. "Introduction." In *Global Pentecostal and Charismatic Healing*, edited by Candy Gunther Brown, 3–26. New York: Oxford University Press, 2011.

———. *Testing Prayer: Science and Healing*. Cambridge, MA: Harvard University Press, 2012.

Brown, Mory, et al. "Study of the Therapeutic Effects of Proximal Intercessory Prayer (STEPP) on Auditory and Visual Impairments in Rural Mozambique." *Southern Medical Journal* 103 (2010) 864–69.

Brümmer, Vincent. "Farrer, Wiles and the Causal Joint." *Modern Theology* 8 (1992) 1–14.

Bunch, Wilton H. "Theodicy through a Lens of Science," *Perspectives on Science and Christian Faith* 67 (2015) 189–99.

Burnett, Joel S. *Where is God? Divine Absence in the Hebrew Bible*. Minneapolis: Fortress, 2010.

Butterfield, Herbert. "God in History," in *God, History and Historians*, edited by C. T. McIntire, 193–204. New York: Oxford University Press, 1977.

Byrd, Randolph C. "Positive Therapeutic Effects of Intercessory Prayer in a Coronary Care Unit Population." *Southern Medical Journal* 81 (1988) 826–29.

Caird, G. B. *The Language and Imagery of the Bible*. London: Duckworth, 1980.

Carey, Philip. "No Secret Plan: Why You Don't Have To 'Find' God's Will for Your Life." *Christian Century* October 5 (2010) 20–23.

Cartwright, Nancy. *The Dappled World: A Study of the Boundaries of Science*. Cambridge: Cambridge University Press, 1999.

Cartwright, Nancy and Keith Ward, eds. *Rethinking Order after the Laws of Nature*. New York: Bloomsbury Academic, 2016.

Cavalcanti, Zampieri, et al. "Hydroxychloroquine with or without Azithromycin in Mild-to-Moderate Covid-19." *New England Journal of Medicine*, July 23, 2020. Nejm.org, DOI: 10.1056/NEJMoa2019014

Chambliss, Daniel F. and Russell K. Schutt. *Making Sense of the Social World: Methods of Investigation*. 2nd ed. Thousand Oaks, CA: Pine Forge/Sage, 2006.

Clayton, Philip. "Natural Law and Divine Action: The Search for an Expanded Theory of Causation." *Zygon* 39 (2004) 615–36.

Clifton, Shane. "The Dark Side of Prayer for Healing: Toward a Theology of Well-Being." *Pneuma* 36 (2014) 204–25.

Clore, Gerald. "Psychology and the Rationality of Emotion." In *Faith, Rationality and the Passions*, edited by Sarah Coakley, 209–22. Chichester, Suffox: Wiley-Blackwell, 2012.

Clouser, Roy. *Knowing with the Heart: Religious Experience and Belief in God*. Downers Grove: InterVarsity, 1999.

Coakley, Sarah. "Introduction." In *Faith, Rationality and the Passions*, edited by Sarah Coakley, 1–12. Chichester, Suffox: Wiley-Blackwell, 2012.

Cohen, Jack and Ian Stewart. *The Collapse of Chaos: Discovering Simplicity in a Complex World*. London: Penguin, 1994.

Cohen, S. Marc. "Aristotle's Metaphysics," *The Stanford Encyclopedia of Philosophy* (Winter 2016 Edition), Edward N. Zalta, ed. https://plato.stanford.edu/archives/win2016/entries/aristotle-metaphysics/.

Cohoe, Caleb Murray. "God, Causality, and Petitionary Prayer." *Faith and Philosophy* 31 (2014) 24–45.

Coles, Peter. *From Cosmos to Chaos: The Science of Unpredictability*. Oxford: Oxford University Press, 2006.

Cook, Harry. "Emergence: A Biologist's Look at Complexity in Nature." *Perspectives on Science and Christian Faith* 65 (2013) 233–41.

Cooper, Terry D. *Sin, Pride and Self-Acceptance: The Problem of Identity in Psychology and Theology*. Downers Grove: InterVarsity Press, 2003.

Craig, William Lane. *The Only Wise God*. Eugene, OR: Wipf & Stock, 1999.

Damasio, Antonio. *Descartes' Error: Emotion, Reason, and the Human Brain*. New York: Putnam, 1994.

Daube, David. *The Deed and the Doer in the Bible: David Daube's Gifford Lectures, Vol 1*. Edited and compiled by Calum Carmichael. West Conshocken, PA: Templeton Foundation, 2008.

Davies, Oliver. *The Creativity of God: World, Eucharist, Reason*. Cambridge: Cambridge University Press, 2004.

Davies, Paul. *The Mind of God: The Scientific Basis for a Rational World*. New York: Simon & Schuster, 1992.

De Berker, Rutledge, et al. "Computations of Uncertainty Mediate Acute Stress Responses in Humans." *Nature Communications* 7, 10996 (2016) https://doi.org/10.1038/ncomms10996

Deviant, Stephanie. "Statisticshowto." https://www.statisticshowto.datasciencecentral.com/

Diaconis, P. and Mosteller, F. "Methods of Studying Coincidences." *Journal of the American Statistical Association* 84 (1989) 853–61.

Donovan, Denise and Ian McDowell, eds. *Association of Faculties of Medicine Canada (AFMC) Primer on Population Health: A Virtual Textbook on Public Health*. Ottawa, ON: AFMC, 2020. http://phprimer.afmc.ca/Part1-TheoryThinkingAboutHealth/Chapter1ConceptsOfHealthAndIllness/IllnessSicknessandDisease

Dougherty, Rose Mary. *Discernment: A Path to Spiritual Awakening*. New York: Paulist, 2009.

Douglas, Mary. *Purity and Danger*. London: Routledge & Kegan Paul, 1966.

Drummond, Henry. *Natural Law in the Spiritual World*. London: Hodder & Stoughton, 1884.

Du Toit, Cornel. "Human Freedom and the Freedom of Natural Processes: On Omnicausality, A-Causality and God's Omnipotence." *Religion and Theology 20* (2013) 36–59.

Duffin, Jacalyn. *Medical Miracles: Doctors, Saints and Healing in the Modern World*. Oxford: Oxford University Press, 2009.

Dumbrell, William H. *The Search for Order: Biblical Eschatology in Focus*. Grand Rapids: Baker, 1994.

Eagle, Antony "Randomness Is Unpredictability." *British Journal for the Philosophy of Science* 56 (2005) 749–90.

Edelman, G. M. and J. A. Gally. "Degeneracy and Complexity in Biological Systems. *Proceedings of the National Academy of Sciences* 98 (2001) 13763–68.

Ehrenreich, Barbara. *Natural Causes: An Epidemic of Wellness, the Certainty of Dying, and Killing Ourselves to Live Longer*. New York: Metropolitan, 2018.

Ellis, Albert. *Reason and Emotion in Psychotherapy*. New York: Stuart, 1962.

Ellis, George. *How Can Physics Underlie the Mind? Top-down Causation in the Human Context*. Heidelberg: Springer-Verlag, 2016.

Ellis, Ralph. D. and Natika Newton. *How the Mind Uses the Brain: To Move the Body and Image the Universe*. Chicago: Open Court, 2010.

Engel, Christoph and Wolf Singer, eds. *Better than Conscious? Decision Making, the Human Mind and Implications for Institutions*. Cambridge, MA: MIT, 2008.

English, Lars Q. *There Is No Theory of Everything: A Physics Perspective on Emergence*. New York: Springer, 2017.

Evans, Ian and Nicholas D. Smith. *Knowledge*. Cambridge: Polity, 2012.

Evans, John G. "The Notion of Cause in Biomedicine." In *Questioning Causality: Scientific Explorations of Cause and Consequence across Social Contexts*, edited by Rom Harré and Fathali Moghaddam, 169–83. Santa Barbara: ABC-CLIO, 2016.

Eve, Eric. *The Healer from Nazareth: Jesus' Miracles in Historical Context*. London: SPCK, 2009.

Ewart, Paul. "The Necessity of Chance: Randomness, Purpose, and the Sovereignty of God." *Science and Christian Belief* 21 (2009) 111–31.

Ewart, Winston and Robert J. Marks II. "A Mono-Theism Theorem: Gödelian Consistency in the Hierarchy of Inference." *Perspectives on Science and Christian Faith* 66 (2014), 103–12.

Eysenck, Michael W. and Mark T. Keane. *Cognitive Psychology: A Student's Handbook*. London: Psychology Press/Taylor & Francis, 2015.

Falcon, Andrea. "Aristotle on Causality." *The Stanford Encyclopedia of Philosophy* (Spring 2019 Edition), Edward N. Zalta, ed. https://plato.stanford.edu/archives/spr2019/entries/aristotle-causality/

Falconer, Kenneth. *Fractals: A Very Short Introduction*. Oxford: Oxford University Press, 2013.

Fales, Evan. *Divine Intervention: Metaphysical and Epistemological Puzzles*. London: Routledge, 2010.

Falk, Ruma and Don Macgregor. "The Surprisingness of Coincidences." *Advances in Psychology* 14 (1983) 489–502.

Fanthorpe, Lionel and Patricia. *Mysteries and Secrets of Time*. Toronto: The Dundurn Group, 2007.

Farrer, Austin. *Faith and Speculation*. London: Adam & Charles Black, 1967.

———. *A Science of God?* London: Geoffrey Bles, 1966.

Fee, Gordon D. *God's Empowering Presence: The Holy Spirit in the Letters of Paul*. Peabody, Mass: Hendrickson, 1994.

Fee, Gordon D. and Douglas Stuart. *How to Read the Bible for All Its Worth*. 3rd ed. Grand Rapids: Zondervan, 2003.

Festinger, Leon. *A Theory of Cognitive Dissonance*. California: Stanford University Press, 1957.

Festinger, Riecken, et al. *When Prophecy Fails: A Social and Psychological Study of a Modern Group That Predicted the Destruction of the World*. Minneapolis: University of Minnesota Press, 1956.

Firth, Cox, et al., eds. *Oxford Textbook of Medicine*. Oxford: Oxford University Press, 2020.

Fischer, Kane, et al. *Four Views on Free Will*. Oxford: Blackwell, 2007.

Fisher, Len. *The Perfect Swarm: The Science of Complexity in Everyday Life*. New York: Basic, 2009.

Fisher, Matthew and Frank C. Keil. "The Curse of Expertise: When More Knowledge Leads to Miscalibrated Explanatory Insight." *Cognitive Science 40* (2016) 1251–69.

Fiske, Susan T. and Shelley E. Taylor. *Social Cognition*. 2nd ed. New York: McGraw-Hill, 1991.

Foster, George M. "Disease Etiologies in Non-Western Medical Systems." *American Anthropologist 78* (1976) 773–82.

Francis, Williams, et al. "The Unconventional Beliefs of Conventional Churchgoers: The Matter of Luck." *Implicit Religion 9* (2006) 305–14.

Frankl, Viktor E. *Man's Search for Meaning*. Translated by Ilse Lasch. Boston: Beacon, 1959.

Fretheim, Terence E. *Creation Untamed: The Bible, God and Natural Disasters*. Grand Rapids: Baker Academic, 2010.

———. *God and World in the Old Testament*. Nashville: Abingdon, 2005.

Friesen, Gary with J. R. Maxson. *Decision Making and The Will of God: A Biblical Alternative to the Traditional View*. Portland, OR: Multnomah, 1980.

Frijda, Antony, et al., eds. *Emotions and Beliefs: How Feelings Influence Thoughts*. Cambridge: Cambridge University Press, 2000.

Fringer, Rob A. and Jeff K. Lane. *Theology of Luck: Fate, Chaos, and Faith*. Kansas City, MO: Nazarene, 2015.

Gaiser, Frederick J. *Healing in the Bible: Theological Insight for Christian Ministry*. Grand Rapids: Baker Academic, 2010.

———. "Why Does It Rain? A Biblical Case Study in Divine Causality." *Horizons in Biblical Theology 25* (2003) 1–18.

Gallagher, Timothy M. *The Discernment of Spirits*. New York: Crossroad, 2005.

Gilbert, Brown, et al. "The Illusion of External Agency." *Journal of Personality and Social Psychology* 79 (2000) 690–700.

Gilovich, Thomas and Lee Ross. *The Wisest One in the Room: How You Can Benefit from Social Psychology's Most Powerful Insights.* New York: Free Press, 2015.

Gilovich, Vallone, et al. "The Hot Hand in Basketball: On the Misperception of Random Sequences." *Cognitive Psychology* 17 (1985) 295–314.

Goldstein, E. Bruce. *Sensation and Perception.* 8th ed. Belmont, CA: Wadsworth, 2010.

Goleman, Daniel. *Emotional Intelligence: Why it Can Matter More Than IQ.* New York: Bantam, 1995.

————. *Social Intelligence: The New Science of Human Relationships.* New York: Bantam, 2006.

Gordon, Kerry. "The Impermanence of Being: The Psychology of Uncertainty." *Journal of Humanistic Psychology* 43 (2003) 96–117.

Gorman, Sara E. and Jack M. Gorman. *Denying to the Grave: Why We Ignore the Facts That Will Save Us.* Oxford: Oxford University Press, 2017.

Grad, Bernard. "Some Biological Effects of Laying-On of Hands: A Review of Experiments with Animals and Plants." *Journal of the American Society for Psychical Research* 59 (1965) 95–127.

Greear, J.D. "What if You Really Believed God Has a Plan and is with You? *Church Leaders* https://churchleaders.com/outreach-missions/outreach-missions-articles /279656-believed-god-jd-greear.html

Gregersen, Niels Henrik. "Risk and Religion: Toward a Theology of Risk Taking." *Zygon* 38 (2003), 355–76.

Grenz, Stanley J. *Theology for the Community of God.* 2nd ed. Grand Rapids: Eerdmans, 2000.

Gribbin, John. *Deep Simplicity.* New York: Random House, 2004.

Griffin, David Ray. *Parapsychology, Philosophy and Spirituality: A Postmodern Exploration.* Albany: State University of New York Press, 1997.

Groopman, Jerome. *Second Opinions. Stories of Intuition and Choice in the Changing World of Medicine.* New York: Penguin, 2001.

Gruning, Herb. *How in the World Does God Act?* Lanham, MD: University Press of America, 2000.

Gundry, Stanley N. and Dennis W. Jowers, eds. *Four Views on Divine Providence.* Grand Rapids: Zondervan, 2011.

Gunther, York, ed. *Essays on Nonconceptual Content.* Cambridge, MA: MIT, 2003.

Haarsma, Deborah and Scott Hoezee, eds. *Delight in Creation: Scientist Share Their Work with the Church.* Grand Rapids: Center for Excellence in Preaching, 2012.

Haidt, Jonathan. *The Righteous Mind: Why Good People Are Divided by Politics and Religion.* New York: Vintage, 2012.

Hand, David J. *The Improbability Principle: Why Coincidences, Miracles, and Rare Events Happen Every Day.* New York: Scientific American/Farrar Straus Giroux, 2014.

Haroutunian, Joseph, ed. *Calvin: Commentaries.* Library of Christian Classics. Philadelphia: Westminster John Knox, 1958.

Harré, Rom. "The Discourse Frame." In *Questioning Causality: Scientific Explorations of Cause and Consequence across Social Contexts*, edited by Rom Harré and Fathali Moghaddam, 3–19. Santa Barbara: ABC-CLIO, 2016.

Harrison, Peter. "Introduction." In *Science Without God?: Rethinking the History of Scientific Naturalism,* edited by Peter Harrison and Jon H. Roberts, 1–25. Oxford: Oxford Scholarship Online, 2019.

Hart, David Bentley. *The Doors of the Sea.* Grand Rapids: Eerdmans, 2005.

Hasker, William. *Metaphysics: Constructing a Worldview.* Downers Grove: InterVarsity, 1983.

Hassin, Bargh, et al. "Spontaneous Causal Inferences." *Journal of Experimental Social Psychology* 38 (2002) 515–22.

Hastie, Reid and Robyn M. Dawes. *Rational Choice in an Uncertain World: The Psychology of Judgment and Decision Making.* 2nd ed. Newbury Park, CA: Sage, 2010.

Hawking, Stephen. *Black Holes and Baby Universes and Other Essays.* New York: Bantam, 1994.

Heaney, John J. *The Sacred and the Psychic: Parapsychology and Christian Theology.* New York: Paulist, 1984.

Heider, Fritz and Marianne Simmel. "An Experimental Study of Apparent Behavior." *The American Journal of Psychology* 57 (1944) 243–59.

Heider, Fritz. *The Psychology of Interpersonal Relations.* New York: Wiley, 1958.

Heisenberg, Werner. *Physics and Beyond: Encounters and Conversations.* Translated by Arnold J. Pomerans. New York: Harper & Row, 1971.

———. *Physics and Philosophy: The Revolution in Modern Science.* 1958. Reprint. New York: Penguin, 2000.

Highfield, Ron. *The Faithful Creator: Affirming Creation and Providence in an Age of Anxiety.* Downers Grove: InterVarsity, 2015.

Hill, Austin B. "The Environment and Disease: Association or Causation?" *Proceedings of the Royal Society of Medicine* 58 (1965) 295–300.

Hitchcock, Christopher. "Causal Models." *The Stanford Encyclopedia of Philosophy* (Summer 2020 Edition), Edward N. Zalta, ed. https://plato.stanford.edu/archives/sum2020/entries/causal-models/

Hoffman, Peter M. *Life's Ratchet: How Molecular Machines Extract Order from Chaos.* New York: Basic, 2012.

Hofstadter, Douglas. *I Am a Strange Loop.* New York: Basic, 2007.

Holmes, Jamie. *Nonsense: The Power of Not Knowing.* New York: Broadway, 2015.

Howard, Evan B. *Affirming the Touch of God: A Psychological and Philosophical Exploration of Christian Discernment.* Lanham, MD: University Press of America, 2000.

———. *The Brazos Introduction to Christian Spirituality.* Grand Rapids: Brazos, 2008.

Huff, Darrell. *How to Lie with Statistics.* New York: Norton, 1954.

Illari, Russo, et al. "Why Look at Causality in the Sciences? A Manifesto." In *Causality in the Sciences,* edited by Phyllis McKay Illari et al., 3–22. Oxford: Oxford University Press, 2011.

Irwin, Harvey J. and Caroline A. Watt. *An Introduction to Parapsychology.* 5th ed. Jefferson, NC: McFarland & Company, 2007.

Jaccoby, Brown, et al. "Becoming Famous Overnight: Limits on the Ability to Avoid Unconscious Influences of the Past. *Journal of Personality and Social Psychology* 56 (1989) 326–38.

James, William. *The Varieties of Religious Experience: A Study in Human Nature.* New York: Penguin, 1902.

Jeeves, Malcolm and Warren S. Brown. *Neuroscience, Psychology, and Religion: Illusions, Delusions, and Realities about Human Nature.* West Conshocken, PA: Templeton Foundation, 2009.

Jensen, Alexander S. *Divine Providence and Human Agency: Trinity, Creation and Freedom.* Burlington, VT: Ashgate, 2014.

Jenson, Philip P. *Graded Holiness: A Key to the Priestly Conception of the World.* JSOTSup 106, Sheffield: Sheffield Academic Press, 1992.

Jersak, Brad. *Can You Hear Me? Tuning in To the God Who Speaks.* Abbotsford, BC: Fresh Wind, 2003.

Johnson, Luke T. *Scripture and Discernment: Decision Making in the Church.* 2nd ed. Nashville: Abingdon, 1996.

Johnson, Valenti, et al. "Simplicity and Complexity Preferences in Causal Explanation: An Opponent Heuristic Account." *Cognitive Psychology* 113 (2019) doi: 10.1016/j.cogpsych.2019.05.004.

Jones, Kanouse, et al. *Attribution: Perceiving the Causes of Behavior.* New York: General Learning, 1972.

Jung, Carl G. *Synchronicity: An Acausal Connecting Principle.* Bollingen, Switzerland: Bollingen Foundation, 1952.

Kahneman, Daniel. *Thinking, Fast and Slow.* Toronto: Doubleday Canada, 2011.

Kalat, J. W. *Biological Psychology.* 12th ed. Toronto: Thomson-Wadsworth, 2016.

Kauffman, Stuart A. *Reinventing the Sacred.* New York: Basic, 2008.

Kee, Howard Clark. *Medicine, Miracle and Magic in New Testament Times.* Cambridge: Cambridge University Press, 1986.

Keil, Frank C. "Explanation and Understanding." *Annual Review of Psychology* 57 (2006) 227–54.

———. "Running on Empty? How Folk Science Gets by With Less." *Current Directions in Psychology* 21 (2012) 329–34.

Keil, Frank C. and George E. Newman. "Order, Order Everywhere, and Only an Agent to Think: The Cognitive Compulsion to Infer Intentional Agents." *Mind and Language* 30 (2015) 117–39.

Keil, Frank C. and Robert A. Wilson, eds. *Explanation and Cognition.* Cambridge, MA: MIT, 2000.

Kelemen, Deborah. "Why Are Rocks Pointy? Children's Preference for Teleological Explanations of The Natural World." *Developmental Psychology* 35 (1999) 1440–52.

Kelsey, Morton T. *Psychology, Medicine and Christian Healing.* New York: Harper & Row, 1988.

Kierkegaard, Søren. *The Concept of Anxiety: A Simple Psychologically Oriented Deliberation in View of the Dogmatic Problem of Hereditary Sin.* Translated by Alastair Hannay. 1844. Reprint. New York: Liveright, 2014.

Kim, Luhmann, et al. "The Conceptual Centrality of Causal Cycles." *Memory and Cognition* 6 (2009) 744–58.

Kirkpatrick, Frank G. *The Mystery and Agency of God: Divine Being and Action in the World.* Minneapolis: Fortress, 2014.

Knight, Christopher. *The God of Nature: Incarnation and Contemporary Science.* Theology and the Sciences. Minneapolis: Fortress, 2007.

Koenig, King, et al. *Handbook of Religion and Health.* Oxford: Oxford University Press, 2012.

Koren, Steve and Michael O'Keefe. *Bruce Almighty*. Directed by Tom Shadyac. Universal City, CA: Universal Pictures, 2003.

Kruglanski, Arie W. and Donn M. Webster. "Motivated Closing of the Mind: 'Seizing' and 'Freezing.'" *Psychological Review 103 (1996) 263–83.*

Kuhn, Thomas, *The Structure of Scientific Revolutions*. Chicago: Chicago University Press, 1967.

Kydd, Ronald A. N. *Healing through the Centuries: Models for Understanding*. Grand Rapids: Baker Academic, 1995.

Lakoff, George and Mark Johnson. *Metaphors We Live By*. Chicago: University of Chicago Press, 1980.

Lang, Amanda. *The Beauty of Discomfort: How What We Avoid Is What We Need*. Toronto: HarperCollins, 2017.

Langer, Ellen J. "The Illusion of Control." *Journal of Personality and Social Psychology* 32 (1975) 311–28.

Laszlo, Ervin. *The Connectivity Hypothesis*. Albany: State University of New York Press, 2003.

Lazarus, Richard S. *Psychological Stress and the Coping Process*. New York: McGraw-Hill, 1966.

Lazarus, Richard S. and Susan Folkman. *Stress, Appraisal, and Coping*. New York: Springer, 1984.

Leary, Diebels, et al. "Cognitive and Interpersonal Features of Intellectual Humility." *Personality and Social Psychology Bulletin* 43 (2017) 793–813.

Lehrer, Jonah. *How We Decide*. Boston: Houghton Mifflin Harcourt, 2009.

Leibovici, Leonard. "Effects of Remote, Retroactive Intercessory Prayer on Outcomes in Patients with Bloodstream Infection: Randomized Controlled Trial." *British Medical Journal* 323 (2001) 1450–1.

Lerner, Small, et al. "Heart Strings and Purse Strings: Carryover Effects of Emotions on Economic Decisions." *Psychological Science* 15 (2004) 337–41.

Lerner, Melvin J. *The Belief in a Just World: A Fundamental Delusion*. Perspectives in Social Psychology. New York: Plenum, 1980.

Leslie, Alan M. and Stephanie Keeble. "Do Six-Month-Old Infants Perceive Causality?" *Cognition* 25 (1987) 265–88.

Lett, Jacof. "Jürgen Moltmann's Theology of Divine Action: Towards A More Integrative Understanding of His Doctrine of Creation." *Wesleyan Theological Journal* 49 (2014) 205–42.

Levison, Jack. *Inspired: The Holy Spirit and the Mind of Faith*. Grand Rapids: Eerdmans, 2013.

Lichtenstein, Slovac, et al. "Judged Frequency of Lethal Events." *Journal of Experimental Psychology, Human Learning and Memory* 4 (1978) 551–78.

Little, William. *Introduction to Sociology*. 1st Canadian Edition. Victoria, BC.: BCcampus, 2014. https://opentextbc.ca/introductiontosociology/

Livio, Mario. *Brilliant Blunders: From Darwin to Einstein—Colossal Mistakes by Great Scientists That Changed Our Understanding of Life and the Universe*. New York: Simon & Shuster, 2014.

Loikkanen, Juuso. "Does Divine Action Require Divine Intervention? God's Actions in the World and the Problem of Supernatural Causation." *Research and Science Today* 2 (2015) 17–27.

Luhrmann, Tanya M. *When God Talks Back: Understanding the American Evangelical Relationship with God.* New York: Alfred Knopf, 2012.

Mackie, J. L. *Cement of the Universe: A Study of Causation.* 2nd ed. Oxford: Clarendon, 1980.

MacNutt, Francis. *Healing.* Notre Dame: Ava Maria, 1974.

Mazur, Joseph. *Fluke: The Math and Myth of Coincidence.* New York: Basic, 2016.

McDonald, George. *The Princess and the Goblin.* 1872. Reprint. Middlesex: Puffin, 1979.

McGilchrist, Iain. *The Master and His Emissary: The Divided Brain and the Making of the Western World.* New Haven, CT: Yale University Press, 2009.

McGrath, Alister. *The Science of God.* Grand Rapids: Eerdmans, 2002.

McIntosh, Mark. *Discernment and Truth.* New York: Crossroad, 2004.

McNamara, Patrick. *The Neuroscience of Religious Experience.* New York: Cambridge University Press, 2009.

McNeil, Pauker, et al. "On the Elicitation of Preferences for Alternative Therapies." *New England Journal of Medicine* 306 (1982) 1259–62.

Michotte, Albert. *The Perception of Causality.* Translated by T. R. Miles and E. Miles. New York: Basic, 1946.

Mientka, W. E. "Professor Leo Moser—Reflections of a Visit." *The American Mathematical Monthly* 79 (1972) 609–14.

Molina, van de Walle, et al. "The Animate-Inanimate Distinction in Infancy: Developing Sensitivity to Constraints on Human Actions." *Journal of Cognition and Development* 5 (2004) 399–426.

Moltmann, Jürgen. *The Crucified God: The Cross of Christ as the Foundation and Criticism of Christian Theology.* Translated by R. A. Wilson and John Bowden. London: SCM Press, 1974.

———. *God in Creation.* 2nd ed. Translated by Margaret Kohl. Minneapolis: Fortress, 1993.

———. *The Spirit of Life: A Universal Affirmation.* Translated by Margaret Kohl. Minneapolis: Fortress, 1992.

Morowitz, Harold J. *The Emergence of Everything: How the World Became Complex.* Oxford: Oxford University Press, 2004.

Mumford, Stephen and Rani Lill Anjum. *Causation: A Very Short Introduction.* Oxford: Oxford University Press, 2013.

Murphy, George L. "Divine Action and Divine Purpose." *Currents in Theology and Mission* 36 (2009) 32–38.

Murphy, Nancey and George F. R. Ellis. *On the Moral Nature of the Universe: Theology, Cosmology, and Ethics.* Minneapolis: Fortress, 1996.

Myers, David G. *The Inflated Self: Human Illusions and the Biblical Call to Hope.* New York: Seabury, 1980.

———. *Intuition: Its Powers and Perils.* New Haven: Yale University Press, 2002.

Myers, David and Jean Twinge. *Social Psychology,* 13th ed. New York: McGraw-Hill, 2019.

Navilon, Genefe. "Everything Happens for a Reason: 7 Reasons to Believe This Is True," Ideapod, Mar 28, 2020, https://ideapod.com/everything-happens-for-a-reason-7-reasons-to-believe-in-this-philosophy/

Newberg, Andrew B. *Why We Believe What We Believe: Uncovering Our Biological Need for Meaning, Spirituality and Truth.* New York: Free Press, 2006.

Newsome, William T. "Human Freedom and 'Emergence.'" In *Downward Causation and the Neurobiology of Free Will: Understanding Complex Systems*, edited by Nancey Murphy et al, 53–62. Berlin: Springer, 2009.

Nichols, Natalie. "Filtered through His Fingers of Love"; *Shades of Grace Ministries*, 2018. https://www.shadesofgrace.org/2018/03/09/filtered-through-his-fingers-of-love-gods-sovereign-rule-part-2/

Niebuhr, Reinhold. *The Nature and Destiny of Man*, Vol. 1. New York: Charles Scribner's, 1964.

Nisbett, R. E. and T. D. Wilson. "Telling More Than We Can Know: Verbal Reports on Mental Processes." *Psychological Review* 84 (1977) 231–59.

Nouwen, Henri J. M. *Lifesigns: Intimacy, Fecundity, and Ecstasy in Christian Perspective.* Toronto: Doubleday, 1989.

O'Neil, Cathy. *Weapons of Math Destruction: How Big Data Increases Inequality and Threatens Democracy*. New York: Crown, 2016.

Oord, Thomas Jay. *The Uncontrolling Love of God: An Open and Relational Account of Providence.* Downers Grove: InterVarsity Academic, 2015.

"Optical Illusions." N.a, n.d. https://www.123opticalillusions.com/

Outler, Albert C., *ed. John Wesley*. Oxford: Oxford University Press, 1964.

Paley, William. *Natural Theology.* London: Wilks and Taylor, 1802.

Pannenberg, Wolfhart. *Systematic Theology Vol. 1 and 2.* Translated by Geoffrey W. Bromiley. Grand Rapids: Eerdmans, 1991, 1994.

Pargament, Kenneth I. *The Psychology of Religion and Coping: Theory, Research, Practice.* New York: Guilford, 1997.

Parker, Stephen E. *Led by the Spirit: Toward a Pentecostal Theology of Discernment and Decision Making.* JPT supplement. Sheffield: Sheffield Academic, 1996.

Paul, L. A., and Ned Hall. *Causation: A User's Guide.* Oxford: Oxford University Press, 2013.

Peacocke, Arthur R. *Creation and the World of Science.* Oxford: Oxford University Press, 2004.

———. *God and the New Biology.* London: J.M. Dent & Sons, 1986.

———. *Theology for a Scientific Age: Being and Becoming—Natural, Divine, and Human.* Minneapolis: Fortress, 1990.

Pearcey, Nancy R. *Total Truth: Liberating Christianity from Its Cultural Captivity.* Wheaton: Crossway, 2004.

Pearl, Judea and Dana Mackenzie. *The Book of Why: The New Science of Cause and Effect.* New York: Basic, 2018.

Perkins, David. *Outsmarting IQ: The Emerging Science of Learnable Intelligence.* New York: Free Press, 1995.

Pinnock, Clark H. "Divine Election as Corporate, Open, and Vocational." In *Perspectives on Election: Five Views,* edited by Chad Brand, 276–313, Nashville: Broadman & Holman, 2006.

———. *Flame of Love: A Theology of the Holy Spirit.* Downers Grove: InterVarsity, 1994.

———. *Most Moved Mover: A Theology of God's Openness.* Grand Rapids: Baker, 2001.

Pinnock, Rice, et al. *The Openness of God: A Biblical Challenge to the Traditional Understanding of God.* Downers Grove: InterVarsity, 1994.

Piper, John. *Coronavirus and Christ.* Wheaton: Crossway, 2020.

Polanyi, Michael. *Personal Knowledge: Towards a Post-Critical Philosophy.* Chicago: University of Chicago Press, 1958.

————. *The Tacit Dimension*. New York: Doubleday, 1966.

Polkinghorne, John C. "The Credibility of the Miraculous." *Zygon* 37 (2002) 751–57.

————. *Exploring Reality: The Intertwining of Science and Religion*. New Haven, CT: Yale University Press, 2005.

————. "Is Science Enough?" *Sewanee Theological Review* 39 (1995) 11–26.

————. *Quantum Theory: A Very Short Introduction*. Oxford: Oxford University Press, 2002.

————. *Quarks, Chaos and Christianity*. 2nd ed. New York: Crossroad, 2005.

————. *Science and Providence: God's Interaction with the World*. 2nd ed. West Conshocken, PA: Templeton Foundation, 2005.

————. *Science and Theology: An Introduction*. London: SPCK, 1998.

Pollard William G. *Chance and Providence: God's Action in a World Governed by Scientific Law*. London: Faber and Faber, 1959.

Porterfield, Amanda. *Healing in the History of Christianity*. Oxford: Oxford University Press, 2005.

Powell, Diane Hennacy. *The ESP Enigma: The Scientific Case for Psychic Phenomena*. New York: Walker & Co., 2009.

Poythress, Vern S. *Chance and the Sovereignty of God*. Wheaton: Crossway, 2014.

Psillos, Stathis. *Causation and Explanation*. Montreal: McGill-Queens University Press, 2002.

Rabins, Peter V. *The Why of Things: Causality in Science, Medicine, and Life*. New York: Columbia University Press, 2013.

Radin, Dean. *The Conscious Universe: The Scientific Truth of Psychic Phenomena*. New York: HarperOne/HarperCollins, 1997.

————. *Entangled Minds: Extrasensory Experiences in a Quantum Reality*. New York: Paraview, 2006.

————. "Exploring Relationships between Random Physical Events and Mass Human Attention: Asking for Whom the Bell Tolls." *Journal of Scientific Exploration* 16 (2002) 533–47.

Rankin, Lissa. *Mind over Medicine: Scientific Proof That You Can Heal Yourself*. New York: Hay House, 2013.

Redman, Matt. "10000 Reasons." Track 1 on *10000 Reasons*, 2012.

Reichard, Joshua. "Beyond Causation: A Contemporary Theology of Concursus." *American Journal of Theology and Philosophy* 34 (2013) 117–134.

————. "From Causality to Relationality: Toward a Wesleyan Theology of *Concursus*." *Wesleyan Theological Journal* 49 (2014) 122–38

Rescher, Nicholas. *The Limits of Science*. Revised ed. Pittsburgh: University of Pittsburgh Press, 1999.

Rice, Richard. "Biblical Support for a New Perspective." In *The Openness of God: A Biblical Challenge to the Traditional Understanding of God*, edited by Clark H. Pinnock et al, 11–58. Downers Grove: InterVarsity, 1994.

Ricoeur, Paul. *The Rule of Metaphor: Multi-disciplinary Studies of the Creation of Meaning in Language*. Translated by Robert Czerny. Toronto: University of Toronto Press, 1977.

Risen, Jane L. and Clayton R. Critcher. "Visceral Fit: While in A Visceral State, Associated States of The World Seem More Likely." *Journal of Personality and Social Psychology* 100 (2011) 777–93.

Rolls, Edmund. T. *Emotion and Decision-Making Explained*. Oxford: Oxford University Press, 2014.

Rosenblatt, R. "The 11th Commandment." *Family Circle* December 21 (1993) 30–32.

Rosenthal, Jeffrey S. *Struck by Lightning: The Curious World of Probabilities*. Toronto: Harper Perennial, 2005.

Ross, Greene, et al. "The False Consensus Effect: An Egocentric Bias in Social Perception and Attribution Processes." *Journal of Experimental Social Psychology* 13 (1977) 279–301.

Ross, Michael and Fiore Sicoly. "Egocentric Biases in Availability and Attribution." *Journal of Personality and Social Psychology* 37 (1979) 322–36.

Rothan, H.A. and S. N. Byrareddy. "The Epidemiology and Pathogenesis of Coronavirus Disease (Covid-19) Outbreak." *Journal of Autoimmunology* (2020). Feb 26:102433. doi: 10.1016/j.jaut.2020.102433

Rothman, Kenneth J. *Epidemiology: An Introduction*. 2nd ed. Oxford: Oxford University Press, 2012.

Rotter, Julian B. "Generalized Expectancies for Internal Versus External Control of Reinforcement." *Psychological Monographs: General and Applied* 80 (1966) 1–28.

Rozenblit, Leonid R. and Frank C. Keil. "The Misunderstood Limits of Folk Science: An Illusion of Explanatory Depth." *Cognitive Science* 26 (2002) 521–62.

Russell, Robert J. *Cosmology: From Alpha to Omega*. Minneapolis: Fortress, 2008.

———. "Does the 'God Who Acts' Really Act in Nature?" In *Science and Theology: The New Consonance*, edited by Ted Peters, Boulder, CO.: Westview Press, 1998.

Saunders, Nicholas. *Divine Action and Modern Science*. Cambridge: Cambridge University Press, 2002.

Sayers, Dorothy L. *The Mind of the Maker*. New York: Living Age, 1956.

Scherer, Shorr, et al., eds. *Appraisal Processes in Emotion: Theory, Methods, Research*. Canary, NC: Oxford University Press, 2001.

Schulz, Kathryn. *Being Wrong: Adventures in the Margin of Error*. New York: HarperCollins, 2010.

Schwartz, Bless, et al. "Ease of Retrieval as Information: Another Look at the Availability Heuristic." *Journal of Personality and Social Psychology* 61 (1991) 195–202.

Schwebel, Lisa J. *Apparitions, Healings and Weeping Madonnas: Christianity and the Paranormal*. New York: Paulist, 2004.

Sears, Robert E. "The Nature of Experience: Empirical Considerations and Theological Ramifications." *Perspectives on Science and Faith* 69 (2017) 13–26.

Seligman, Martin E. *Depression and Learned Helplessness*. New York: John Wiley & Sons, 1974.

Selye, Hans. *The Stress of Life*. New York: McGraw-Hill, 1956.

Senter, Philip J. "Leviathan, Behemoth, and Other Biblical Tannînim: Serpents, not Dinosaurs. *Perspectives on Science and Faith* 71 (2019) 218–32.

Serban, George. *The Tyranny of Magical Thinking*. New York: E. P. Dutton, 1982.

Seybold, Klaus and Ulrich B. Mueller. *Sickness and Healing*. Translated by Douglas W. Stott. Nashville: Abingdon, 1978.

Shauf, Scott. *The Divine in Acts and in Ancient Historiography*. Minneapolis: Fortress, 2006.

Sherlock, William. *A Discourse Concerning the Divine Providence*. London: William Rogers, 1702.

Shuster, Marguerite. *Power, Pathology, Paradox: The Dynamics of Evil and Good.* Grand Rapids: Academie, Zondervan, 1987.

Simons, Daniel J. and Christopher F. Chabris. "Gorillas in Our Midst: Sustained Inattentional Blindness for Dynamic Events." *Perception* 28 (1999) 1059–74.

Simons, Daniel J. and Ronald A. Rensink. "Change Blindness: Past, Present, and Future." *Trends in Cognitive Sciences* 9 (2005) 16–20.

Skinner, B. F. "'Superstition' in the Pigeon." *Journal of Experimental Psychology* 38 (1948) 168–172.

Slick, Matt. "Does Everything Happen for a Reason?" *Christian Apologetics and Research Ministry*, 2015. https://carm.org/does-everything-happen-for-a-reason

Sloan, Richard P. *Blind Faith: The Unholy Alliance of Religion and Medicine.* New York: St Martins, 2006.

Sloman, Steven. *Causal Models: How People Think about the World and Its Alternatives.* Oxford: Oxford Scholarship Online, 2007.

Smith, Gordon T. *The Voice of Jesus.* Downers Grove: InterVarsity, 2003.

Smith, Leonard. *Chaos: A Very Short Introduction.* Oxford: Oxford University Press, 2007.

Smith, Mark S. *The Priestly Vision of Genesis 1.* Minneapolis: Fortress, 2010.

Smith, Nicholas D. and Andrew Yip. "Partnership with God: A Partial Solution to the Problem of Petitionary Prayer." *Religious Studies* 46 (2010) 395–410.

Spelke, Elizabeth and Katherine Kinzler. "Core Knowledge." *Developmental Science* 10 (2007) 89–96.

Sproul, R. C. *Not a Chance: The Myth of Chance in Modern Science and Theology.* 2nd ed. Grand Rapids: Baker, 2014.

Stanovich, Keith E. *What Intelligence Tests Miss: The Psychology of Rational Thought.* New Haven: Yale University Press, 2009.

Statistics Canada, "Crude Birth Rate." Table 13-10-0418-01. Crude Birth Rate, Age-Specific Fertility Rates and Total Fertility Rate (live births); https://doi.org/10.25318/1310041801-eng

Stauss, Sharon E. and Finlay A. McAlister. "Evidence-Based Medicine: A Commentary on Common Criticisms." *Canadian Medical Association Journal* 163 (2000) 837–41.

Stein, Alex. "Are People Probabilistically Challenged?" *Michigan Law Review* 111 (2013) 855–76.

Stevens, Bruce A. "Grounded Theology: A New Method to Explore Luck." *Theology Today* 73 (2016) 117–28.

Stewart, Ian. *Does God Play Dice? The New Mathematics of Chaos.* 2nd ed. New York: Penguin, 1997.

Strom, Bill. "Weathering Well: Predictors of Resilient Pluck during COVID Isolation." Paper presented at Trinity Western University Research and Creativity Symposium, 2020.

Taijfel, Henri. "Experiments in Intergroup Discrimination." *Scientific American* 223, 5 (1970) 96–102.

Taleb, Nassim Nicholas. *The Black Swan: The Impact of the Highly Improbable.* 2nd ed. New York: Random House, 2010.

————. *Fooled by Randomness: The Hidden Role of Chance in Life and in the Markets.* New York: Random House, 2004.

Tetlock, Philip E. *Expert Political Judgment: How Good Is It? How Can We Know?* Princeton: Princeton University Press, 2005.

Tetlock, Philip E. and Dan Gardner. *Superforecasting: The Art and Science of Prediction.* New York: Crown, 2015.

Thiessen, Terrance L. *Providence and Prayer: How Does God Work in the World?* Downers Grove: InterVarsity, 2000.

Thomas, John Christopher. *The Devil, Disease and Deliverance: Origins of Illness in New Testament Thought.* 2nd ed. Sheffield: Sheffield Academic Press, 2011.

Thompson, Paul R. "Causality, Theories and Medicine." In *Causality in the Sciences,* edited by Phyllis McKay Illari et al., 25–45. Oxford: Oxford University Press, 2011.

Toolan, David. *At Home in the Cosmos.* New York: Orbis, 2001.

Tornau, Christian. "Saint Augustine." *The Stanford Encyclopedia of Philosophy* (Summer 2020 Edition), Edward N. Zalta, ed. https://plato.stanford.edu/archives/sum2020/entries/augustine/

Torrance, Thomas F. *The Christian Frame of Mind.* Edinburgh: Handsel Press, 1985.

———. *Divine and Contingent Order.* Oxford: Oxford University Press, 1981.

———. *Space, Time and Incarnation.* London: Oxford University Press, 1969.

Tracy, Thomas F. "Divine Action, Created Causes, and Human Freedom." In *The God who Acts: Philosophical and Theological Explorations,* edited by Thomas Tracy, 77–102. Pennsylvania: Pennsylvania University Press, 1994.

———. "God and Creatures Acting: The Idea of Double Agency." In *Creation and the God of Abraham,* edited by David B. Burrell et al., 221–27. Cambridge: Cambridge University Press, 2010.

Trivers, Robert. *The Folly of Fools: The Logic of Deceit and Self-Deception in Human Life.* New York: Basic, 2013.

Tulving, Schacter, et al. "Priming Effects in Word-Fragment Completion Are Independent of Recognition Memory. *Journal of Experimental Psychology: Learning, Memory, and Cognition* 8 (1982) 336–42.

Turner, Denys. *The Darkness of God: Negativity in Christian Mysticism.* Cambridge: Cambridge University Press, 1995.

Tversky, Amos and Daniel Kahneman. "Belief in The Law of Small Numbers." *Psychological Bulletin* 76 (1971) 105–10.

———. "Extensional Versus Intuitive Reasoning: The Conjunction Fallacy in Probability Judgment." *Psychological Review* 90 (1983) 293–315.

Twelftree, Graham H. *In the Name of Jesus: Exorcism Among Early Christians.* Grand Rapids: Baker, 2007.

———. *Jesus the Miracle Worker.* Downers Grove: InterVarsity, 1999.

Van Berkum, Jos J. A. "Understanding Sentences in Context: What Brain Waves Can Tell Us." *Current Directions in Psychological Science* 17 (2008), 376–80.

Van Inwagen, Peter. "The Place of Chance in a World Sustained by God." In *Divine and Human Action: Essays in the Metaphysics of Theism,* edited by Thomas V. Morris, 211–35. Ithaca: Cornell University Press, 1988.

Van Wolde, Ellen. "The Limits of Linearity: Linear and Non-Linear Causal Thinking in Biblical Exegesis, Philosophy and Theology." *Bijdragen, International Journal in Philosophy and Theology* 63 (2001) 371–92.

Vigen, Tyler. *Spurious Correlations.* New York: Hachette, 2015.

Von Harnack, Adolf. *The Mission and Expansion of Christianity in the First Three Centuries.* London: G. P. Putnam's Sons, 1908.

Vyse, Stuart A. *Believing in Magic: The Psychology of Superstition.* Updated ed. Oxford: Oxford University Press, 2014.

Wagner, Gregory A. and Edward K. Morris. "'Superstitious' Behavior in Children." *The Psychological Record* 37 (1987) 471–88.

Walls, Jerry L. and Joseph R. Dongell. *Why I Am Not a Calvinist.* Downers Grove: InterVarsity, 2004.

Waltke, Bruce. *Finding the Will of God: A Pagan Notion?* 2nd ed. Grand Rapids: Eerdmans, 2002.

Walton, John H. *Ancient Near Eastern Thought and the Old Testament: Introducing the Conceptual World of the Hebrew Bible.* Grand Rapids: Baker Academic, 2006.

Warren, E. Janet. *Cleansing the Cosmos: A Biblical Model for Conceptualizing and Counteracting Evil.* Eugene, OR: Pickwick, 2012.

———. "'I Do Not Do What I Want': Commonalities in Addiction and Sin." *Perspectives on Science and Christian Faith* 70 (2018) 252–263.

———. "When Pneumatology Meets Demonology: Options for Reconciling Divine Omnipresence and Divine Absence." *Canadian Journal of Pentecostal-Charismatic Christianity* 6 (2015) 22–42.

Warren, Rick. *The Purpose Driven Life.* Grand Rapids: Zondervan, 2002.

Wason, P. C. "On the Failure to Eliminate Hypotheses in a Conceptual Task." *Quarterly Journal of Experimental Psychology* 12 (1960) 129–40.

Watts, Fraser. "Cognitive Neuroscience and Religious Consciousness." In *Neuroscience and the Human Person: Scientific Perspectives on Divine Action,* edited by Robert J. Russell et al., 327–46. Vatican City State: Vatican Observatory Publications, 1999.

Wegner, Lars H. and Ulrich Lüttge, eds. *Emergence and Modularity in the Life Sciences.* New York: Springer, 2019.

Weiner, Bernard. *An Attributional Theory of Motivation and Emotion.* New York: Springer-Verlag, 1986.

Westerholm, Martin. "On Christian Discernment and the Problem of the Theological." *International Journal of Systematic Theology* 16 (2014), 454–69.

White, Curtis. *The Science Delusion.* Brooklyn, NY: Melville House, 2013.

White, J. Wesley. "The Personality of Sin: Anxiety, Pride, and Self-Contempt." *Mid-America Journal of Theology* 27 (2016) 85–97.

White, Vernon. *The Fall of a Sparrow: A Concept of Special Divine Action.* Exeter: Paternoster, 1985.

Wildman, Wesley J. *Religious and Spiritual Experiences.* Cambridge: Cambridge University Press, 2011.

Wiles, Maurice. *God's Action in the World.* London: SCM Press, 1986.

Wilkinson, John. *The Bible and Healing: A Medical and Theological Commentary.* Grand Rapids: Eerdmans, 1998.

Willard, Dallas. *Hearing God: Developing a Conversational Relationship with God.* 4th ed. Downers Grove: InterVarsity, 2012.

Williams, Joseph W. *Spirit Cure: A History of Pentecostal Healing.* New York: Oxford University Press, 2013.

Wilson, Timothy D. and Jonathan W. Schooler. "Thinking Too Much: Introspection Can Reduce the Quality of Preferences and Decisions." *Journal of Personality and Social Psychology* 60 (1991) 181–92.

Wolters, Albert M. *Creation Regained: Biblical Basics for a Reformational Worldview.* 2nd ed. Grand Rapids: Eerdmans, 2005.

Wood, John R. "An Ecological Perspective on the Role of Death in Ecology." *Perspectives on Science and Christian Faith* 68 (2016) 74–86.

World Health Organization. "Coronavirus Disease (COVID-19) Advice for the Public: Mythbusters." World Health Organization, updated 4 June 2020. https://www. who.int/emergencies/diseases/novel-coronavirus-2019/advice-for-public/myth-busters

Worthing, Mark William. "Divine Action and the Problem of Miracles." *Christian Perspectives on Science and Technology* ISCAST Online Journal (2009) 1–16.

———. *God, Creation and Contemporary Physics.* Minneapolis: Fortress, 1994.

Wright, N. T. *God and the Pandemic: A Christian Reflection on the Coronavirus and Its Aftermath.* Grand Rapids: Zondervan, 2020.

Wright, Terry J. *Providence Made Flesh: Divine Presence as a Framework for a Theology of Providence.* Paternoster Theological Monographs. Eugene, OR: Wipf & Stock, 2009.

———. "Reconsidering Concursus." *International Journal of Systematic Theology* 4 (2002) 205–15.

Yamagishi, Kimihiko. "When a 12.86% Mortality Is More Dangerous Than 24.14%: Implications for Risk Communication." *Applied Cognitive Psychology* 11 (1997) 495–506.

Yancey, Philip. *Prayer: Does It Make Any Difference?* Grand Rapids: Zondervan, 2006.

———. *The Question That Never Goes Away.* Grand Rapids: Zondervan, 2013.

Yanofsky, Noson S. *The Outer Limits of Reason: What Science, Mathematics, and Logic Cannot Tell Us.* Cambridge, MA: MIT, 2013.

Yerkes, R.M. and J.D. Dodson. "The Relation of Strength of Stimulus to Rapidity of Habit-Formation." *Journal of Comparative Neurology and Psychology* 18 (1908) 459–482.

Yong, Amos. *The Spirit of Creation: Modern Science and Divine Action in the Pentecostal-Charismatic Imagination.* Grand Rapids: Eerdmans, 2011.

Young, Wm. Paul. *Lies We Believe about God.* New York: Atria, 2017.

Zajonc, Robert B. "Attitudinal Effects of Mere Exposure." *Journal of Personality and Social Psychology* 9 (1968) 1–27.

Zaleski, Philip. "The Saints of John Paul II." *First Things*, March (2006) https://www. firstthings.com/article/2006/03/the-saints-of-john-paul-ii

Zheng, Elmer, et al. "Wuhan Coronavirus: China Will Contain 'Demon' Outbreak, Xi Jinping Says as Death Toll Mounts." *South China Morning Post*, Jan 28, 2020. https://www.scmp.com/news/china/society/article/3047849/china-coronavirus-death-toll-climbs-106-confirmed-cases-surpass

Index